The most amazing places of folklore & legend in Britain

The most amazing places of folklore & legend in Britain

PUBLISHED BY
THE READER'S DIGEST ASSOCIATION, INC.
LONDON • NEW YORK • SYDNEY • MONTREAL

Contents

INTRODUCTION 6–7
THE FOLKLORE YEAR 8–11

SOUTHWEST ENGLAND 12–47
Cornwall 14–25
Devon 26–33
FEATURE: CELEBRATING MAY 30–31
Dorset 34–38
Somerset 39–45
Channel Islands 46–47

SOUTHERN ENGLAND 48–81
Bedfordshire 50–51
Berkshire 52–53
Buckinghamshire 54–55
Hampshire & Isle of Wight 56–58
Hertfordshire 59–60
Kent 61–67
FEATURE: THE OLD AND THE NEW 68–69
Oxfordshire 70–73
Surrey 74
Sussex 75–79
Wiltshire 80–81

LONDON 82–93
FEATURE: TRADITIONS OF A CITY 90–91

EAST ANGLIA 94–109
Cambridgeshire 96–99
Essex 100–103
FEATURE: THE MADNESS OF THE MORRIS 104–105
Norfolk 106–107
Suffolk 108–109

CENTRAL ENGLAND 110–139
Derbyshire 112–113
Gloucestershire 114–117
Herefordshire 118–119
Leicestershire & Rutland 120–121
Lincolnshire 122–125
Northamptonshire 126–127
FEATURE: SPORTS AND MERRYMAKING 128–129

Nottinghamshire 130–131
Shropshire 132–133
Staffordshire 134–135
Warwickshire 136–137
Worcestershire 138–139

NORTHWEST ENGLAND 140–157
Cheshire & The Wirral 142–145
Cumbria 146–149
FEATURE: CHRISTIAN PAGEANTS 150–151
Lancashire, Liverpool & Manchester 152–155
Isle of Man 156–157

NORTHEAST ENGLAND 158–173
Durham & Teesside 160–161
Northumberland & Tyneside 162–167
FEATURE: PROUD INDUSTRIAL HERITAGE
164–165
Yorkshire 168–173

WALES 174–191
North & Mid Wales 176–183
FEATURE: THE GREAT SITTING TOGETHER
184–185
South Wales 186–191

SCOTLAND 192–215
Southwest Scotland 194–197
FEATURE: THE FIRES OF MIDWINTER 198–199
Fife & Southeast Scotland 200–203
Central & Northeast Scotland 204–207
North Highlands & Islands 208–211
Orkney Islands 212–213
Shetland Islands 214–215

INDEX 216–223

ACKNOWLEDGMENTS 224

Introduction

From the mighty Shetland fire festival of Up Helly Aa to the mermaid of Zennor's tale of love and loss, let the amazing folklore and legends of Britain add a new dimension to your journeys around England, Scotland and Wales.

Britain's folklore – its stories, customs and popular beliefs – is as much a part of the nation's character as the landscape itself. Deeply rooted in the pre-industrial age, these fables and traditions arose when pastoral demands shaped the year and seasonal celebrations played their practical part. Travelling fairs, such as the 700-year-old Nottingham Goose Fair, were great venues for trade. Parades, such as the rushbearing festivals of Northern England and well dressing in many counties, were a thank you to God (and once an earlier deity) for another year's harvest and water. Very few rituals can be traced back to pre-Christian times with any certainty, but there are some events, among them the May fires of Beltane and the Abbots Bromley Horn Dance, which have genuinely ancient origins. Many – Devon's Hunting of the Earl of Rone, for example, and Oxford's May Day Morning – have lost sight of their beginnings but have gathered new myth and meaning over time.

Attempts to trace folklore and traditions to their source are often fruitless, and historical research can sometimes drain the exuberance from the original event or story. Tales of sleeping knights and ghostly kings were told

to thrill and entertain, and annual gatherings were usually high-spirited feasts of revelry and ale. If the myths and rituals have survived, it's not out of some worthy sense of duty to maintain our culture – it's because they are fun.

Orkney Islands
Shetland Islands
SCOTLAND 192-215
NORTHEAST ENGLAND 158-173
NORTHWEST ENGLAND 140-157
CENTRAL ENGLAND 110-139
WALES 174-191
EAST ANGLIA 94-109
LONDON 82-93
SOUTHWEST ENGLAND 12-47
SOUTHERN ENGLAND 48-81
Isles of Scilly
Channel Islands

This guidebook seeks to capture that fun, offering an insight into the most amazing folklore and legends of town and country, from ancient tales of megalithic monuments to an accursed urban underpass. There are nine chapters: Southwest England, Southern England, London, East Anglia, Central England, Northwest England, Northeast England, Wales and Scotland. Each chapter begins with a regional map divided by county, or in the case of Wales and Scotland, by area. Numbers on the map show the geographical location of each entry, and act as a useful touring guide. Directions at the end of each entry lead you by road or landmark to each destination. Events linked to a specific date are listed in 'The Folklore Year' on pages 8–11. Most festivals and events have their own websites or are listed on regional tourism sites. Always check dates and times before visiting, as these can be subject to change at short notice.

Many of the places listed in this book are easy to reach by car or public transport; others are more remote and are accessible only on foot. When walking to outlying sites and locations, be sure to wear appropriate clothing for the weather and terrain, and always tell someone where you're going.

Almost all of the destinations featured are open to the public. Where places or properties are privately owned, always respect the owners' privacy and don't stray on to private land to view or photograph the site.

Useful websites

Much of the British countryside together with older buildings in towns and cities are owned or managed by heritage organisations, notably English Heritage, the National Trust, the National Trust for Scotland and Cadw in Wales. Many properties and destinations have associated myths and legends, and all organisations host a number of events and celebrations throughout the year at key sites, most notably at Stonehenge (English Heritage), starting on the eve of the Summer Solstice, June 20. Check websites regularly for news and details of events.
www.english-heritage.org.uk
www.cadw.wales.gov.uk
www.nationaltrust.org.uk
www.nts.org.uk

The Folklore Society is devoted to the study of all aspects of folklore, in Britain and abroad, including music, dance and drama, custom and belief, arts and crafts and folk medicine.
www.folklore-society.com

The Museum of British Folklore is an online museum that aims to draw greater public attention to the folklore of the British Isles, to encourage its study and promote education, and to maintain an extensive collection of artefacts and photographs.
http://museumofbritishfolklore.com

The folklore year

January

1st Truro, Cornwall,
Truro Wassailers, p18

Hubberholme, Yorkshire,
Candle Auction, The George, p168

Tenby, Pembrokeshire,
Raindrop sprinkling, p188

Cwm Gwaun, Pembrokeshire,
Calennig and Noson Lawen, p188

6th Aconbury, Herefordshire,
Rising waters in St Anne's Well, p118

Haxey, Lincolnshire,
Haxey Hood game, p122

11th Burghead, Moray,
The Burning of the Clavie, p206

Old Twelfth Night
Carhampton, Somerset,
Wassailing the Apple Trees, p39

Twelfth Night is a Christian festival marking the end of the Twelve Days of Christmas and the coming of Epiphany. It is celebrated in Europe on January 6th. Old Twelfth Night, January 17, is a relic of the Julian calendar observed in Britain before 1752.

First Tuesday after Twelfth Night
Whittlesea, Cambridgeshire,
Straw Bear Day, p99

Last Tuesday
Lerwick, Shetland,
Up Helly Aa, p198

February

Monday of Candlemass Week
St Ives, Cornwall,
Hurling the Silver Ball, p16

Candlemass, February 2nd, once the Roman festival of Februa when candles were paraded through the streets, is the Christian 'festival of light'.

Shrove Tuesday

St Colomb Major, Cornwall,
Hurling the Silver Ball, p21

Corfe Castle
Freemen of the Ancient Order of Purbeck Marblers Annual Court and football match, p35

Ashbourne, Derbyshire,
Shrovetide football, p113
(afternoon, for two days)

Winster, Derbyshire,
Pancake Race between the Crown Inn and Market House, p113

Atherstone, Warwickshire,
Atherstone Ball Game p136

Sedgefield, County Durham,
Sedgefield Football, p161

Alnwick
Shrovetide Football, p166

Scarborough, Yorkshire,
Pancakes and Skipping Festival, p170

Shrove Tuesday falls 40 days before Easter and is the last day before Lent; Shrovetide is traditionally a time of feasting and merrymaking before the abstemious period of Lent. On Shrove Tuesday anything that will not last or cannot be consumed during Lent is made into pancakes.

Various dates
Jedburgh, Borders,
Jethart Handba' p203

March

1st Lanark, South Lanarkshire,
Whuppity Scoorie Day, p196

Third Thursday
Market Weighton, Yorkshire,
Kiplingcotes Derby, p172

Easter

Easter marks the end of Lent and is not fixed in the calendar. It succeeded pre-Christian celebrations of spring and is the most important Christian celebration of the year, commemorating Jesus' crucifixion. The date of Easter Sunday is calculated as the first Sunday after the full moon following the spring equinox. Palm Sunday, when Jesus entered Jerusalem, is the Sunday before Easter Sunday.

Palm Sunday
Fintstock, Oxfordshire,
Spanish Liquor Day, p70

Hentland church, Herefordshire,
Hentland Cakes, p118

Monday before Easter
Bourne, Lincolnshire,
Whitbread Meadow Auction, p125

Second Tuesday after Easter
(sometimes in April)
Hungerford, Berkshire,
Hocktide Festival, p52

Good Friday Morning
Brighton, Sussex,
Bat-and-trap ball game, p76

Good Friday
Tinsley Green, Sussex,
British and World Marbles championship, p75

St Bartholomew-the-Great, Smithfield, London,
The Poor Widows bun, p88

Bromley-by-Bow, London,
The Widow's Son, hot cross bun custom, p93

Good Friday and after
Workington, Cumbria,
Uppies and Downies, p146

Easter Saturday
Bacup, Lancashire,
Britannia Coconut Dancers Nut Dance, p154

Easter Monday
Biddenden, Kent
Distribution of Old Workhouse Wheaten Cake, p67

Hallaton, Leicestershire & Rutland,
Bottle kicking, p121

Ashton-under-Lyne, Manchester,
Riding the Black Lad, p155

Winter: Ring of Brodgar, Orkney

April

14th Heathfield, Sussex,
Heathfield Fair, p78

25th Whittlesford, Cambridgeshire,
the rising of the wraiths, p96

30th Carlton Hill, Edinburgh,
Beltane Fire Festival, p200

May

1st Eve and for three days after
Minehead, Somerset,
Hobby Horse, p39

1st (midnight)
Padstow, Cornwall,
Obby Oss ceremony, p22

1st Longwick Village Fete,
Buckinghamshire,
May Day Garlands, p54

Magdalen College, Oxford,
Oxfordshire,
May Morning, p72

May Day
Charlton, Otmoor, Oxfordshire,
May Day Procession, p72

Knutsford, Cheshire,
Sanding Ceremony, p142

May Day is superimposed on the festival of Beltane, when pre-Christian societies marked the beginning of summer with bonfires and celebrations. In Britain, May 1st is officially designated May Day and is still taken as holiday, as is the Spring Bank Holiday at the end of the month.

May Day Weekend
Rochester, Kent,
Sweeps Festival, p62

May Day Bank Holiday
Hastings, Sussex,
Jack-in-the-Green Festival, p79

Stilton, Cambridgeshire,
Stilton rolling, p99

First Saturday
Belton, Leicestershire,
Maypole dancing, p120

First Sunday
St Anne, Alderney,
Milk-O-Punch celebration, p46

First Sunday
St Albans, Hertfordshire,
Beating the Bounds, p60

8th Helston, Cornwall,
Helston Furry Dance, p16

Second Saturday
Hayes Common, Kent,
May Queen Festival, p93

Spring: Maypole dancing, London

Randwick, Gloucestershire,
Randwick Wap, p114

13th Abbotsbury, Dorset,
Blessing the Garlands, p34

Rogation Sunday
Oddington, Otmoor, Oxfordshire,
Blessing of the Crops, p72

Rogationtide Sunday and the following three days before Ascension Day. A time of blessing the crops, springing from Roman feast of Terminus, god of fields and landmarks.

Rogation Monday
Leighton Buzzard,
Beating the Bounds, p51

Whit Sunday
St Briavels, Gloucestershire,
Bread and cheese dole, p114

Sileby, Leicestershire, Victory oranges distributed in the churchyard, p120

Whitsuntide is derived from the celebrations of Summer Day, the beginning of the summer half-year. Falls on the seventh Sunday after Easter, generally in May.

Whit Monday
Great Dunmow, Essex,
Dunmow Flitch Trial (once every four years), p100

Enderby, Leicestershire,
The selling of the keep of the Wether (hay crop) p120

Barwick in Elmet, Yorkshire,
Raising the maypole, p172

Whit Tuesday
St Ives, Cambridgeshire,
Dice throwing, p98

Friday following Whit Sunday
Ashton-under-Lyne,
Annual Band Contest, p155

29th Chelsea, London,
Oak Apple Day: Chelsea Pensioners' Parade, p85

Castleton, Derbyshire,
Oak Apple Day, p112

Oak Apple Day on May 29 commemorates the Restoration of Charles II who hid in an oak tree to avoid capture, though it is thought the original rites stem from tree worship.

Day before Ascension Day
Whitby, Yorkshire,
Horngarth: the Planting of the Penny Hedge, p170

Ascension Day
Bisley, Gloucestershire,
Well dressing, p116

Ascensiontide is the ten days after Ascension Day, the day on which Jesus is said to have ascended to heaven. It falls on a Thursday, 40 days after Easter Sunday.

Spring Bank Holiday
Combe Martin, Devon,
The Hunting of the Earl of Rone, p27

Bampton, Oxfordshire,
Bampton Morris Men performance, p70

Tetbury, Gloucestershire,
Woolsack Race, p114

Cooper's Hill, Gloucestershire,
Cheese Rolling (check details annually), p116

Endon, Staffordshire,
Well Dressing, p134

Spring Bank Holiday Monday
Kingsteignton, Devon,
Ram Roasting Fair, p29

Late May (or early June)
Thaxted, Essex,
Thaxted Morris Meet, p100

Southwold, Suffolk,
Trinity Fair (for three days) p109

Various dates
Malvern Hills, Worcestershire,
Well dressing, p139

9

June

First Saturday
Chawleigh, Devon,
Chawleigh Village Friendly Society
Club Walk, p28

Early June
Hastings, Sussex,
Blessing of the Sea, p79

4th Eton, Berkshire,
Eton College's Fourth of June Holiday,
p53

17th Hartland Point, Devon,
St Nectan's Mass, St Nectan's Well,
p26

19th Abingdon, Oxfordshire,
Election of the Mayor of Ock Street,
p73

20th Stonehenge, Wiltshire,
Summer Solstice celebrations, p81

Summer Solstice is the moment of
the year when the tilt of the earth is
most inclined towards the sun in the
Northern Hemisphere, creating the
longest day and shortest night. It
generally occurs on June 21st and is
usually celebrated in Britain as night
falls on the 20th until dawn on 21st.
Midsummer Day is June 24, the feast
of St John the Baptist.

23rd Chapel Carn Brea, Cornwall,
Midsummer bonfire ceremony, p17

24th Guildhall, London,
Election of Sherrifs, p92

24th Winster, Derbyshire,
Winster Wakes celebrations, p113

Midsummer
Penzance, Cornwall,
Golowan (ten-day midsummer festival)
p14

**Closest Saturday to
Midsummer's Day**
Appleton Thorn,
Bawming the Thorn, p142

Summer: Morris dancing,
solstice dawn, Derbyshire

Sunday following June 29
(St Peter's Day)
**St Peter's Church, Wingrave,
Buckinghamshire**
Hay strewing festival, p54

Folkestone, Kent,
Blessing of the Sea and Fisheries, p66

Braunstone Church, Leicestershire,
Hay strewing festival, p120

Late June (or early July)
Wisbech, Cambridgeshire,
Wisbech Rose Fair, p96

Late June
Macclesfield, Cheshire,
Barnaby Festival, p145

Late June for two weeks
Jedburgh, Borders,
Callant's Festival, p203

June (check for dates)
St Dogmaels, Pembrokeshire,
Blessing the fleet, p188

July

4th Whalton, Northumberland,
Whalton Bale, p166

5th St John's, Isle of Man,
Meeting of the Tynwald, p158

Thursday after July 4
Garlick Hill, London,
Vintners' Procession, p92

Second Saturday
Durham, County Durham,
Durham Miners' Gala p164

Mid July
Innerleithen, Borders,
St Ronan's Border Games, p203

25th (every five years)
St Ives, Cornwall,
John Knill's Will Ceremony, p16

Last Friday
Langholm, Dumfries & Galloway,
Langholm's Fair and Common Riding,
p196

31st Tenby, Pembrokeshire,
St Margaret's Fair Procession, p188

Late July
Castletown, Isle of Man,
World Tin Bath Championships, p159

August

5th (feast of St Oswald)
Guiseley, Yorkshire,
Clipping the Church, p172

First Sunday
Horning, Norfolk,
Blessing the Norfolk Broads, p107

Early August
Marldon, Devon,
Apple Pie Fair, p29

St Andrews, Fife,
Lammas Fair, p200

Lammastide begins on August 1,
marking the start of the harvest.

Queensferry, City of Edinburgh,
August Ferry Fair, p200

Weekend after August 12
Saddleworth, Greater Manchester,
Saddleworth Rushcart, p152

Wednesday in August
(check before visiting)
**St Margaret's Hope, South
Ronaldsay, Orkney,**
Ploughing contest, p213

24th Sandwich, Kent,
St Bartholomew's Day, p66

St Bartholomew's Day, August 24, is
a traditional day for fairs and markets.

Saturday closest to August 24,
West Witton, Yorkshire,
Burning the Bartle, p168

August Bank Holiday
**Bourton-on-the-Water,
Gloucestershire,**
Football match in the River Windrush,
p117

Grasmere, Cumbria,
Grasmere Lakeland Sports, p149

August Bank Holiday weekend
Waen Rhydd, Powis,
Bog Snorkelling Championships, p179

Last Sunday
Glasserton, Dumfries & Galloway
Catholic Diocese of Galloway's
Pilgrimage to St Ninian's Cave, p195

Third Saturday after first Monday
Irvine, North Ayrshire,
Marymass Fair, p196

September

Monday following the first Saturday after September 4
Abbots Bromley, Staffordshire,
Horn Dance, p134

Second Tuesday
Widecombe in the Moor, Devon,
Widecombe Fair, p29

Early September (last day of harvest) **St Keverne, Cornwall,**
Crying the Neck, p17

Early September
Pyfleet Creek, Colchester,
Colchester Oyster Festival, p101

Wednesday before September 20
Barnstaple, Devon,
Barnstaple Fair, p28

19th **Painswick, Gloucestershire,**
Clipping the Church, p115

End of September (every three years),
Poole, Dorset,
Beating the Bounds, p37

29th **Guildhall, London,**
Election of the Lord Mayor, p92

Every alternate September (no fixed date)
Avening, Gloucestershire,
Pig Face Day, p114

October

First Thursday
Nottingham, Nottinghamshire,
Goose Fair, p130

Last Thursday
Bampton, Devon,
Bampton Charter Fair, p28

Hinton St George, Dorset,
Punky Night Celebrations, p44

Monday after October 10
Sherborne, Dorset,
Pack Monday Fair, p38

2nd **Braughing, Hertfordshire,**
Old Man's Day, p60

20th (generally, but check before visiting as date may change from year to year)
Colchester, Essex,
Oyster Feast p101

Late October to Early November
Antrobus and surrounding villages, Cheshire,
Soul Caking, p143

November

1st **Wicken, Northamptonshire,**
Love Feast, p126

5th **Shebbar, Devon,**
Turning the stone, p28

Ottery St Mary,
Guy Fawkes Celebrations, p32

Lewes, Sussex,
Lewes Bonfire, p78

Nearest Wednesday to November 5
Hatherleigh, Devon,
Hatherleigh Carnival, p29

Second Saturday
Guildhall and London,
The Lord Mayor's Show, p92

Third Wednesday
Sidbury, Devon,
Annual Court Leet and Court Baron, p32

Four evenings before the last Friday
Wareham, Dorset,
Wareham Court Leet, p37

Closest Friday to November 5
Bridgwater, Somerset,
Guy Fawkes Carnival, p40

Early November
Burnham-on-Sea, Somerset,
Highbridge and Burnham Carnival, p41

11th **Stretton-on-Dunsmore, Warwickshire,**
Payment of Wroth Silver, Knightlow Hill, p136

First Sunday after November 12
Broughton, Northamptonshire,
Tin Can Band Parade, p127

November (or December)
Laxton, Nottinghamshire,
Laxton Court Leet, p130

December

First Monday
Brightlingsea, Essex,
Election of Deputy of the Cinque Port Liberty, p102

21st **Penzance, Cornwall,**
Montol Festival, p14

21st **Brighton, Sussex,**
Burning the Clocks, p77

Winter Solstice generally occurs on December 21st or 22nd and is celebrated in Britain on the 21st.

23rd **Mousehole, Cornwall,**
Tom Bawcock's Eve, p14

Autumn: Tar Barrel Rolling, Ottery St Mary, Devon

Christmas (check for dates)
Pencoed, Bridgend,
Mari Lwyd – the Grey Mare Ceremony, p191

24th **Dunster, Somerset,**
Burning the Ashen Faggot, p39

Dewsbury, Yorkshire.
Tolling the Devil's Knell, p173

25th **Queen's College, Oxford,**
Boars Head Ceremony, p72

26th **Cathedral forecourt, Gloucester,**
Performances by City of Gloucester Mummers, p116

Marshfield, Gloucestershire,
Performances by the Marshfield Mummers, p117

31st **Allendale Town, Northumberland,**
Allendale Tar Barrels, p166

Biggar, South Lanarkshire,
Biggar Bonfire, p202

Comrie, Perth & Kinross,
Comrie Flambeaux, p207

Stonehaven, Aberdeenshire,
Stonehaven Fireballs, p207

Yuletide and Hogmanay
Kirkwall, Orkney,
Kirkwall Ba', p213

Yule a pagan winter festival celebrated by northern tribes and later absorbed into Christianity.

Hogmanay a Scottish festival celebrating the end of the year, thought to have Norse origins.

Times and dates of events are subject to change. Always confirm with the local tourist office or website before planning a trip.

Southwest England

Legends cast their shadow over the shores of the southwest, while folklore lives and thrives in spirited seasonal revels. Here, in this land of gods and giants, visitors get a glimpse of the old ways in stories and celebrations that pay little heed to the modern world.

KEY

1 Main entry
County boundary
Motorway
Principal A road

Bristol
11
10
A38
16 A37
15
Bath
Weston-super-Mare
9
Mendip
Hills
8
17
Frome
A361
Minehead
Exmoor
National
Park
2 1 3
12 4 A39
13
Somerset
Levels
A361
19 Glastonbury
Bridgwater
5
A361
7
Taunton
M5
A303
7
SOMERSET
39-45
A37
A303
14
Shaftesbury
A396
6
A303
Yeovil
A30
13
A350
A354
Tiverton
18
Honiton
A30
18 A35
14
Lyme
16
Regis
15
17
1
A37
Blandford
Forum
11
A431
DORSET
34-38
12
Exeter
10
6
A35
A348
A338
9
Poole
Exmouth
Dorchester
Bournemouth
13
Weymouth
7
8
2
4
5
9
A38
12 A380
3
Swanage
Torquay
A385 11
10
Dartmouth
Alderney
5
Salcombe
Guernsey
Herm
St Peter
3 4 Port
Sark
CHANNEL ISLANDS
46-47
Jersey
2
1
St Helier

CORNWALL

The ancient land of Kernow, or Cornwall, retains its distinct
Celtic identity. Many of its legends and customs survive from
a time beyond memory, relics of a proud pre-Christian past.

❶ Land's End

**In 1998, a team of Russian researchers
from the Institute of Metahistory in
Moscow claimed that they had discovered**
the lost city of Atlantis 100 miles off the coast of
Land's End. This drowned city lay on Little Sole
Bank, a rise of land out in the Atlantic Ocean on
the edge of the Celtic Shelf. The researchers at
the institute had studied ancient texts, in which
the Greek philosopher Plato claimed that Atlantis
lay beyond the Pillars of Hercules – today's straits
of Gibraltar. The team also considered the myths
of the sunken land of Lyonesse, said to have
stretched from Land's End to the Isles of Scilly
and been submerged in a mighty flood at the
time of King Arthur.

   Cornwall has a rich body of tales in which
church bells are said to ring below the waters and
for centuries Cornish fishermen have reported
glimpsing spires and castles beneath the waves. The
Isles of Scilly are thought to be the old Lyonesse
mountain tops; the last time the land was exposed
was during the last Ice Age around 20,000 years ago.
▶ *9 miles SW of Penzance on A30.*

❷ St Buryan

**The 14th-century church, despite its granite
dourness, provides a moment of humour. In
folklore, lawyers are generally portrayed** as
dishonest. A churchyard epitaph mentions two
exceptions: 'Here lie John and Richard Benn Two
lawyers and two honest men. God works miracles
now and then.'

   The circular graveyard is a relic of the original
church, said to have been founded in the 6th
century by the Irish saint, Buriana, who died
– according to legend – during a kidnap attempt
by a local Cornish king and was buried on the
site. Today's church has a ring of six bells, which is
reputed to have the heaviest peel in the world.
▶ *On B3283 S of A30, 4 miles SW of Penzance.*

❸ Mousehole

**In 1595, a fleet of Spanish ships appeared
and burnt the village of Mousehole to the
ground.** Only the Keigwin Arms, now a private
house, survived. Near the quay is a stone called
Merlin's Rock, and the Spanish attack was
regarded locally as the fulfilment of a prophecy
by the wizard. An old saying of the district, is:
'There shall land on the Rock of Merlin Those
who shall burn Paul, Penzance and Newlyn.'

   Merlin's other prophecies have still to be
fulfilled. He said, for instance, that: 'When the
Rame Head and Dodman meet, Man and woman
will have cause to greet (cry).' The two headlands
remain 40 miles apart.

   Mousehole is also famous for its celebrations
on Tom Bawcock's Eve, which take place on
December 23. Tom Bawcock was a legendary
fisherman and widower who lived in the village
during a time of terrible famine several centuries
ago. Old and with little to lose, Tom braved
terrible storms with his faithful cat to bring back
a mighty catch for the starving villagers. The
celebrations of this heroic event include a lantern
procession, followed by a supper of stargazey pie
– a dish of potatoes, eggs and pilchards, their
heads poking out of the top, gazing at the stars.
All of Mousehole harbour is illuminated with
lights installed for the celebrations.
▶ *On minor roads off B3315, 3 miles S of Penzance.*

❹ Penzance

**The Montol festival is held every year in
Penzance on the winter solstice, December
21, which is known as 'Montol' in Cornish.**
This date is traditionally believed to be King
Arthur's birthday, and the celebrations include
Cornish carols and Mummers' plays. There are
also guise dancers – 'disguised' in traditional
costumes – who parade through the town by
torchlight. A beacon burns at Lescudjack Castle,
and the festivities culminate in the lighting of the
Mock, or Cornish Yule Log, in the town centre.
They are overseen by the Penzance Obby Oss,
a creature that goes by the name of Penglaz.

   The Obby Oss is also present at Golowan
(Cornish for the Feast of St John), a ten-day
midsummer festival culminating in Mazey Day, a
costumed celebration of dance and arts that takes
place on the Saturday closest to midsummer.
Golowan is one of the last survivors of the old
midsummer fire festivals of the southwest, and
until the 1890s burning tar barrels were carried
through the streets and fires set on hilltops.
▶ *On A30, 20 miles SW of Redruth and 15 miles
W of Helston.*

⑤ Madron

The granite Men-an-Tol, or stone-and-hole, lies to the northwest of Madron, near Penzance. Originally forming the entrance to a chambered tomb, the stone was thought to possess curative powers. Even in the 20th century, it was customary for young children to be passed naked through the hole nine times as a cure for scrofula, rickets and other diseases. Pregnancy was guaranteed to married women who wriggled through backwards at full moon. It was also believed that the stone would answer questions, by means of two brass pins laid across each other near its edge. The pins would pivot of their own accord, although folklore leaves interpretation of the pins' movement open to the observer.

The stone's original purpose is unknown, but holed stones are not uncommon in the region. Another, the Tolven, can be seen in a garden near Helston.

▶ *On minor roads off A30 and A3071, 1 mile N of Penzance.*

⑥ St Michael's Mount

The Cornish name for St Michael's Mount is 'Carrick luz en cuz', which means 'the ancient rock in the wood'. At low tide, it is possible to glimpse the fossilised remains of a forest that once covered the coastal area. Its current name dates from early Christian times, when, according to legend, St Michael himself appeared to a group of fishermen on the Mount.

In 1044, Edward the Confessor founded a chapel on the Mount; later, the Normans built a fortress there, which exists today as a magnificent castle. Within its walls is a rough-cut stone seat known as Michael's Chair. St Keyne, on a pilgrimage to the Mount, is said to have endowed the seat with the same power that she gave to her holy well at St Keyne (page 20) – the first of a married couple to drink from the well (or sit on the seat) will dominate the partnership for life.

▶ *St Michael's Mount is off Marazion, S of A394, 4 miles E of Penzance. Reached on foot via causeway at low tide or ferry (summer only) at high tide.*

THE MAGICAL RING HAS CURATIVE POWERS
MEN-AN-TOL, MADRON

❼ Longrock

The Cornish 'Carrek Hyr', or Long Rock, is a small village situated between Penzance and Marazion. In February 1990, a sperm whale was stranded on the beach there and died. Its stomach was later found to contain the beaks of 47 giant squid – a carnivorous mollusc that can grow to the size of a bus. These squid are creatures of legend, depicted as attacking ships and dragging them under the waves. Sightings are rare – only about 250 have ever been recorded, and most of these creatures were found dead.
▶ *On A30, 3 miles E of Penzance.*

❽ St Ives

Every fifth year on July 25, a fiddler and his entourage fulfil the terms of John Knill's will. Knill, mayor of the town in 1767, requested that ten small girls in white should dance through the streets to his hilltop mausoleum on the feast of St James the Apostle; here, at the three-sided granite obelisk, the mayor and two widows were to join them and dance round the monument, after which the spectators were to sing the hundredth psalm.

Another tradition, Hurling the Silver Ball, usually takes place in February, on the Monday of Candlemas week. The mayor starts it off at 10.30am, and the ball is passed from hand to hand along the streets and the beach until noon, when the holder receives a small cash prize.
▶ *At junction of A3074 and B3306, 9 miles NE of Penzance.*

ST IVES

❾ Zennor

The beautiful 12th-century church of St Senara in Zennor has a 600-year-old carved bench end that features a mermaid holding a comb and a mirror. The carving evokes a local legend that involved a chorister of the local church called Matthew Trewella, the squire's son. He sang so beautifully that his voice attracted a mermaid from the sea. Using all her charms, she lured him back to her deep domain, from which he never returned. His voice, legend says, can still be heard from beneath the waves.

Outside the local Wayside Museum is the Plague Stone, which marks the boundary beyond which villagers could not go during the Black Death in the 14th century. The hollow in the top of the stone was filled with vinegar, which was used to steep coins thought to be contaminated by the plague.

Zennor Quoit, a Neolithic burial chamber, lies a mile from the village on Amalveor Downs. The huge capstone has fallen, but the chamber is still clearly visible, surrounded by seven uprights. The entire chamber was once covered by a cairn, and was reported by early investigators to have held cremated bones, pottery and flint.
▶ *On B3306, 4 miles W of St Ives. Zennor Quoit 1 mile SE of Zennor, access by footpaths off B3306.*

❿ Helston

According to one legend, the Devil was flying across Cornwall carrying a boulder to block the entrance to Hell, when he was challenged by St Michael. In the ensuing battle, the Devil dropped the rock, and the place where it fell became known as Hell's Stone or Helston. It is said that a large rock built into the wall of the Angel Hotel in Coinagehall Street is this very stone. To celebrate St Michael's victory over the Devil, the inhabitants danced through the streets and thereby originated the famous Furry Dance, which still takes place on the nearest Saturday to the feast day of the town's patron saint, St Michael the Archangel (May 8). The name of the dance is possibly derived either from the Middle English word 'ferrie', implying a church festival, or the Celtic 'feur' meaning a holiday or fair. However, its seasonal setting suggests the dance may once have been a pagan spring festival.

The ceremony that precedes the Furry Dance is probably more significant than the dance itself. It is a true relic of ancient May games, designed to greet the summer with song and drama, the aim being to induce crop fertility. Known as the Hal-an-Tow, this mumming play features the older children. Garlanded and carrying branches of sycamore, they sing an ancient song, part of the chorus of which runs:

Welcome is the Summer, the Summer and the May-O,
For Summer is a-come-O, and Winter is a-gone-O.

▶ *15 miles E of Penzance on A394.*

⑪ Penhale Sands

Penhale Sands is one of the largest areas of sand dune in Britain. This wonderful natural habitat hides a secret – a religious centre once thrived here, but was engulfed by Atlantic-blown sands in the 18th century. Legend recalls the beautiful town of Langarroc, made rich by mining, but buried by sand as God's punishment for its moral decline.

About 100 years ago, a small 7th-century oratory was discovered beneath the sands at nearby Perranzabuloe, and restored. This name in old Cornish means 'the church of St Piran in the sands', and the oratory is believed to mark the spot where St Piran landed from Ireland.

▶ *Penhale Sands are N of Perranporth on B3285, off A3075.*

⑫ St Keverne

The harvest custom of Crying the Neck, which is associated with the ancient belief that the corn-spirit is embodied in the last-cut wheatsheaf, has been revived in this village. On the last day of harvest at the end of September, as the reaper cuts the final swathe, the workers divide into three groups. The first group calls three times: 'We have it!' The second replies: 'What have 'ee?' – again three times – and the third group answers: 'A neck!' – also three times. The 'neck' or wheatsheaf is then carried to the farmhouse, where it is plaited and suspended above the fireplace until spring, when it is ploughed into the ground.

▶ *At end of B3293 off A3083, 10 miles SE of Helston.*

⑬ Falmouth

Morgawr – Cornish for sea giant – is the name given to the monster of Falmouth Bay. This modern legend was first sighted in 1876, when fishermen out in their boat caught something strange in their net. Then a peculiar creature became tangled in fishing nets in 1926, and again in 1975 near Pendennis Point, where it was described by offshore fishermen as a hump-backed creature with horns and with bristles down its back. Several witnesses have since succeeded in photographing the creature, their blurry images evoking a lumpy Loch Ness monster. In 1999, Morgawr was caught on video by John Holmes, who had formerly worked at London's Natural History Museum.

▶ *At end of A39, 12 miles S of Truro.*

⑭ Penryn

A legend tells that, after years at sea, a young sailor of Penryn went back to his parents' inn. In order to surprise them even more on his return, he decided to play a joke on the old people, and arrive in disguise. He went first to see his sister, who lived in another street, and told her of the ruse. However, his plan to celebrate a joyful homecoming backfired, because his parents, seeing only a rich stranger, succumbed to temptation and murdered the young man. The full horror of the parents' situation was revealed next morning when their daughter came in search of her brother. Overcome with remorse, both parents committed suicide and their daughter died soon after. This sad story was turned into a successful play called 'The Penryn Tragedy' in the 18th century.

▶ *Off A39, 10 miles S of Truro and 3 miles N of Falmouth.*

⑮ Chapel Carn Brea

The Midsummer Bonfire ceremony, performed on June 23, was a pagan festival centuries before it was hallowed by the Church to celebrate the Eve of St John. The first fire, kindled at Chapel Carn Brea near Land's End, said to be the most westerly hill in England, is the signal for other fires to be lit through Madron, Sennen, Sancreed Beacon, Carn Galver and St Agnes Beacon to Kit Hill in Callington and the Tamar. Each fire is blessed by a local clergyman in the Cornish language, and herbs and wild flowers are burnt. Once, when only embers remained, young people leapt across them to drive away evil and bring good luck.

It is thought that the fires were originally lit to worship the sun; another theory is that the flames were supposed to ward off witchcraft. At St Cleer the fire is still crowned with a broomstick, and a sickle with a newly cut oak handle is thrown into the flames to ensure fertility, both of crops and humans. Since the 1920s, the lighting of the fires has been organised by the Old Cornwall Society.

▶ *Close to junction of A30 and B3306, 3 miles NE of Land's End.*

16 Truro

An ancient Christmas season custom still survives. The Truro Wassailers circulate the city at New Year, drinking beer or cider from a gaily decorated bowl, and collecting money for charity. The Old English word wassail means 'be of good cheer', although the original ceremony was designed to drive off evil spirits.

Less happy is the story of Comprigney, a field outside the town. Reports of spectres and rattling chains are a grim reminder of the site's history – in Cornish, 'Gwel Cloghprenyer' means 'the field of the gibbet'.

▶ *At junction of A39 and A390, 16 miles SW of St Austell.*

17 Castle Dore

An old weathered needle of stone known as the Tristan stone stands beside the road to Fowey. It was once part of a cross, and is inscribed with the words 'Drustans hic iacet Cunomori filius', or 'Drustanus lies here, the son of Cunomorus'. It is believed that this is the grave of Tristan (Drustanus), who was actually the nephew of Mark (Cunomorus), an unpopular, some say wicked, 6th-century ruler of Cornwall. Tristan's story is a tragic tale of love.

Mark sent Tristan to seek out a bride on his behalf. He wanted the owner of a golden hair that had fallen from the beak of a dove for his queen. Tristan embarked for Ireland on his quest, and discovered that the hair belonged to Iseult the fair, the king's daughter, who had been promised in marriage to Tristan himself many years before. Despite their strong affection for one another, the young prince and princess knew that it was their duty to obey the king of Cornwall, and they began their sea voyage back, so that Mark could claim his bride. On board ship, Tristan and Iseult drank a love potion made for Iseult and the king. Now their love was deeper than ever, but still Iseult remained dutiful and married Mark.

Years passed. Tristan married in a kingdom across the sea, but when he was wounded in battle, he sent for his true love, Iseult. The returning ship was to bear a white sail if Iseult was aboard and a black sail if she had failed to come. When the ship was spied approaching port, the white sail was billowing, but Tristan's wife, jealous of his old love, reported that the sail was black. On hearing the news, Tristan died, and when Iseult came ashore, she died, too, of a broken heart.

▶ *Close to B3269, 1 mile E of village of Tywardreath. 3 miles E of St Austell.*

18 Veryan

The pretty parish of Veryan on the Roseland peninsula contains five strange thatched cottages. Each one is entirely circular, with a pointed roof surmounted by a cross. They were built in the early 19th century by the Reverend Jeremiah Trist who, it was said, believed that their shape would prevent the Devil from hiding in any corners. The Reverend had married a girl from Tregamenna. They had five daughters and one story is that he built a house for each of them.

About a mile from the village, on the St Mawes road, Melinsey Mill, an old water mill once used for corn, has been restored and turned into a museum and traditional craft centre.

Also about a mile from Veryan, overlooking Gerrans Bay to the south, stands Carne Beacon, a Bronze Age burial mound. Legend relates that the body of Gerennius, a 5th-century king of Cornwall, was rowed across the bay in a golden boat with silver oars, and buried in full regalia under the mound. Excavations, however, have not proved the theory.

Gerrans Bay and Veryan Bay were notorious hazards for any sailing vessels heading for Falmouth and both have had their fair share of shipwrecks. In 1914, a German boat, *Hera*, came to grief off Nare Head and quickly sank. Just a mast remained above the waves and five survivors managed to cling on until they were rescued some hours later. The bodies of 12 of the crew were recovered and lie buried together in a single grave in Veryan's parish churchyard.

▶ *On minor roads off A3078, 7 miles NE of St Mawes.*

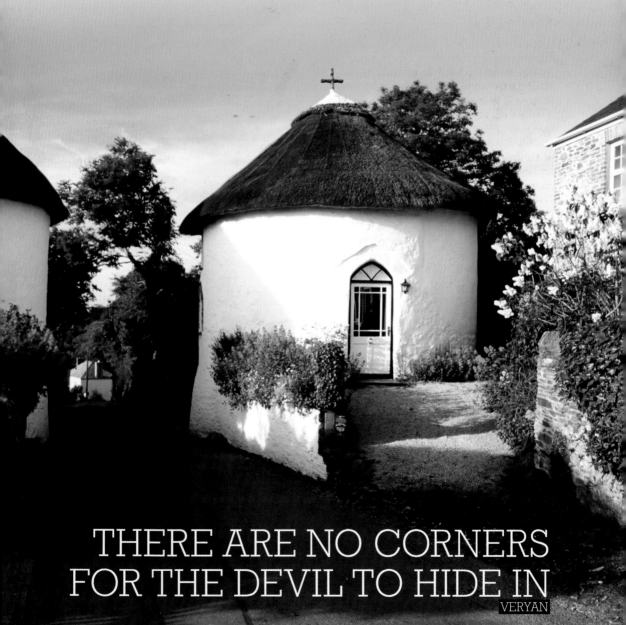

THERE ARE NO CORNERS FOR THE DEVIL TO HIDE IN
VERYAN

⓳ St Germans

The old church in St Germans was said to contain a chair on which a carving depicted the story of Dando, a dissolute 14th-century priest from the priory near by. One Sunday, Dando forsook his devotions and went hunting with his wild friends. After a successful chase, he called for a drink. A stranger riding a fiery black horse came forward and offered him a richly carved drinking horn. Having quenched his thirst, Dando saw the stranger stealing his game, and despite the priest's curses, the stranger refused to return it. In a drunken frenzy, Dando rushed at him and cried, 'I'll go to Hell after them, but I'll get them from thee.' 'So thou shalt,' replied the stranger and, tossing Dando across his horse, he galloped off, hotly pursued by the hounds and Dando's hunting companions. On reaching the River Lynher, the horse never hesitated, and while Dando's horrified friends watched, horse, riders and dogs all disappeared amid flames and a hiss of steam.

▶ *On B3249 2 miles S of junction with A38, 7 miles SE of Liskeard.*

⓴ St Keyne

Some time during the 5th century, St Keyne – one of 15 daughters of a Welsh king – settled here. Water from her well is said to bestow supremacy in a marriage upon the first partner to drink from it. Eighteenth-century poet laureate Robert Southey recalled this in his ballad 'The Well of St Keyne'. The last verse reads:

I hastened as soon as the wedding was done,
And left my wife in the porch;
But i' faith she had been wiser than me,
For she took a bottle to church.

▶ *3 miles S of Liskeard on B3254.*

㉑ St Neot

This pretty village on the edge of Bodmin Moor takes its name from a saint, said to be just 38cm (15in) tall. St Neot found fame with his miracles involving animals. One day an angel appeared and gave Neot three fishes for his well, saying that so long as he ate only one a day, their number would never decrease. When Neot was sick, however, his servant took two of the fish and cooked them. Horrified, the saint prayed over the dead fish, and ordered them to be returned to the well. As they touched the water, they completely revived.

Another story tells of a hunted doe that, totally exhausted, ran to Neot's side. The saint's stern look turned the hounds back to the forest, while the huntsman dropped his bow and became the saint's faithful disciple. A holy well lies a short distance from St Neot's church beside the river Loveny.

▶ *5 miles NW of Liskeard, on minor roads 2 miles N from A38.*

THE GIANTS OF CORNWALL

THE BRITISH CHRONICLER Geoffrey of Monmouth, writing in 1136, describes how Brutus and the Trojans, after many years of wandering following the fall of Troy, finally landed at Totnes in Devon. Britain 'was uninhabited except for a few giants'. Brutus divided the country among his followers, and Corineus was given Cornwall, the land that still bears his name. Corineus 'experienced great pleasure in wrestling with the giants of whom there were far more there than in any other district'.

Cornwall retains what is said to be evidence of these huge people in such ancient rock formations as the Giant's Cradle on Trencrom (or Trecobben) Hill – a legendary fortress to which the giants dragged their victims before murdering them. Lamorna has a mythical Giant's Cave and there is a Giant's Chair 3 miles southeast of Land's End.

One of the best-known stories tells of a giant named Cormoran and his wife Cormelian. They lived in the thick forest that once covered Mount's Bay between Penzance and Marazion. Cormoran resolved to build himself a mighty fortified tower, and set his wife the task of gathering the white granite in her apron. One day when her husband was sleeping, Cormelian gathered greenstone instead, which was closer than the granite and easier to carry. Cormoran awoke, saw her and gave her a kick that caused her apron strings to break. A block of greenstone is still visible on the causeway to St Michael's Mount, the legendary site of Cormoran's fortress.

Cormoran's reign of terror was not to last. One night, a young Cornishman named Jack crept up to the Mount and dug a huge pit, which he covered with twigs and straw. Then he blew his hunting horn, waking the giant who blundered into the pit. Jack struck off the giant's head with an axe, a feat that earned him a magnificent sword, and a belt embroidered with gold.

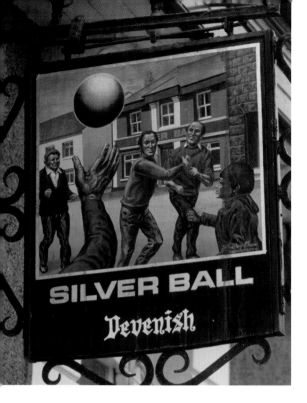

㉒ St Columb Major

Hurling the Silver Ball is a game played annually here each February, on Shrove Tuesday. The ancient sport resembles football, but its rules are vague. Two teams are formed. Any number can participate and the goals are 2 miles apart. Before the game is started, the ball, made of apple wood and coated with silver, is passed from hand to hand, to bring luck to all who touch it. The silver ball is believed to embody a relic of long-forgotten sun-worship.

▶ *On A39, 9 miles SW of Wadebridge.*

㉓ Rillaton

The Bronze Age round barrow of Rillaton on Bodmin Moor was opened in 1837, revealing a skeleton accompanied by grave goods, which included a bronze dagger, a cup of corrugated sheet gold, a decorated pot, pieces of ivory and glass beads. Local legend tells of the ghost of a druid priest who would waylay any passer-by and offer him a magic potion from a golden cup that could never be drained. The legend is thought to be a work of Victorian fancy, invented after the discovery of the treasures, although the cup itself became the subject of a real mystery when it went missing shortly after its discovery. The finds had been sent as Duchy Treasure Trove to William IV (1831-7) shortly before his death, after which they could no longer be located. A century later, on the death of King George V in 1936, the cup was rediscovered

in his dressing room, being used as a receptacle for cufflinks. Today, the cup is kept in the British Museum, and the county museum in Truro has an exact copy.

▶ *On minor roads between B3254 and B3257, 7 miles NE of Liskeard*

㉔ Bodmin

The old Cornish town of Bodmin was mainly an ecclesiastical settlement until the Dissolution of the Monasteries by Henry VIII in the mid 1500s. The original monastery, a few traces of which remain, was founded in the 6th century by St Petroc, a Celtic missionary from Wales. In the crypt of St Petroc's Church lies an ivory casket thought to have contained the saint's bones. During the reign of Henry II, these were stolen by a Breton priest and taken to St Meen Abbey in Brittany. Henry, who was overlord of Brittany, forced the Bretons to return the casket and its contents to Bodmin. The bones are thought to have been removed from the casket and buried during the Reformation.

A stone well house dedicated to St Guron, a holy man who lived around AD 500, stands in the churchyard. Water from the same source flows from two 16th-century gargoyles beside the church steps. Until recent times, the well was the source of the town's main water supply.

Bodmin has a number of other holy wells, including Bree Shute Well near the town centre, which is also known as the Eye Well for its curative properties. Scarletts Well was famed for its iridescent water and wonderful healing powers.

▶ *Just W of A30, 7 miles SE of Wadebridge and 13 miles W of Liskeard.*

㉕ Egloshayle

The village had the finest bell-ringers in the county in the early 19th century, when bell-ringing competitions were held between rival villages. The team is still remembered in a local song 'The Ringers of Egloshayle', a verse of which runs:

> There's Craddock the cordwainer first who rings the treble bell,
> The second is John Ellery who none could ever excel,
> The third is Pollard, carpenter, the fourth is Thomas Cleave,
> And Goodfellow the tenor-man who rings 'em round so brave.

The bodies of all five ringers lie in Egloshayle churchyard, their epitaphs carved in stone.

▶ *Just S of Wadebridge on A389 towards Bodmin.*

SOUTHWEST ENGLAND

㉖ Padstow

The town is famous for the colourful 'Obby Oss' ceremony, the origins of which are lost in antiquity. It commences at midnight on the first day of May, when the townspeople walk through the streets singing the Morning Song, which lasts until about 2 o'clock on May morning. After a few hours, they are out again, collecting greenery to decorate the town, and flowers for the maypole in the square.

The climax arrives when the Oss – represented by a man in a black frame-hung cape and gruesome mask – emerges from its stable. The Day Song is then struck up as the Oss prances through the narrow lanes, bowing and leaping before his 'teasers' or attendants, and trying to catch young girls beneath his cape. Finally, at midnight, the Oss dies and the crowd sings its farewell – until the Oss is resurrected the following May Day. The ceremony is believed to be based on a pre-Christian spring fertility rite with the dying Oss representing the passing of the old year.

The village was originally named Petroc-stow after Welsh missionary St Petroc, who landed at nearby Trebetherick around AD 500. Petroc arrived during a hot summer, and made many converts to Christianity by striking a rock with his staff and producing a stream of cool water.

▶ *On Camel estuary at junction of A389 and B3276, 8 miles W of Wadebridge.*

PADSTOW OBBY OSS

㉗ St Teath

The village of St Teath was the birthplace of Anne Jeffries, a maidservant who became embroiled in one of the most famous – and strangest – witch trials of the 17th century. In 1645, when Anne was 19 years old, she entered the service of a Mr Moses Pitt. One day, while sitting in her employer's garden, she encountered a group of tiny men, whom she befriended. When one of them touched her eyes she found herself flying through space until she came to a beautiful country. When she returned to the garden, she found herself surrounded by anxious members of the household, who thought she had fallen into a fit.

This was the first of many meetings Anne was to have with the 'airy people'. They taught her the arts of healing and herbal lore, which she practised on members of the household and villagers. Understandably, she was accused of witchcraft, and committed to Bodmin gaol by the notoriously cruel Jan Tregeagle, then the local magistrate. While in prison Anne neither ate nor drank the food and water offered to her, claiming that the little people fed her with morsels they bought her themselves. Eventually she was released for lack of evidence. Records of the trial and letters from Moses Pitt to the Bishop of Gloucester, describing her experiences, are in the Bodleian Library at Oxford.

▶ *Just W of A39, 7 miles NE of Wadebridge.*

㉘ Tintagel

Spectacular Tintagel Castle, perched high on precipitous cliffs above the Atlantic coastline, is suffused with myth. The island, joined to the mainland by a narrow rocky pass, is the legendary birthplace of King Arthur. It was here that King Uther Pendragon deceived the beautiful Igerna, wife of Gorlois, Earl of Cornwall. The king, with magical assistance from his wizard Merlin, disguised himself as Igerna's husband. Entering the fortress in this guise, he seduced Igerna, who later gave birth to the boy who became King Arthur.

The castle was, in fact, built by Reginald of Cornwall, the illegitimate son of Henry I, in 1141 – long after the historical Arthur lived. At one time it belonged to Edward, Prince of Wales, otherwise known as the Black Prince after his distinctive black armour. By the mid 16th century it had fallen into disrepair. The cavern below the castle is known as Merlin's Cave, and

the wizard's ghost is said to wander in its echoing recesses. According to another local story, Arthur himself is reincarnated in the form of the rare Cornish chough, a bird that may sometimes be seen perched on the wave-lashed cliff ledges.

▶ *Off B3263 4 miles SW of Boscastle.*

㉙ Boscastle

A small museum by the harbour contains the world's largest collection of artefacts related to witchcraft in the world. Inside is a huge collection of spells and charms, many purchased by the museum's founder, Cecil Williamson, from practitioners across Britain in the early 20th century. They include mole's feet for cramp, stolen meat for warts and knotted lengths of rope, sold by witches to sailors. The ropes were said to contain the wind – when the sailors needed the wind for their sails, they untied a knot – one for a breeze, two for a strong wind and three for a tempest. There are wands and cauldrons, curse dolls and witch mirrors, plus important European acquisitions. The museum is open to the public, but check times first. The extensive library of occult works may be visited by appointment.

▶ *W of A39 at junction of B3263 and B3266. 15 miles N of Wadebridge.*

㉚ St Nectan's Glen

This beautiful rocky glen conceals a waterfall that cascades 12m (40ft) into a rock basin known locally as the Kieve. The 5th century holy man St Nectan, on his deathbed, threw his silver chapel bell into this torrent. In an instant it vanished into the rock bed, and the saint declared that it would reappear only when true religion had been restored to what was, at the time, a dissident Church.

After his death the saint's body was placed in a chest, along with the sacramental plate, and the chest was hidden in the Kieve. Hundreds of years later, according to local stories, miners tried to blast their way through the Kieve in order to recover the tresure. Their efforts led to nothing, and after much toil the miners were unsettled by the sound of a bell. This eerie tinkling was followed by a whispering, that became louder, until they could hear the words: 'The child is not yet born who shall recover this treasure.' The miners fled the Kieve in terror. The prophecy of the Glen has never been fulfilled.

▶ *Inland from B3263, 2 miles NE of Tintagel.*

SOUTHWEST ENGLAND

㉛ The Cheesewring

This natural pile of granite slabs takes its name from its similarity to a cheese-press. It is associated with Daniel Gumb, a local stonecutter, whose work can still be seen in Linkinhorne churchyard. Daniel was of unusually high intelligence and, although his parents were uneducated, he taught himself mathematics, became deeply interested in astronomy and was an avid reader. He and his wife, a local girl, set up home in a cave beneath the Cheesewring, where they raised numerous children, baptising them on prehistoric altars nearby. Until the cave collapsed, many of Gumb's intricate geometrical designs could be seen carved in the granite, with the inscription 'D. Gumb 1735' cut above the cave entrance.

▶ *On minor roads off B3254, 6 miles N of Liskeard.*

㉜ Altarnun

The name Altarnun derives from 'altar of St Non'. Both the 15th-century church – known as the cathedral of the moor – and the holy well nearby are dedicated to St Non. Non was a princess born in AD 475 who took holy orders, but she was cruelly seduced by Prince Sandde of Ceredigion and had a son, who later became St David of Wales. The waters of the well were once used to cure madness. Lunatics would be dipped in the pool by the well and then carried to the church for masses to be said. When they regained their wits, prayers would be offered to the saint. The Cornish cross at the churchyard entrance is believed to date from the 6th century, the time of St Non.

▶ *1 mile off A30, 9 miles SW of Launceston.*

THE GRANITE SLABS RESEMBLE A CHEESE PRESS
THE CHEESEWRING

㉝ Stratton

In this small village near Bude was born a real Cornish giant. During the Civil War, the 2.2m (7ft 6in) Anthony Payne was enlisted as bodyguard to the Royalist Sir Bevil Grenville. He fought beside Sir Bevil, who commanded the king's army, at Stamford Hill, and later at the battle of Lansdown Hill, near Bath. Here, Sir Bevil was killed, but at once Payne set up the general's 16-year-old son beside the standard, crying out 'A Grenville still leads you!' to the Cornishmen around him. The men rallied and the fight was a Royalist victory; afterwards Payne sorrowfully carried his master's dead body home to Stratton.

Payne lived and died in the Grenville's manor house at Stratton – now the Tree Inn – where an inscription on the wall tells of the great victory at nearby Stamford Hill. It is said that when the giant died, the house had to be re-structured to allow his huge coffin to be carried in and out. His body lies in the local churchyard where an inscribed tombstone marks his final resting place.
▶ *On A39, 1 mile NE of Bude.*

㉞ Morwenstow

David 'Cruel' Coppinger was a Dane who is said to have settled near Morwenstow in the 18th century, and whose exploits became the stuff of local legend. Most accounts tell how he landed on the Cornish coast during a terrible storm. Unable to make safe haven, the captain, Coppinger, dived into the mountainous seas. Fighting his way through the waves, he finally reached the shore. He leapt on to a horse ridden by a young woman, Dinah Hamlyn, who had come to the beach to see the stormbound ship. Turning the double-laden horse, he urged it away at full speed, and forced it homeward. Coppinger installed himself at Dinah's home and, on her father's death a year later, married the girl.

His criminal career now began. The house became the headquarters of a gang of smugglers – with Coppinger as their ruthless captain. No authority dared take action, since he was merciless in his treatment of anyone who offended him. So Coppinger pursued his vicious way of life with no check or restraint. He assumed control over some of the local roads and issued orders that no one should use them by night. These roads, still known as 'Coppinger's Tracks', converged on the 90m (300ft) headland of Steeple Brink. Below this cliff, in a practically inaccessible cove, the gang stored their contraband and caroused at night.

Coppinger's domestic life was no less evil and he treated his wife with appalling cruelty. When she bore him a deaf-mute son, people said the child had been born without a soul.

Eventually, the revenue men concentrated their forces in a final effort to destroy the gang. Many of the gang were killed, and the treasures of the cave were captured. Coppinger realised his days were numbered. Again a strange vessel appeared off Harty Race. It lowered a boat and the crew rowed through the boiling surf to where Coppinger stood cursing, and waving his cutlass. As the boat grounded, he leapt aboard and took command. The boat fought its way back through the raging seas and Coppinger and his crew flung themselves aboard the parent ship. In an instant the vessel vanished into the flying spray and Cruel Coppinger was never seen again.
▶ *On minor roads 4 miles W of A39. 6 miles N of Bude.*

㉟ Scilly Isles: Tresco

The sub-tropical isle of Tresco in the Scilly Isles is the mythical haunt of mermaids, particularly around Piper's Hole, a cave on the northern coast with a freshwater pool. This cave is believed to have a legendary passage to the adjacent island of St Mary's; apparent proof of this was provided when a Tresco dog emerged from a cave on St Mary's.

One story says that during the Civil War (1642-51), when the Royalists held the Isles, a Roundhead avoided capture by hiding in Piper's Hole. He was discovered by a Cavalier's daughter who fell in love with him and arranged his escape to the mainland. After the war he returned to marry her.
▶ *The Isles of Scilly lie 30 miles off Land's End. Access Tresco by boat from St Mary's or by helicopter from Penzance.*

DEVON

Historic county fairs offer spectacle and entertainment from late summer, while outside the towns, Devon's rocky shores and ancient stones hold fast to old legends.

❶ Hartland Point

This promontory was once called the Headland of Hercules. There is a legend that Hercules landed there, fought the British giants, and for some years successfully governed the whole country. During the 6th century, a Welsh hermit named St Nectan settled there. On St Nectan's Day (June 17), mass is still celebrated beside his holy well, after which the local children march in procession carrying foxgloves, the saint's special flower. It is said that after being decapitated by robbers, the saint picked up his head, carried it to a particular spot and set it on the ground, whereupon water sprang forth. Wherever the saint's blood fell, foxgloves sprang up.

▶ *6 miles W of Clovelly via minor roads off A39.*

❷ Braunton

The original church, and the hillside chapel, were both founded by St Brannoc, a 6th-century missionary who was said to have sailed from Wales in a stone coffin. Some of his many miracles, mostly concerned with animals, are depicted in carvings in the church where the holy man is also buried. St Brannoc taught the local people how to till the soil, and used wild deer to pull his plough. On one occasion, someone stole his cow, and killed, dismembered and cooked it. However, at the saint's call, the cow emerged from the pot, reassembled itself, and continued to supply him with milk for many years afterwards.

▶ *8 miles W of Barnstaple on A361.*

❸ Combe Martin

The celebration of the Hunting of the Earl of Rone is a traditional Combe Martin festival that takes place over the Spring Bank Holiday. It was revived in 1974, having been banned as a result of the drunken and licentious behaviour of the revellers in 1837. During the weekend the villagers, together with the Hobby Horse, Fool and Grenadiers, hunt the Earl, who sits back to front on a donkey and rides through the village and on to the shore, during which time he is shot, revived and shot again, until he is finally thrown into the sea.

The real earl was, according to legend, a man called Hugh O'Neill, Earl of Tyrone, who fled to England from Ireland in 1607 and was shipwrecked locally. He survived for a while in the woods, before being captured by Grenadiers. Historians have found no proof in the legend, for apparently the real O'Neill was washed up in Spain. It may be that the custom is a vestige of medieval games that were played locally, or a pre-Christian celebration of early summer.

Along the long and winding main street of the village, stands a most unusual inn, called the Pack o' Cards. The Ley family owned land in the area, and in 1690 George Ley, a relative of the first Earl of Marlborough, apparently decided to build himself a house after a big win at cards. It was built on four floors, had 13 rooms, 52 windows and 52 stairs, and the original building covered an area of 52 sq ft. It's not clear when the building was turned into an inn, but today it is a well-known and popular feature of the village.

▶ *4 miles E of Ilfracombe on A399.*

HERCULES
LANDED HERE AND
FOUGHT THE
BRITISH GIANTS
HARTLAND POINT

❹ Barnstaple

Barnstable fair, whose charter dates from the early Middle Ages, is held each year on the Wednesday before September 20. Once its main function was trading and the selling of livestock, but today it is primarily a funfair laid on by travelling showpeople. Its opening is heralded by a ceremony at the Guildhall, where spiced ale brewed from a closely guarded Elizabethan recipe is ladled into silver cups from which all present must drink success to the fair. A large white glove is hung from the Guildhall – an ancient symbol once used to show that outsiders could enter and trade freely within the town. A similar custom applies to the fair held at Honiton on the last Tuesday in July.
▶ *At junction of A39 and A361, 7 miles NE of Bideford.*

❺ Shebbear

The Devil is believed to lie trapped beneath a large boulder resting under an ancient oak in the village square. Every November 5, local bell-ringers use crowbars to lever the stone over before ringing a peal on the church bells. The ritual ensures that the Devil is kept down for the next 12 months. Another story says that the stone is the foundation stone of Henscott church across the River Torridge, but the Devil moved it.
▶ *On minor roads 8 miles NE of Holsworthy.*

❻ Chawleigh

The village Friendly Society, which was founded in 1870, is probably the last of its kind in the West Country. Friendly Societies were parish-based welfare schemes that sprang up throughout Britain at the beginning of the 19th century. Each had an annual 'walk' in which members marched through the parish, holding wands tipped with the society's badge cast in brass. Chawleigh still holds its 'Club Walk' on the first Saturday in June, headed by members carrying the Society's banner. The walk is followed by a church service, sports events and plenty of eating and drinking.
▶ *2 miles E of A377 on B3042, 15 miles SE of Barnstaple.*

❼ Bampton

Granted a Royal Charter by Henry III in 1258, Bampton Charter Fair is one of the oldest in the country. It was originally known as St Luke's Fair since the charter stipulated it was to be held on the 'vigil, day, and the morrow' of St Luke, October 18. Now the fair starts on the last Thursday of October. For centuries it was a trading post for sheep and cattle – and in the 19th century Exmoor ponies. The fair is still a showcase for livestock and bloodstock, plus local crafts, food producers and entertainers.
▶ *Just off A396, 6 miles N of Tiverton.*

DEVIL'S BOULDER, SHEBBEAR

8 Hatherleigh

The annual town carnival is held on the nearest Wednesday to November 5. Just before daybreak, burning tar barrels are drawn through the streets by 12 to 20 townsmen. The ceremony is repeated at nightfall, when there is also a torchlight procession. Although these activities are now linked with Guy Fawkes day, they may have evolved from the fires that were lit during the Celtic festival of Samhain (November 1).
▶ *At junction of A386 and A3072, 7 miles N of Okehampton.*

9 Widecombe in the Moor

Widecombe Fair – which still takes place on the second Tuesday in September – is famed the world over for the song that recounts the adventures of Uncle Tom Cobleigh, his friends and the unfortunate grey mare. The song was once widespread throughout the West Country, and was freely adapted to suit any locality and personalities.

Nevertheless, Uncle Tom Cobleigh was a real farmer from Spreyton in North Devon, 12 miles north of Widecombe. It is uncertain which Tom has been immortalised – there were several of that name in the family – but it was probably the one who died in 1794 and is buried in an unmarked grave in Spreyton churchyard. The Thomas Cobleigh whose tombstone is outside the south porch was his nephew.

Old 'Uncle Tom' was an amorous bachelor, and when he was young he had bright red hair. This characteristic seems to have been to his advantage, for when paternity orders came in thick and fast, he refused to maintain any babies that did not have red hair like he had.

Early in the 20th century, the novelist Beatrice Chase presented an 'Uncle Tom' smock to the organisers of the fair, and now Uncle Tom appears at the festivities every year, complete with his grey mare.
▶ *At end of B3387, 7 miles W of Bovey Tracey.*

10 Totnes

The Brutus Stone, is set into the pavement in Fore Street near the East Gate of Totnes. According to legend, Brutus, leader of the survivors of the Trojan garrison, sailed with his followers up the River Dart, stepped off his boat on to a rock and proclaimed:

'Here I am and here I rest,
And this town shall be called Totnes.'

The myth says that the country around was inhabited by giants, and having captured a pair named Gog and Magog, he took them to London where they stood guard outside his palace. The effigies of the two giants still stand in the Guildhall, replacements of earlier effigies destroyed by fire during the Second World War.
▶ *At junction of A385 and A381, 6 miles W of Paignton.*

11 Marldon

The Apple Pie Fair takes place at the beginning of August. It was founded in 1888, lapsed during the Second World War, and was revived in 1958. Quantities of small pies are baked and concealed under a vast imitation pie-crust, and the whole edifice is drawn by a donkey to the fairground where the pies are sold. The ceremony originates from the time when poor labourers supplemented the family diet with such perquisites as fallen fruit. At some unknown period the community decided, for economy, to make one huge pie in the village bakehouse and turned the occasion into a party.
▶ *Just W of A380, 2 miles W of Torquay.*

12 Kingsteignton

A whole ram is roasted and served at the Ram Roasting Fair that takes place on Spring Bank Holiday Monday. In the distant past, it is said, the stream that flows through the churchyard suddenly dried up. The waters reappeared when a ram was sacrificed, and the custom still continues.
▶ *1 mile N of Newton Abbot.*

13 Powderham

Since the Middle Ages, Powderham Castle has had within its possession a unicorn's horn that could apparently detect poison. When the horn was dipped into a poisoned drink, the liquor was said to change colour. In fact, the 'unicorn's horn' is the 2.7m (9ft) long tusk of a narwhal.

In the 18th century, the castle was owned by the Courtenay family, and, during renovations, the third viscount commissioned a floor covering from the newly formed Axminster Carpet Company. This was the largest carpet ever made, until the Prince Regent, hearing of it, promptly commissioned a larger one. The castle, gardens and deer park are open to the public.
▶ *Beside the Exe estuary off A379, 8 miles S of Exeter.*

Celebrating May

New life and new beginnings – this deep-rooted cause for celebration is well appreciated in the southwest.

The pagan fire festival of Beltane dates back to the Celtic culture that held sway in these islands long before the Romans invaded. The equivalent of May Day, Beltane represented the death of winter and the coming of spring. Cattle that had been penned all winter were prepared for the high pastures where they would spend summer. With garlands twined in their horns and round their necks, the beasts were symbolically purified by being driven between giant bonfires ignited by Druid priests. Then it was party time, with drinking, dancing and love-making. Sometimes there was a darker side. One individual might be selected as a ritual scapegoat, whom the participants would beat or pretend to throw into the fires. In some cases, the scapegoat had to bear a cursed name and undergo year-long humiliation until freed by the choosing of a new victim when Beltane came round once more.

Hot fires and hot blood

The optimism and joy of living engendered by the coming of spring found expression in the emergence from dull constriction and narrow routine into frolics and freedom all over Britain. This was nowhere more so than in the southwest, where a lively agricultural heritage mingled with strong Celtic ties of blood and tradition. Today, as well as the Padstow Obby Oss and the Helston Furry Dance, the region hosts several other highly flavoured May ceremonies, most of them the pride of seaside communities. At Abbotsbury on the west Dorset coast, garlands of flowers made by the children are paraded through the village; in Millbrook, Cornwall, a boat decorated with flowers is carried to the sea and launched into the waves. On the Somerset coast at Minehead, three separate Hobby Horses – more like brightly coloured ships, in fact – parade the streets for the three days of the May holiday, culminating in Bootie night, when victims are snatched out of the crowds, prostrated before the Horse and given a ritual pretend kicking. This ceremony has been recorded in Minehead for at least 500 years.

In a ritual at the end of May in the North Devon village of Combe Martin, farther west along the same coast, a sinister fugitive in a weird baggy suit and clown-painted mask, the 'Earl of Rone', is hunted by Grenadiers and a Fool for three days. Once captured in his traditional hiding place of Lady's Wood, the Earl is subjected to a backwards-facing donkey ride through the village during which he is shot off his steed, to be revived and restored by the Fool. Finally, the Grenadiers finish him off on the beach, and he is hurled into the sea.

Light and dark

Several common threads emerge from these present-day May ceremonies of the southwest. They all reinforce the notion of community – prescribed costumes carefully adhered to, everyone united in singing and dancing. Yet there is a notably dark strand to the rituals. Some involve partisanship and adherence to one group or another – the Horses of Minehead, for example. Others concentrate the united community on a single central figure, some of whom, such as the Padstow Obby Oss, look fierce but seem to be objects of love and reverence. Others undergo a ritualised humiliation, as the scapegoat did in the ancient Beltane ceremonies – the victims of Minehead's Bootie Night, for example, and the Earl of Rone. Ending up in the sea, that symbol of cleansing and renewal, is another common theme in this maritime part of the world – the Millbrook boat for one, and the Abbotsbury flower garlands used to be rowed out and thrown into the sea.

Some of the festivals have links, tenuous if not mythical, to historical events featuring the repelling of sea-borne foes – Minehead's Hobby Horse is said to commemorate a triumphant scaring of the Danes at sea by a fearsomely decorated ship, and there is a legend that the women of Padstow and their Oss did the same to would-be French invaders while the men were away fishing.

Lusty cavorting

Often the dancers and other attendants at these May festivals seem to act out a chase or hunt. The central figure is vigorous and fertile – the Obby Oss was known for whipping young ladies under his skirts, releasing them with blackened faces and reputations – but in the end the god becomes a victim, weakens, dies and is reborn. Although Beltane fires are rare these days, their vestigial presence comes in the form of fireworks.

Many of the traditional May ceremonies practised in the southwest fell into disuse over the years but were revived during the 20th century. Incomers were the catalyst in some places, locals in others. But whatever the reason, young children and teenagers are enthusiastically singing and capering again, maintaining the southwest's May traditions for the future.

HOBBY HORSE IN DUNSTER, SOMERSET

⑭ Ottery St Mary

On the evening of November 5 the roads are barred to traffic and flaming tar barrels are carried or rolled down the main street, guided by men whose hands are bound with protective sacking. Although now part of Guy Fawkes' commemorations, the event may have originated as an ancient fire festival. During the 19th century the party occasionally got so out of hand that police reinforcements had to be sent from Exeter; but despite all efforts, the authorities were unable to put an end to this popular tradition.
▶ *On B3177 2 miles off A30. 12 miles E of Exeter.*

⑮ Sidbury

The annual Court Leet and Court Baron – a form of manorial court – is traditionally held in Sidbury Manor on the third Wednesday of November. It elects manorial officers whose ancient responsibilities include ale-tasting, bread-weighing and meat-tasting.
▶ *On A375 6 miles S of Honiton.*

⑯ Southleigh

A local legend concerns the Hangman's Stone on the south side of the A3052, by the crossroads to Beer and Southleigh. The story goes that a sheep-stealer, carrying a heavy carcass on a rope over his shoulder, decided to rest in this quiet spot. Setting the dead sheep on the stone, he sat down with his back against the rock and fell asleep. As the thief slept, the carcass slipped off the stone and pulled the cord tight around his neck, strangling him to death.
▶ *Hangman's Stone at junction of A3052 and B3174, 9 miles W of Lyme Regis. Southleigh on minor road 2 miles N of junction.*

MEN HEAVE FLAMING TAR BARRELS DOWN THE STREET
OTTERY ST MARY

⑰ Uplyme

The Old Black Dog Guest House in Uplyme is named after a legendary black dog that once plagued the village. A farm worker living in a cottage became so sick of the phantom that one day, in desperation, he took a poker and chased the ghost into his attic where it leapt through the roof. Hitting at the thatch, the man found a hoard of Stuart coins, which helped to buy a house on the other side of the road. He converted the house into an inn and, in gratitude, named it 'The Black Dog'. The guest house stands on the site of the old inn, and the dog continues to haunt the neighbourhood, particularly Haye Lane (once called Dog Lane) behind the inn. In 1959 the spectre was seen by three holidaymakers simultaneously one evening. In January 2010 a man walking his dog reported being disturbed by an unusual shadow. His dog fled. He had previously been unaware of the legend.
▶ *On B3165 1 mile NW of Lyme Regis.*

⑱ Axminster

Newnham Abbey ruins of are associated with a strange story concerning its founder, Reginald de Mohun. As he lay dying in 1257, he reported his dream of a boy 'more radiant than the sun' who walked from the abbey font to its altar. De Mohun's followers saw the dream as evidence of his saintliness and his acceptance into the next world.

Seventy-five years later, when the paving over his grave was removed for repair, the workers found his body perfectly preserved and exuding a fragrant floral odour. Several medieval saints were reputedly distinguished by this 'odour of sanctity'. Such preservation is usually the result of perfect – if unintentionally created – environmental conditions, which can occur when well-made coffins seal the body from the effects of bacteria and water.
▶ *At junction of A35 and A358, 10 miles E of Honiton. Newnham Abbey is SW of the town centre.*

SOUTHWEST ENGLAND

DORSET

Rural customs and seafaring traditions still flourish in Dorset's villages and towns, altered and embellished down the ages. Old tales of a cursed field persist but an ancient stone pillar remains a mystery.

❶ Bettiscombe

The old manor in the hamlet of Bettiscombe – now a private house – is famous for a strange legend connected to a human skull. The skull is said to have been part of the contents of the manor since the 17th century, and is said to have belonged to a slave, who was buried against his dying wish in the local churchyard, rather than his native land. Upon his burial, terrible screams and moans were heard throughout the house, which only ceased when the body was disinterred and brought back into the manor. The house never regained its former peace, and it was whispered that if ever the skull was removed, a terrible fate would befall the occupants.

In the early 19th century, a tenant tried to rid the house of the skull by throwing it into a nearby pond. For days the house was shaken by screams and tremors, until the tenant was forced to retrieve the relic from the muddy depths.

Analysis has shown that the skull is about 2,000 years old, and is that of a woman in her twenties. It is believed to have come from Pilsdon Pen, a local hill on which an Iron Age settlement has been found.

▶ *9 miles NE of Axminster, close to junction of B3164 and B3165.*

❷ Abbotsbury

An ancient custom thought to be a survival of pagan sea-god worship is still observed in this old fishing village. On May 13, fishermen's families attach garlands of flowers to wooden frames and parade them round the streets. In days gone by, after a blessing on the beach, each boat carried its garland out to sea and cast it overboard. Now the flowers are placed on the war memorial as a tribute to the dead.

▶ *At N end of Chesil Beach on B3157, 8 miles NW of Weymouth.*

❸ Isle of Portland

Until the early part of the 20th century, buying and selling land on Portland was done by means of 'Church Gift'. The people involved in the transaction went to the church and made a verbal declaration of the transfer, which was considered legal and binding. Records of land ownership were kept by means of notches cut in a 'reed-pole', and each area had its own pole, kept in the church or pub. The distance between notches showed how much land each man owned.

▶ *6 miles S of Weymouth on A354.*

❹ Bincombe

The village of Bincombe lies just under the Ridgeway, and Bincombe Down was extensively settled during the Stone and Bronze Ages, evidence of which is provided by the many burial mounds – or barrows – in the district. Tradition insists that these hillocks, known locally as the Music Barrows, are actually the houses of the fairy-folk. It is said that if you put your ear to the top of one of them at midday, you will hear the sound of a fairy orchestra.

▶ *1 mile E of A354, 4 miles S of Dorchester.*

❺ Corfe Castle

On Shrove Tuesday, the Freemen of the Ancient Order of Purbeck Marblers hold their annual court to introduce new Freemen at the castle. After the ceremony, a game of street football is played along the road from Corfe to Swanage and back to the castle. The purpose is to maintain an ancient right of way to Swanage Harbour, from where valuable Purbeck marble was once shipped.

A flock of ravens has recently taken up residence in the keep, much to the delight of the castle's current guardians, the National Trust. According to an old legend, if the ravens leave, disaster will not be long in coming. The ravens did leave in 1638 and just eight years later, during the Civil War, the besieged castle fell to Cromwell's men.

▶ *4 miles S of Wareham, on A351 Swanage road.*

THE CASTLE FELL WHEN THE RAVENS TOOK FLIGHT
CORFE CASTLE

❻ Cerne Abbas

The image of a naked, club-wielding giant cut into the chalk on the Dorset hillside is one of the enduring 'ancient' symbols of southern Britain. The 55m (180ft) giant is argued to be an Iron Age symbol or a depiction of the Roman Hercules. The problem with both of these theories is that earliest written reference to the giant did not appear until 1694; and 80 years later, antiquarian the Reverend John Hutchins referred to the giant as 'a modern thing' that had been cut by Denzil Holles, owner of the hill and a critic of the then military and political leader Oliver Cromwell, sometimes called England's Hercules. The debate can be settled only by using a dating technique known as Optical Stimulated Luminescence, which reveals the date on which buried soil was last exposed to sunlight. The technique has been used effectively on Berkshire's Uffington White Horse (page 70) and dated the horse's construction to the Bronze Age, around 1057 BC.

The giant is rechalked every 25 years to maintain its clarity on the hillside. There is still belief in the legend that if a woman spends the whole night on the giant's penis, she will become pregnant.

▶ *8 miles N of Dorchester on A352.*

THE CERNE ABBAS GIANT

❼ Wareham

On the four evenings before the last Friday in November, a group of strangely dressed men visit many of the public houses in the town, checking on the quality and quantity of the food and drink supplied by each landlord. These men are officials of the Court Leet, which in Norman times was the main judicial and local government court in many parts of the country. A few courts, such as the one at Wareham, still preserve the ceremonies, although their judicial powers have ceased. The officials include the Ale-tasters, who use pewter measures more than 200 years old; the Bread-weighers, who carry an ancient pair of scales; the Carnisters who taste the meat; and the Surveyors and Searchers of Mantles and Chimneys, who check flues for obstructions, since Wareham has a history of serious fires.

▶ *At junction of A351 and A352, 9 miles W of Poole.*

❽ Poole

In 1248, when it received its charter from the Earl of Salisbury, this town was an important fishing and trading port. The earl's name is immortalised in the small, disused lock-up or prison still called 'The Salisbury', situated near the Georgian Customs House. The mayor also has the ancient title of Admiral of the Port of Poole; and every three years, at the end of September, the right of the townspeople to use the harbour is reaffirmed in the ceremony of Beating the Bounds. This entails the admiral's barge sailing round the boundary marks. The Jurymen of the Court of Admiralty scramble ashore to ensure that the marks are visible, and leave a floating buoy at seaward marks. At each shore mark, two children are ceremonially 'beaten' – an age-old custom to remind everyone of the boundaries.

▶ *S of A35, 6 miles W of Bournemouth.*

❾ Godmanstone

The 600-year-old thatched pub, the Smith's Arms, claims to be the smallest public house in England – its front is only 3.3m (11ft) wide. Once the pub was a smithy, and the story goes that one day, Charles II was riding through the village when he stopped at the blacksmith's to have his horse reshod. While he waited, he asked the smith to bring him some ale but the man replied that he had no licence. On hearing this, the king granted him one, and the licence has been kept up ever since.

▶ *On A352, 5 miles N of Dorchester.*

❿ Batcombe

This village, which lies 3 miles northwest of Cerne Abbas, is backed by steep hills from which it is possible to look down on to the flat roof of the church tower. Possibly it was this view that gave rise to the story of Conjuror Mynterne, a 16th-century squire of the manor who was reputed to have dabbled in witchcraft.

One day, as Mynterne rode out along the top of Batcombe Hill, he suddenly remembered that he had left his book of spells open on his desk. Fearing that someone might read it and perhaps come to harm by trying out the spells, he hurried back home. Galloping by the shortest route, he jumped his horse from the top of Batcombe Hill clean across the village. As he sailed over the rooftops, his horse's hoof caught one of the four pinnacles surrounding the church tower and knocked it off. Despite this, the horse made a safe landing on a field called Pitching Plot; but such was the power of the magic that grass would never grow there again.

The broken pinnacle was replaced by a new one about 100 years later. However, the new pinnacle leans out of true, so is easily distinguished from the other three. Also it is not so stained by the weather as they are.

Conjuror Mynterne lived for several years after this incident, and when he died, he left instructions that he was to be buried 'neither within the church nor without it'. So the magician lies buried under the church wall, with half his tomb inside the building and half outside.

On the road across Batcombe Hill there is a stone pillar known as the Cross-and-Hand (or the Cross-in-Hand), which is thought to date from the 7th century although antiquarians have been unable to discover its true history. However, local legends abound.

One story tells of a priest who lost a holy relic while travelling along the road. When he realised his loss, he hurried back, rounding a bend to find hundreds of animals – sheep, oxen, rabbits and badgers – all kneeling in adoration. Suddenly, a shaft of fire from the sky illuminated the place where the lost relic lay, and the pillar was built to commemorate the miracle.

Another story, quoted by Thomas Hardy in *Tess of the d'Urbervilles*, is less pleasant. The pillar marks the grave of a criminal who was tortured and hanged on the site. It is said that the man had sold his soul to the Devil, and sometimes, at night, his ghost is seen near the pillar.

▶ *1 mile E of A37, 11 miles N of Dorchester.*

SOUTHWEST ENGLAND

THE DORSET OOSER

HUNDREDS of years ago, a man wearing a horned mask known as an Ooser may have been a high priest who officiated at pagan fertility rituals; and the mask may have represented a powerful pagan god. But by the 19th century, the Ooser's original meaning had been forgotten, and in Shillingstone, among other places, it had become the 'Christmas Bull', a terrifying creature that roamed through the streets of Dorset villages at the end of the year demanding refreshment from any folk it met. Sometimes, its former sanctity was so far forgotten that it was used to frighten children, or to taunt unfaithful husbands or wives.

At that time, the Ooser almost certainly played a part in a widespread custom known as 'Skimmington Riding' or 'Skimmity'. To express their disapproval of adultery, villagers would troop through the streets, leading a horse or donkey on which two figures, representing a couple suspected of unfaithfulness, were seated back to back.

Sometimes dummies were used, and sometimes a masked man and woman played the parts. The Ooser mask was worn either by the man or by one of the crowd, as a particularly damning gesture of derision. Why the custom was so named is not clear, but it was a strangely ironical use of the symbol of a former god of fertility.

Once every Dorset village may have had an Ooser, but by the beginning of the 20th century only one was left, at Melbury Osmond. Now, even that has been lost, and the ancient Horned God has probably disappeared from Dorset forever.

⑪ Badbury

The Iron Age hillfort known as Badbury Rings lies on a hilltop in the grounds of Kingston Lacy House near Wimborne. It comprises three concentric ramparts and ditches, and is an impressive monument to its architects – the Durotriges tribe – even after 2,000 years of erosion and decay. Arthurian scholars have linked Badbury with the site of Mons Badonicus (Mount Badon), where Arthur was said to have defeated the Angles, Saxons and Jutes in battle in AD 518. According to ancient chroniclers: 'Arthur carried the cross of Our Lord Jesus Christ, for three days and nights on his shoulders, and the Britons were victorious.' The battle was said to have given Britain 21 years of peace that lasted until Arthur took up arms against his treacherous nephew, Modred. There is no evidence to support the legend, although it is thought likely the inhabitants were overcome by invading Romans making their way west. Excavations have shown that the site has been occupied for at least 5,000 years.
▶ *4 miles SE of Blandford Forum on B3082 Wimborne Minster road.*

⑫ Winterborne Whitechurch

A few metres west of the village crossroads is a field known as the Round Meadow. Local legend claims that because the field was once reaped on a Sunday, it was accursed and no crops would grow. Eventually the Round Meadow was chosen as the site of a new church, but no matter how many stones were laid, they were moved each night and found next morning in another field. After weeks of unprofitable labour, the villagers concluded that the curse was still operating and that divine disapproval was being expressed about building the church on such a site. Finally, it was built near the stone quarry, where it still stands. The Round Meadow is still cursed, apparently; it is said that, however brilliant the weather, any attempt to mow the field will always bring rain and storms.
▶ *On A354 6 miles SW of Blandford Forum.*

⑬ Sherborne

Pack Monday Fair, held on the first Monday after October 10, old Michaelmas Day, probably dates from the 13th century. The name may be a corruption of Pact – the agreement made between master and labourer at a hiring fair. At midnight on the night before the fair, a group of people known as Teddy Roe's Band parade and blow horns and whistles, swing rattles and bang kettles and saucepans. This custom dates back to the 15th century, when a serious fire left Sherborne Abbey in need of extensive repairs. After they were completed, the workmen, led by their foreman Teddy Roe, celebrated by going round the town blowing on cows' horns.

In the gardens of nearby Sherborne Castle, the ghost of a former owner, Sir Walter Raleigh, is said to walk on St Michael's Eve (September 28).
▶ *On A30 5 miles E of Yeovil.*

SOMERSET

With celebrations ranging from winter carnivals to the May Day revels, Somerset's old traditions are joyfully observed, while mythical tales of witches and fairies surround its famous caves and marshes.

❶ Dunster

Ash logs and faggots often figure in old customs, probably because ash is one of the few woods that will burn easily when it is still green. An ancient legend says that the baby Jesus was first warmed by a fire of green ash. Until a century ago, Burning the Ashen Faggot was a widespread custom on Christmas Eve, particularly in Somerset; this medieval tradition is still observed at the Luttrell Arms Hotel in Dunster. The faggot is a bundle of 12 ash branches bound with green ash bands. It is burnt in the great fireplace of the hotel, and as each band burns, another round of punch is ordered from the bar. While the wood burns, everyone sings the Dunster Carol, and when the faggot is finally consumed, a charred fragment is taken out to light next year's fire.
▶ *2 miles E of Minehead on A396.*

❷ Minehead

The town's Hobby Horse makes its first appearance on May Day Eve; then, for the next three days at various times, it prances its way around the district accompanied by drum and accordion. The horse consists of a 2.7m (9ft) long frame covered with canvas and ribbons, concealing a dancer. Like other Hobby Horses, the Minehead version is probably the survival of an ancient spring rite, though local legend gives it a different origin. In the 9th century, the town was constantly under attack by Viking pirates. But the raiders fled in terror when a Minehead crew disguised its ship as a sea serpent. The Hobby Horse is a celebration of their victory. It is pointed out that the horse bears some resemblance to a longship.
▶ *Off A39, 26 miles W from the M5 near Bridgwater.*

❸ Carhampton

For hundreds of years the rite of Wassailing the Apple Trees has been observed by the villagers on old Twelfth Night (January 17). Cider is poured on the roots of the finest tree and spiced wassail cake is placed in the branches – a relic of the offerings once made to the tree gods to provide a fruitful harvest. Finally, shotguns are fired through the branches to drive away any evil spirits that may be lurking there and the chant 'Hats full, caps full, three bushel bags full' is sung.
▶ *On A39 3 miles E of Minehead.*

MINEHEAD HOBBY HORSE

❹ Bridgwater

The Guy Fawkes Carnival is a spectacular annual celebration in Bridgwater, and the town has the reputation of hosting the largest illuminated procession in the world. It began, as did all November 5 celebrations, in 1606, the year after the gunpowder plot was foiled. This was the plan by Catholic conspirators to blow up the Houses of Parliament when it was in session and the king, a Protestant, was in attendance. After the conspirators had been brutally dealt with, James I declared that every year on the anniversary of the plot, bonfires should be lit, so that the conspiracy and how it was overcome should never be forgotten. The staunchly Protestant townsfolk of Bridgwater complied with enthusiasm.

Today the event, which takes place on the closest Friday to November 5, comprises a parade with decorated carnival floats, a firework display and 'squibbing' – giant fireworks, or squibs, made to a secret formula and attached to long poles are lit simultaneously. More than 100 squibs create a great trail of fire.

▶ *10 miles NE of Taunton. Access from junctions 23 or 24 of M5.*

❺ Buckland St Mary

According to fairy lore, the village of Buckland St Mary is said to be the last place in Somerset where red-clothed fairies were seen. Nineteenth century folklorists claimed they were defeated in battle with the pixies, so that everywhere west of the River Parret is now Pixyland. These pixies can be recognised by their red hair, pointed ears and green clothing. It is thought that the fairies fled to Ireland, although some say that a few settled in Devon and Dorset.
▶ *Just N of A303, 6 miles SW of Ilminster.*

FIRE RAINS DOWN ON THE GUY FAWKES SQUIBBERS
BRIDGWATER

❻ Athelney

The Isle of Athelney was at one time surrounded by marshes, and it was there that King Alfred sought refuge from the Danes in AD 878. The famous 'burning the cakes' legend belongs to Athelney. The story goes that Alfred was sitting by a peasant's hearth, totally absorbed in his own thoughts, when the housewife saw her loaves burning by the fire. Not recognising the king, she boxed his ears for his inattention.

In the 19th century a stone was placed on the site in memory of the incident. The inscription recalls the king's gratitude for the peasant's hospitality, and records the fact that he erected a monastery and endowed it with all the lands on the Isle of Athelney. Now only a few ruined stone walls and a pond mark the site of this foundation, the once-wealthy Edington Monastery, northeast of Frome.
▶ *Just off A361, 9 miles NE of Taunton.*

❼ Burnham-on-Sea

The winter carnivals of Highbridge and Burnham-on-Sea are part of a wider winter carnival circuit. The festivities are held annually in November, when decorated floats parade through the towns, followed by displays of fireworks.
▶ *W off A38, 8 miles N of Bridgwater.*

❽ Bleadon

It is said that the place was originally called 'Bleed Down' in commemoration of a bloody skirmish between the local people and Danish raiders. The story goes that one morning in the 7th century; six Danish longboats came sweeping up the Severn on the strong spring tide. The local fishermen ran to nearby Uphill to rouse the farming people, leaving behind one old, lame woman, who was by the riverside gathering rushes. Hidden by the tall reeds, she watched the marauders land and scatter in search of plunder, leaving their boats unguarded. The old woman noticed that the tide that had brought the raiders up the estuary was now on the turn, so hobbling from mooring to mooring, she cut each longboat adrift.

Meanwhile, the Uphill men had rallied and driven the Danes, encumbered by their loot, back towards the landing place. There was no escape for the pirates, and not one of them survived.
▶ *3 miles S of Weston-super-Mare on A370.*

9 Bristol

King Brennus, the mythical founder of Bristol, and his brother Belinus are commemorated with small statues, which stand on the medieval St John's Gate. The brothers were princes, and when their father, King Malmutius died, he left his kingdom north of the Humber to Brennus, and south to Belinus. But the southern lands were colder and less fruitful, and only the intervention of their mother, Queen Conwenna, prevented war between them. As an act of reconciliation Brennus came south and built Bristol, the 'place of the bridge'.
▶ *6 miles from M5 and 6 miles from M4 (via M32).*

10 Bristol Channel

The Green Meadows of Enchantment is the name once given to the islands that supposedly lie out in the water somewhere between Somerset and Pembrokeshire. These fairy islands are not usually visible to humans, and certainly not to those who seek them. They are said to be glimpsed by chance, and can disappear at will. Fairies reputedly came and went from the mainland using a secret passage under the sea.

Many seafaring nations can trace magical islands in their folklore – often islands of the dead upon which only blessed mortals could set foot. In reality, many islands, such as the Canaries – or Fortunate Islands – were discovered then lost again by ancient sailors and navigators, adding to their mythical status.
▶ *Lies N of coast of Devon and Somerset, and S of coast of Wales.*

11 Croydon Hill

According to legend, a terrifying horned devil haunts the lane close to Croydon Hill, talk of which caused a local tragedy. The awful event took place in the 19th century when a ploughboy went to the smithy at Rodhuish for a plough-blade repair. While he waited, the smiths recounted tales of the mythical beast, and the butcher's boy took it into his head to play a practical joke. As the ploughboy made his way home along the lane, he was suddenly set upon by a horned monster, bellowing furiously. He lashed out with the plough-blade, then ran. Later the villagers found nothing more than a bullock's hide with a gash in it. The butcher's boy was never seen again. It is said the Devil took him, and he can be heard howling on stormy nights as his and other lost souls are hounded by demons.
▶ *4 miles S of Minehead on minor road off A396.*

12 Kilve

An extraordinary shale and limestone pavement on the sea shore at Kilve recalls the legend of a huge fiery dragon called Blue Ben that lived within nearby Putsham Hill. He used to cool himself by swimming in the sea, and in order to avoid the mudflats as he emerged from his cavern below Kilve and Putsham, he built a causeway of rocks into the water.

Having discovered Blue Ben's lair, the Devil used to harness him and ride him round Hell – much to the dragon's disgust because he got far too hot. One day, hurrying to cool off after a sortie, he slipped on the causeway, fell into the mud and drowned. As proof of the legend, people used to say that the fossilised ichthyosaurus (a prehistoric sea-creature) found near Glastonbury in the 19th century, and now in the county museum in Taunton, is really Blue Ben.
▶ *On A39 12 miles W of Bridgwater.*

13 Cadbury Castle

The ramparts of the Iron Age hillfort of Cadbury Castle, near Yeovil, enclose an area of almost 7.2 ha (18 acres). From the summit there are impressive views of central Somerset and Glastonbury Tor some 12 miles away.

Medieval chroniclers identified the hillfort with Camelot, from where Arthur was believed to have led the Britons to victory against Saxon invaders. Archaeological evidence shows that during the 6th century, the time of Arthur, earth defences were reinforced with timber and stone, converting the existing fort into a stronghold.

Myths claim that the hill is hollow and that within, Arthur and his knights lie sleeping until such times as Britain will call upon their services.
▶ *On minor roads 2 miles E of A359, 9 miles NE of Yeovil.*

14 Bath

The famous healing waters of the ancient Roman city are said to have been discovered by King Bladud. Before his accession, Bladud, contracted leprosy, and one day plunged into a black, evil-smelling bog that cured him. Wells were sunk into the bog, and the curative properties of the waters of Bath gained fame and fortune.

The Romans believed in their magic and in the course of recent excavations a number of 'curse' tablets have been discovered – invocations to Minerva written on thin strips of lead by victims of wrongdoing, seeking retribution.
▶ *12 miles SE of Bristol.*

THE SEA SHORE AT KILVE

⓯ Stanton Drew

Three massive prehistoric stone circles close by the River Drew are believed to date from the same period as Avebury in Wiltshire. For centuries they have been known as 'The Devil's Wedding' after the story of a fateful village wedding that was followed by wild revels that went on late into the night. As the clock struck midnight the piper refused to play on, because the following day was Sunday. The bride declared that the dancing would continue if she had to go to hell to find a piper – and with that an old man introduced himself and said he would play for the celebrants. The music was sweet and the dancers were compelled to follow his tune, although he played faster and faster and they were dancing to the point of exhaustion. As day broke, the villagers found that the wedding party had been turned to stone.

▶ *On B3130 1 mile W of junction with A37,*
6 miles S of Bristol.

⓰ Wookey Hole

The series of caves known as Wookey Hole were carved out of the limestone over millions of years by the River Axe. Within are many stalagmite and stalactite formations, with one oddly shaped stalagmite said to be the Witch of Wookey, turned to stone as a result of her evil deeds. The witch was said to have set up home in the cavern with her familiars, a goat and its kid. She had once been crossed in love, according to the legend, and out of bitterness cast spells on the villagers of Wookey. So the people appealed to the Abbot of Glastonbury to rid them of the hag.

A monk attempted to confront the witch and such was his piety, she knew her evil magic was powerless against him and tried to flee. The quick-thinking monk sprinkled the witch with holy water, instantly turning her to stone. She has remained petrified ever since, on the bank of the Axe in the Great Cave at Wookey Hole.

In another story, the wicked witch directed her malevolence against lovers in particular – even the monk who turned her to stone. for the poor young man was once engaged to a local girl, before their wedding plans were wrecked by the witch. In sorrow, he took holy vows.

In 1912, excavations in the caves uncovered the bones of a Romano-British woman. Close to her grave were the bones of a goat and kid, and a comb, a dagger and a polished alabaster ball. These relics are now in Wells and Mendip Museum in the Wookey Hole room.

▶ *On minor road 1 mile N of Wells.*

⓱ Hinton St George

The Punky Night celebrations, on the last Thursday in October, may have some link with the ancient fire rites of Celtic Samhain (November 1). On this night, children go around the village begging for candles, which they place inside scooped-out mangel-wurzels. These lanterns, called 'punkies', are carved to represent faces, trees or houses. The children parade up and down the village streets, singing the traditional 'punky' song. It has been suggested that this old tradition was carried to America and re-imported with the modern Halloween tradition of pumpkin lanterns.

Strange creatures called hunky punks appear all over Somerset, clinging to the perpendicular towers of the county's 15th and 16th-century churches. In other counties they are known as 'grotesques', stone-carved monsters wrought from the imagination of medieval stonemasons.

▶ *On minor roads 2 miles NW of Crewkerne.*

⑱ Glastonbury

Before the Somerset marshes were drained, flooding turned Glastonbury into an island each winter. An old legend says that Christ himself visited Glastonbury as a boy; and after Joseph of Arimathea had placed Jesus in his own tomb, he too came to England bringing with him the Holy Grail, the cup used at the Last Supper. On Wearyall Hill, near the Tor, Joseph thrust his staff into the earth where it took root and grew into a Holy Thorn tree, which blossomed only at Christmas. Cuttings from this tree, *Crataegus oxyacantha*, still flourish in the neighbourhood and blossom around Christmas time, although the original was cut down in Cromwell's day because it was considered to be an idolatrous image.

Church chronicles record that Joseph built a chapel of wattle and daub on the site where now stands the ruined abbey's Lady Chapel, and there baptised the first British converts to Christianity. Many legends owe their inspiration to this old chapel, which was still standing when the eastern Saxons overran central Somerset in the 7th century. Hermits worshipped there until the 5th century, when St Patrick, it is said, formed them into a monastic community. The monastery survived Saxon and Danish conquests and was a rich Benedictine abbey until the Dissolution of 1539, when Henry VIII hanged the last abbot.

As far as is known, the Iron Age monks encountered by the Saxons did not tell them who had built the chapel – perhaps they did not know. Its origin, and the reason why Joseph came to be regarded as its founder, remain a mystery. The source of the extraordinary story of Christ's visit cannot be traced, either, but a Saxon legend speaks of the church as 'not built of man but prepared by God himself'.

Sometime after Joseph had built his chapel, another was constructed on top of the Tor and dedicated to St Michael, soldier of God and victor over paganism.

For centuries, stories of Melwas, Guinevere's abductor, and the discovery of Arthur's grave in the abbey, were dismissed as tales concocted by monks to attract more pilgrims to Glastonbury. Then, in the 1960s, excavations showed that a fortress existed on the Tor during the 6th century, suggesting at least the possibility of truth in the Melwas legend. The monks' account of the grave is correct, too. It had been opened in the 12th century and the bones lost in the 16th with the Dissolution. Scholars agree that its style belongs to a period later than Arthur's; on the other hand, it seems too ancient to be a 12th-century fake.

▶ *5 miles S of Wells at junction of A39 and A361.*

GLASTONBURY TOR

CHANNEL ISLANDS

Echoes of the long-distant past abound in the island traditions, whether in the form of tributes to a pagan statue, blessed church foundations or toasting the arrival of summer.

❶ St Brélades Bay, Jersey

The parish of St Brélades in southwest Jersey is named after a wandering Welsh saint, said to be the son of Kenen, a Cornish king. The Norman church stands at the end of the bay, some way away from the main settlement. It is said that when work began on building the church, the site was to be a mound close to the parish centre. The builders gathered all the wood and stone together on the mound, but the next morning, everything had disappeared, and they found it half a mile away on a clifftop near the sea. The workmen carried the materials back, but the next morning, everything had been moved to the clifftop once again. They accepted this as God's will, and built the church on the imposing clifftop where it stands today.

Several possible explanations for these strange events were put forward: that the original site near the village was a pagan shrine; that the Devil wanted the church to be located away from the parishioners so as to inconvenience them; that God preferred the beautiful coastal location.

The small fisherman's chapel next to the church is filled with medieval wall paintings, including a wise man, the Blessed Virgin and Adam and Eve.

▶ *On S coast of Jersey, 5 miles W of St Helier. Reach Jersey by ferry from Poole, Portsmouth and Weymouth. Also by air from UK airports.*

❷ St Mary, Jersey

Le Creux du Vis, or Devil's Hole, in St Mary is a rock funnel more than 60m (197ft) deep, the result of a collapsed cave roof. A steep path leads down to the hole, passing a metal sculpture of the Devil, standing in a pool. An old legend tells of a wrecked ship, the fragments of which, including the figurehead, were washed into the hole. The figurehead was either devil-like, or carved into the form of a devil upon recovery, according to conflicting versions of the story. The sculpture commemorates the diabolical find.

Another story claims that the strange and spine-tingling noises made by the sea as it is sucked and blown from the hole gave the place its name.

▶ *On N coast of Jersey, 7 miles NW of St Helier.*

❸ Pezeriez Point, Guernsey

The Pleinmont Fairy Ring at Pezeriez Point is locally known as a wishing ring – walk around it three times and the fairies will make your wishes come true. But the ring's real name – Le Table des Pions – reveals its origins. It was made during the early 18th century for an event that took place every two years, the Chevauchee. The king and his courtiers travelled around the island to ensure the Chemin du Roi (Path of the King) was well maintained. Dining tents were put up for the elite at rest stops, and the ordinary folk, pions, dug themselves a table on the grassy sward.

▶ *On SW coast of Guernsey. Reach Guernsey by ferry from Poole, Portsmouth and Weymouth. Also by air from UK airports.*

❹ St Martin's, Guernsey

Visitors to the church of St Martin are greeted by a strange stone figure at the gate. Known as 'La Gran'mere du Chimquiere (the Grandmother of the Churchyard), this Neolithic menhir is around 4,000 years old, although the head, which has an inscrutable expression that changes with the light, is thought to have been modelled in Roman times. The statue once stood at the church door, but was broken by a churchwarden, angry at the parishioners veneration of the godless figure. Such was the outcry that it was repaired and moved to its current position. Offerings, such as money and flowers, are still made to the statue, especially by brides. In the past, the gran'mere was believed to have ensured fertility or cured sickness.

▶ *In centre of St Martin's village, 2 miles SW of St Peter Port.*

❺ St Anne, Alderney

This small island maintains the tradition of Milk-o-Punch, a celebration held on the first Sunday in May, during which punch is served free from all pubs and clubs. The special 'secret' recipe comprises rum, eggs, nutmeg and milk from the island's dairy. The custom is a modern echo of what happened when the cattle were put out to summer pasture and toasts were drunk in the fields to the prosperity of the season.

▶ *Reach Alderney by ferry or air from Guernsey.*

THE
ENIGMATIC
CIRCLE HAS
A PRACTICAL
ORIGIN
PEZERIEZ POINT

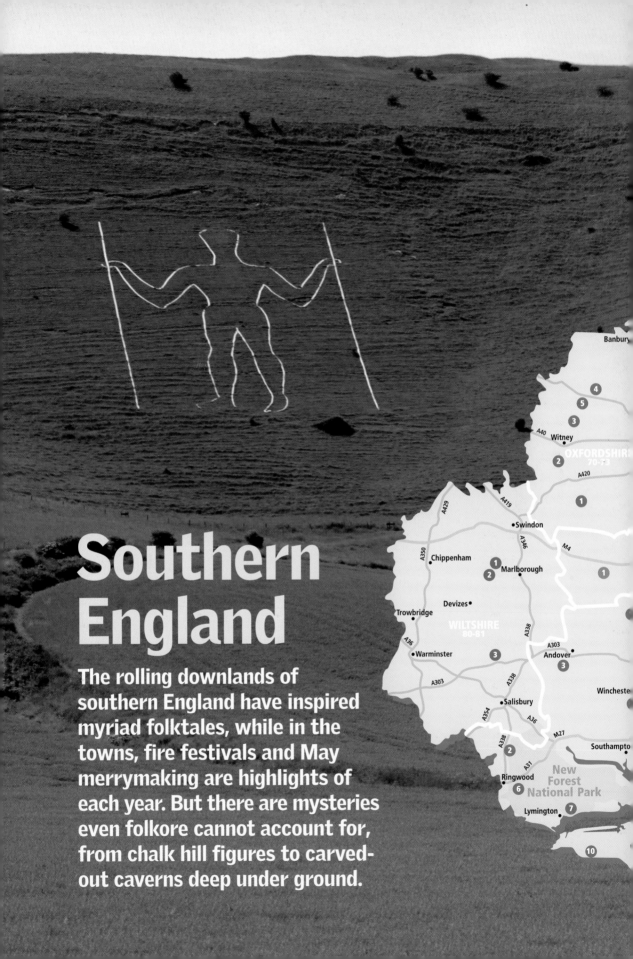

Southern England

The rolling downlands of southern England have inspired myriad folktales, while in the towns, fire festivals and May merrymaking are highlights of each year. But there are mysteries even folkore cannot account for, from chalk hill figures to carved-out caverns deep under ground.

Banbury

4

5

3

A40 · Witney

2 · OXFORDSHIRE 70-73

A420

1

A429 · A419

· Swindon

A346

M4

A350 · Chippenham

1 · Marlborough
2

1

Devizes ·

Trowbridge

WILTSHIRE 80-81

A338

A303

· Andover

· Warminster

3

3

A303

A338

· Salisbury

Winchester

A354

A36

A338

M27

Southampton

2

A31

New Forest National Park

· Ringwood

6

Lymington ·

7

10

BEDFORDSHIRE

In this green and pleasant county, tales of healing wells and wealthy benefactors are offset by legends of devilish visitations and witchery, but a charitable society remains intent on curing the world's woes.

❶ Odell

Five scratches on the western door of All Saints Church were allegedly made by the Devil. One of the several Sir Rowland Alstons, barons of Odell, sold his soul, but when the time came to surrender, he fled to the church, and hid cowering inside. Enraged, the Devil descended on Odell and shook the church in fury, scratching the door in the process.

▶ *On minor roads between A6 and A428, 7 miles NW of Bedford.*

❷ Stevington

Those with ailments of the eyes once sought a cure at the holy well near St Mary's Church in Stevington. The church, which dates from Saxon times, is thought to be part of a Christian appropriation of an ancient sacred place, made powerful by its healing waters. The church itself is carved with several expressive medieval stone heads and some comical wooden bench ends. Summer visitors to the well may see a large protected plant, *Petasites Hybridus*, commonly known as butterbur. This medicinal herb has several uses, including the treatment of migraine and hayfever, but is so named because in times past its leaves were used to wrap butter.

▶ *On minor roads 4 miles NW of Bedford.*

❸ Bedford

The town contains the headquarters of the Panacea Society, a Christian organisation and registered charity that is the guardian of a box left by the prophetess Joanna Southcott (1750–1814). It contains writings that were

ENRAGED, THE
DEVIL DESCENDED
ON ODELL
HARROLD ODELL COUNTRY PARK

allegedly dictated to her by Jesus Christ, but under the terms of Joanna's will the box can be opened only in the presence of 24 bishops, who have so far declined to cooperate.

▶ *10 miles NE of Junction 13 of M1 along A421.*

④ Leighton Buzzard

The handsome almshouses in the town were originally built by Edward Wilkes in 1630 for eight elderly poor of the parish. It was a condition of his benefaction that the bounds of the Parish be beaten on Rogation Monday, in May. This condition continues to be honoured, and also on that day a chorister stands on his or her head to hear a reading of Wilkes' will.

▶ *6 miles NW of Dunstable.*

⑤ Chalgrave

The handsome medieval church of All Saints is situated some distance outside the village and, in the 19th century, to protect the earthly remains of their ancestors, the villagers paid an old man one shilling a week 'to purchase gruel with which to warm his inside and to keep a fire burning at night to warm his outside while he watched through the night for body-snatchers in the churchyard'. Body snatching was a great – if slightly exaggerated – fear in Victorian England as anatomists would pay a good price for fresh corpses upon which to practise their art.

▶ *All Saints Church is 1 mile S of Toddington, close to junction of A5120 and Chalgrave Road.*

⑥ Luton

Two miles north of Luton lies Galley Hill, whose earlier name – 'Gallows Hill' – was derived from its being a place of execution in medieval times. The earliest-known structure on the site is an Iron Age hillfort. It was also occupied in Roman and Saxon times. During the 16th and 17th centuries it was used as witches burial ground and may also have been the centre of a witch cult. Archaeological excavations in the 1960s revealed the macabre find of a horse's skull on top of which was placed a bone dice with the '6' uppermost. These objects may have been used in ritual ceremonies and spells.

▶ *2 miles E from Junction 10 of M1. Galley Hill E of A6, 2 miles N of town centre.*

BERKSHIRE

Memories are long in these leafy lowlands. Customs initiated hundreds of years ago are still observed, infamous episodes preserved in place names, and rural traditions kept alive in a modern university.

❶ Hungerford

When John of Gaunt granted Hungerford special fishing and grazing rights in 1364, he also gave the town his hunting horn, which is preserved in the vaults of a local bank. Each year, on the second Tuesday after Easter, his patronage is commemorated at the Hocktide Festival. At 9am a replica of his horn is blown in the Corn Market, summoning commoners to the Hocktide Court, presided over by a jury, which amends the rules governing the town's privileges. Two Tuttimen are elected and given Tutti poles, tall staves festooned with nosegays and ribbons. They are accompanied by the Orange Scrambler, and all by tradition are entitled to a kiss from every woman in the town. Each woman kissed receives an orange. At lunchtime, the Court gathers at the Three Swans Hotel where a Hocktide punch is drunk in memory of John of Gaunt.
▶ *8 miles W of Newbury at junction of A4 and A338.*

❷ Aldworth

In the Middle Ages, Aldworth parish church was the private chapel of the Norman family de la Beche. Inside the church are the 'Aldworth Giants', nine life-size monuments dedicated to men of the family, some of whom, apparently, were over 2m (7ft) tall. Traditionally, three of these statues are called Long John, John Strong and John Neverafraid. A tenth statue, John Everafraid, is now missing, but once stood in an alcove, half inside and half outside the church. John Everafraid was thought to have made a pact with the Devil whereby he received riches in exchange for his soul, which the Devil would take whether John was buried inside or outside the church. He outwitted Satan by being buried in neither place, so saving his soul from damnation.
▶ *5 miles NW of Pangbourne on B4009.*

❸ Aldermaston

Every three years, in Aldermaston Parish Hall, a candle auction is held in January for the lease-rights to lands owned by the Church and known as Church Acre. A horseshoe nail is stuck sideways into a candle, and bidding begins as the candle is lit. The last bid made before the flame reaches the nail and expires secures the lease, and rents so obtained are devoted to charity. Candle auctions are centuries old and this one was revived in 1815.
▶ *On A340, S from A4, 8 miles E of Newbury.*

❹ Reading

During the reign of Henry I (1100–35), nine great cloth merchants prospered in England, including Thomas of Reading. Legend says the king met Thomas and his fellow merchants on the road one day but their many wagons forced him to move aside. At first he was angry, but soon realised how useful the support of such rich men might be. To win their favour, he devised a standard measurement for cloth – the yard, which was exactly the length of his arm.

Today, the Museum of English Rural Life is to be found in the grounds of the University of Reading. Its collections cover all aspects of traditional country life, from bee-keeping to weaving. Check opening times before visiting.
▶ *On A4 40 miles W of London. Access from Junctions 10, 11 and 12 of M4. University lies SE of town centre.*

❺ Colnbrook

The Ostrich Inn at Colnbrook, which dates from 1106, is one of the most ancient of English pubs. King John, it is said, paused here for a glass of ale on his way to Runnymede to sign Magna Carta.

A couple named Jarman, who owned the Ostrich in medieval times, had a gruesome way of increasing their earnings. Any wealthy visitor would be plunged to his death through a concealed trap door, landing in a carefully placed cauldron of boiling ale. The pair dispatched 59 of their guests in this manner, answering awkward questions by saying that the visitors had left early. They were finally exposed when the horse of their 60th victim, a wealthy clothier from Reading, Thomas Cole, was found wandering in the village. A search led to the discovery of Cole's body in a nearby stream. The Jarmans were forced to confess and were executed. It is said that the village takes its name from their final misdeed – Cole-in-the-brook, or Colnbrook.
▶ *Just S of A4, close to Junction 5 of M4.*

ETON, FOURTH OF JUNE

❻ Eton

Eton College's annual Fourth of June holiday commemorates the birthday of George III. 'Speeches' in the morning – readings from great literature delivered to teachers, parents and guests by senior boys dressed in knee-breeches and buckled shoes – are followed in the evening by the Daylight Procession of Boats on the Thames. Dressed as 18th-century sailors, the crews stand precariously to attention in their boats, while the coxswains, wearing admiral's uniform, salute with drawn swords.

'Pop' – the Eton Society – was founded in 1811 as a debating society, but is now an exclusive club of around 12 senior boys. Pop members are entitled to wear wing collars and white bow ties, braided tailcoats, checked trousers, floral waistcoats and flowers in their buttonholes.

A form of football peculiar to Eton is the Wall Game, played on a pitch 109m (120yd) long by just 4.5m (5yd) wide. Players form scrums, or bullies, for attack and defence. Goals are a rarity. In fact, the last goal was scored in 1911.

▶ *N bank of Thames, opposite Windsor. Close to Junction 6 of M4.*

53

BUCKINGHAMSHIRE

Behind the quiet façade of one stately home, the debauched antics of a notorious aristocrat and his cronies have entered the annals of folklore, while elsewhere more innocent rituals continue unabated.

❶ North Marston

Sir John Schorne, or Shorne, rector of North Marston from 1290 to 1314, is credited with originating the medicinal spring that now provides the village with its water. During a drought, Sir John struck the ground near the church of St Mary with his stick and the spring spontaneously burst forth. A well was built around it, and its curative powers – especially for acute fever – attracted sufferers from all over the country, who paid to drink from a gold cup chained to the wall. The proceeds were used to build the chancel of North Marston church. Villagers also bathed their eyes with the water. Although he was never canonised, Sir John was considered a saint by his contemporaries, and pilgrims flocked to his shrine. In 1478 his bones were removed to St George's Chapel, Windsor, where they rest still.

The iron content of the water was said to have increased over time, and when pilgrimages ceased in the 16th century, the water was used to fill cattle troughs. By 1835, though, the mineral taste had apparently lessened, for the spring became the regular source of water for the village. The holy well, called Schorne's Well, which has never run dry through all the centuries, is located a short distance from the church. It is now covered, and operated with a pump, which stands over it.

Sir John's second miracle was to catch the Devil and imprison him in a long boot. This exploit was represented on pewter tokens, made in the locality and sold to pilgrims. It is also commemorated in church paintings.

▶ *On minor roads off A413, 7 miles NW of Aylesbury.*

❷ Quainton

The passing of a former king of the gipsies, thought to be Edward Bozwell, is marked by a rough-hewn stone at the side of the old Roman road that runs below Quainton Hill. Bozwell was executed in 1640 and whether this is his original burial site is doubtful. The road is known locally as Carter's Lane or Gipsy Lane, and the stone, which has the date 1641 crudely carved into it, used to lie in the ditch alongside, shrouded by tangled undergrowth. It has now been set upright.

▶ *On minor roads off A41, 6 miles NW of Aylesbury.*

❸ Wingrave

New-mown hay is spread over the floor of Wingrave church in an annual ceremony that takes place on the Sunday following St Peter's Day (June 29). The custom originated in the ancient practice of rush-spreading, when the earthen floors of churches were covered with fresh rushes once a year. Hay has been substituted for rushes at Wingrave, and is grown in a field that was bequeathed to the church by a local woman. According to legend, this woman lost her way one bitter winter's night and, nearly dead from exposure, was guided to safety by the sound of the church bells.

▶ *Just off A418, 5 miles NE of Aylesbury.*

❹ Longwick

Until the First World War, Longwick was noted for its traditional May Day garlands – circles of saplings covered with a mass of primroses, cowslips and other spring flowers, which children carried from house to house, singing a traditional song. Local children still weave wreaths and garlands of flowers for the village fete, which is generally held on May 1. As well as flower garlands, the fete features country crafts, falconry, morris dancing and maypole dancing. In 1963, author Alison Uttley dedicated her book *Grey Rabbit's May Day* to the children of Longwick school.

▶ *On A4129 5 miles E of Thame.*

❺ Great Kimble

Great Kimble is said to be named after Cunobelinus, King of the Britons, who died c. AD 43. Shakespeare's play *Cymbeline* was based on this half-mythical character, and he was the father of another hero, Caractacus, who led the Britons against the Roman invaders. Caractacus was eventually defeated and taken to Rome in chains. In nearby Chequers Park, the remains of a Norman motte-and-bailey castle, possibly dating from the 12th century, are to be found near Beacon Hill. This is widely known as Cymbeline's Castle and local folklore once had it that if you ran seven times round the mound, the Devil would appear.

▶ *On A4010 5 miles S of Aylesbury. Motte-and-bailey is NE of village.*

❻ West Wycombe

During the mid 18th century, West Wycombe Park, which lies 3 miles west of High Wycombe in Buckinghamshire, was reputed to be the scene of wild orgies and black magic rituals. In about 1755, Sir Francis Dashwood, owner of the Park, founded a private society called the Knights of St Francis. His secret brotherhood was limited to 24 men of high social standing. In summer they met at nearby Medmenham Abbey, where they conducted mock religious ceremonies, but Dashwood had extended the caves in West Wycombe Park and soon the club started meeting there. Before long they became known as the Hellfire Club, with the motto 'Do what you will'. On one occasion, so the story goes, one of their number, reputed to be the radical politician John Wilkes, produced a baboon dressed up with horns at one of the 'services'. Those not party to the joke stampeded in terror, believing the creature to be the Devil.

Exactly above one of the notorious Hellfire Caves, known as the Inner Temple, stands the old parish church of St Lawrence. In 1763, when enthusiasm for his club was beginning to wane, Dashwood had the building renovated in the then popular classical style, and installed what is now a landmark, a hollow golden ball at the top of the tower, with seating for six or eight people. This became an alternative venue for club members to drink and play cards. The church occasionally allows visitors to climb up into the dome, from where the views are spectacular. Inside the church are memorials to the Dashwood family, and the surrounding burial ground is said to be haunted.

▶ *3 miles W of High Wycombe off A40.*

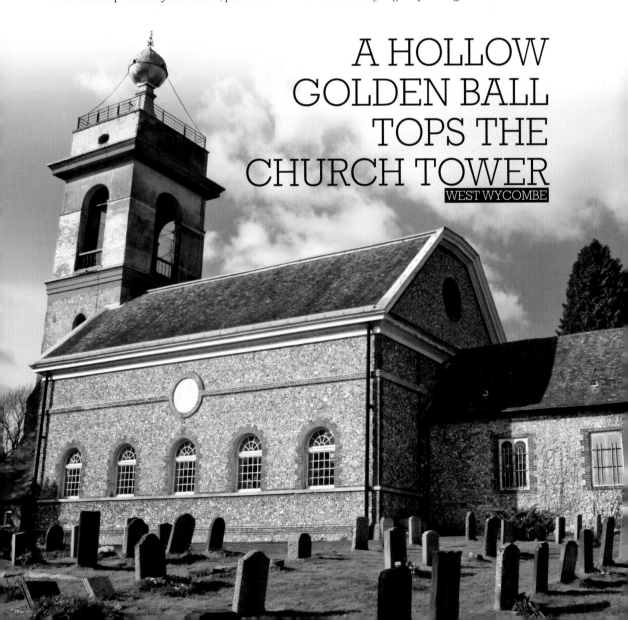

A HOLLOW GOLDEN BALL TOPS THE CHURCH TOWER
WEST WYCOMBE

HAMPSHIRE & ISLE OF WIGHT

Fanciful tales repeated down the years have become part of the history of olde worlde villages and ancient towns. Others, rooted in truth, explain curiosities and give rise to charitable traditions.

❶ Highclere

The grampus is a dolphin-like beast that usually lives in the sea. One is said to have dwelt in the old yew tree by Highclere church, vexing everyone with its noisy breathing. It was fond of chasing the villagers, who retaliated by having it exorcised by a priest who banished the creature to the Red Sea for 1,000 years. The date of its exile is lost, so for all the villagers know, its return could be imminent.
▶ *5 miles SW of Newbury on A343.*

❷ Breamore

On Breamore Down, three-quarters of a mile northwest of Breamore House, is a curious labyrinth of interconnecting paths cut into the turf. Called a miz-maze, it dates from medieval times and is one of seven such constructions scattered throughout England, most notably at St Catherine's Hill, Winchester, Mount Ephram, Faversham, Kent and Leigh in Dorset. The maze is thought to have been associated with an Augustine priory that once stood nearby. As a form of penance, the monks were made to crawl on their knees to the centre of the maze, and then to crawl out again.
▶ *On A338, 7 miles S of Salisbury.*

❸ Abbotts Ann

The custom of hanging Maidens' Garlands from church walls was once widespread. Today garlands can still be seen at St Mary the Virgin, Abbotts Ann. Made of white paper or linen, the garlands are memorials to young virgins of either sex who died within the parish. The garlands resemble a bishop's mitre decorated with paper roses, and they used to be carried in the funeral procession before being placed in the church. They usually have five white paper

gauntlets attached, symbolising a challenge to anyone who disputes the dead person's spotless character. Some 40 garlands hang in St Mary's, the earliest dating from 1716. The most recent was hung in 1953.

▶ *Just off A343, 3 miles SW of Andover.*

❹ Alton

The gruesome event that gave the expression 'Sweet Fanny Adams' to the English language occurred in Alton in 1867. On a warm August afternoon, young Fanny Adams went off with her sister and a friend to play in a hop field. The two other girls later returned home without her. A search party found Fanny's body in a nearby field. Frederick Baker, a local solicitor's clerk, was identified as the killer and was hanged at Winchester on December 24. The Royal Navy at this time was being issued with low-grade tinned meat instead of its traditional salt tack, and the sailors were quick to associate Fanny's disappearance with their new rations. 'Sweet Fanny Adams' soon passed into common usage as a phrase signifying worthlessness.

▶ *Off A31, 16 miles NE of Winchester.*

❺ Winchester

St Swithun was the bishop of Winchester in the 9th century. One of many miracles he is said to have performed concerns a market woman who dropped her basket of eggs near the church after bumping into a monk. Swithun happened to be passing by and was so moved by the poor woman's distress that he made the eggs whole again. On the altar screen in the cathedral, the saint is shown with a pile of eggs at his feet, and each of the four candlesticks in his shrine has a broken eggshell at its base.

When Swithun died in 862, he was buried outside the church of that time, in accordance with his wish to lie where the rain would fall on him. Nearly a century later, the monks decided to move his tomb to a resting place that was deemed worthier, inside the church. Legend has it that St Swithun's spirit, angered by the removal of his remains, made it rain so violently for 40 days that

the monks gave up the plan. Ever since then, rain on St Swithun's Day (July 15) has been regarded as an omen of continuing bad weather.

Castle Hall, near Westgate, is all that remains of William the Conqueror's castle, which was built when Winchester was the capital of England. It contains a round table, alleged to be that of King Arthur and his knights. In fact, it was almost certainly put there in the 12th century by Henry de Blois, who founded the Hospital of St Cross and its almshouses, which lie by water meadows, 1½ miles south of the city centre. For more than 800 years the hospital has dispensed a daily Wayfarer's Dole of bread and ale to all who ask for it. The Hundred Men's Hall, on the site where 100 poor men once received a daily ration of food, is now tearooms.

▶ *W of M3, 12 miles N of Southampton.*

❻ Burley

A legend says that a dragon once lived on Burley Beacon. Every day it flew down to nearby Bisterne to demand a pail of milk. Knowing it was fond of sheep, the villagers willingly provided it with milk, hoping to save their flocks. In time, weary of its extortion, they hired a knight to slay the beast. The knight covered himself with birdlime and ground glass, as a protection against the dragon's fiery breath, and killed it after a fierce battle. There is still a Dragon Lane at Bisterne, and a carved dragon can be seen above the entrance to Bisterne Park.

▶ *On minor roads 2 miles off A31. 4 miles SE of Ringwood.*

❼ South Baddesley

A stream known as 'The Danes' Stream' flows through the parish, and is said to run red with the blood of Danes slaughtered on its banks more than 1,000 years ago. In fact, the colour is probably caused by the iron-rich local soil. According to one tradition, the Knights Templar, and then the Knights Hospitallers of St John, once had a base in South Baddesley, but in fact it was located nearby, in North Baddesley.

▶ *On minor roads 2 miles E of Lymington.*

SOUTHERN ENGLAND

A CURIOUS LABYRINTH OF INTERCONNECTING PATHS
BREAMORE DOWN

⑧ Hambledon

Hambledon is called the 'Cradle of Cricket', although the game had been played in the south of England for years before Hambledon Cricket Club was founded, around 1750. Richard Nyren, landlord of the Bat and Ball Inn and a great cricket enthusiast, was the legendary guiding light, who did much to make the sport nationally popular and who was responsible for the first attempt to formalise the rules of the game. In 1777 he led the team to a resounding victory against an 'All England' side. The club became the most successful in the country and people flocked to Broadhalfpenny Down to watch them. When Nyren moved to take over the George Hotel, the club moved to play on Windmill Down and the George became the headquarters of the game. Today, Hambledon Cricket Club plays at nearby Ridge Meadow, and a monument to the 'Cradle of Cricket' has been erected on Broadhalfpenny Down.
▶ *On B2150, 8 miles NW of Havant.*

⑨ Portsmouth

On stormy winter nights, the bones of Jack the Painter and the chains of his gibbet can be heard clanking in the wind (or so it is said) on Blockhouse Point, which marks the entrance to Portsmouth Harbour. Jack, alias James Aitken, started a fire in the harbour ropehouse in 1776. It is believed that he held anti-monarchist views, and so planned to destroy the Fleet. He was caught, tried and hanged from a ship's mizzen mast. Afterwards, his corpse was gibbeted on Blockhouse Point, and for many years his rotting remains were a familiar warning to all who sailed with the Royal Navy.
▶ *At southern end of Portsea Island. Access via M275 from M27/A27.*

⑩ Mottistone, Isle of Wight

The Long Stone on Mottistone Hill – in fact two local greenstones, one upright, one fallen – is all that remains of a Neolithic long barrow. The name Mottistone suggests that the stone was a 'meeting stone' since it means 'the speaker's stone' in Old English. Mottistone Hill has a long association with druids, who are believed to have worshipped here. Pagan celebrations continue today, with local morris men and many individuals meeting to dance, meditate and make offerings.
▶ *1 mile inland from SW coast of Isle of Wight. 7 miles SW of Newport.*

⑪ Godshill, Isle of Wight

All Saints Church at Godshill owes its magnificent position to an act of God, according to local legend. Shortly after the Christian conversion of the island in the 7th century, the local people decided to build a church in the village at the bottom of the hill. The foundations were marked and the stones prepared. Next morning the villagers awoke to find the stones had been moved to the top of the hill. When this happened twice, they posted a guard to watch the stones, and he saw them moving slowly up the hill of their own accord. Declaring it a miracle, the villagers resolved to build the church where God wanted it – on God's Hill, and declared the land of the orignal site the 'Devil's Acre'. The story of such holy intervention is a common one, but so impressive is its setting that All Saints is among the ten most visited churches in the country.
▶ *5 miles S of Newport on A3020.*

⑫ Gatcombe, Isle of Wight

The Church of St Olave – one of the oldest on the Isle of Wight – was originally built in the 13th century as a chapel for the Estur family. Its legend concerns a young girl, Lucy Lightfoot, who in 1831 fell in love with the effigy of a 14th-century crusader, Edward Estur. She spent many hours in the church, lost in reverie before the object of her love. One June morning she was seen entering the church just as a thunderstorm struck, and at the same time an eclipse of the sun darkened the sky. Lucy was never seen again.

Some years later a churchman on the Isles of Scilly was researching the Crusades when he came across an account of Edward Estur, who embarked for the Holy War accompanied by his mistress, Lucy Lightfoot. She remained in Cyprus, resolved to wait there for his return. But in Syria Edward suffered such severe head injuries that he forgot his mistress and went back to the village of Gatcombe alone. Lucy, meanwhile, remained in Cyprus and married a local fisheman.

Was this a case of time travel, or ghosts made flesh by broken hearts across centuries? The legend has undergone much scrutiny, and its origin appears to have been a pamphlet written – as fiction – by the Reverend James Evans in the 1970s. That the legend should prove so enduring is a testament to popular appetite for mysteries and the Reverend's skill in mixing just enough historical fact with a ripping yarn.
▶ *On minor roads 3 miles S of Newport.*

HERTFORDSHIRE

From a mysterious cave to the ceremonial remembrance of a Christian martyr, evidence of the legendary past is all around. Tales of phantoms and devils keep ancient beliefs alive and give full rein to the imagination.

❶ Royston

One of Hertfordshire's greatest treasures – and most enduring mysteries – lies beneath a High Street shop in Royston. Known as Royston Cave, this bell-shaped chamber was dug from the local chalk by unknown hands, possibly in the 14th century, although there are no records to indicate its origins. A series of images are carved on the walls, from saints to the Holy family, together with indistinct renderings of images more common in ancient times – horses and Sheela-Na-Gig (a stylised woman with exposed genitals). The cave, unique in all of Europe, had lain hidden until the 18th century when workmen erecting a bench discovered a buried millstone, which in turn blocked the entrance to a vertical shaft with toe holds, down which was the chamber itself. It is believed the cave has connections to the Knights Templar as the imagery depicts saints venerated by the order.

The cave is susceptible to flooding, and this, together with changes in the microclimate and worm activity, have caused deterioration to the carvings. It remains open to the public for part of the week from Easter to the last Sunday in September. Check accessibility and opening times before visiting.

▶ *At junction of A10 and A505, 13 miles SW of Cambridge.*

ROYSTON CAVE

❷ Weston

Near the gateway of Weston churchyard two tombstones stand 4m (14ft) apart, which are said to mark the grave of Weston's fabled giant, Jack o' Legs. He is thought to have lived in a cave outside the village some time during the Middle Ages, and was so tall that he could stand in the village street and lean on first-floor windowsills to talk with his friends inside. Jack was famed as an archer and also as a highwayman who robbed the rich to feed the poor. It was said that he could shoot an arrow over 3 miles, and that he was able to bring down a bird half a mile away.

Most of his robberies were carried out at a place that still goes by the name of Jack's Hill, close to the neighbouring village of Graveley. Among his targets were the rich bakers of the nearby market town of Baldock, who resented his charitable gestures at their expense. Eventually, they banded against him, and attacked him as he was passing through Baldock. He was struck from behind with a heavy pole, tied up with strong rope, and then his eyes were put out with a red-hot poker. When he recovered consciousness, the bakers handed him his great bow and told him that he could shoot one last arrow to mark his burial place. Jack did so, and it landed over 3 miles away in Weston churchyard. Jack's picture is incorporated on Weston's village shield.

▶ *On minor roads, 2 miles SE of Baldock town centre.*

❸ Braughing

October 2 is Old Man's Day at Braughing, when the church bells are first muffled and tolled as if for a funeral and then rung joyfully in a wedding peal. The originator of this tradition, Braughing's Old Man, was Matthew Wall, a wealthy 16th-century farmer. He apparently died while still a young man, and as his coffin was being carried to the churchyard it was dropped when a pallbearer slipped on wet autumn leaves. The jolt revived the farmer, who rapped on the coffin to be released. He actually died 24 years later, leaving a bequest for Fleece Lane to be swept every year.

▶ *On B1368, 12 miles S of Royston.*

❹ Stevenage

Along the Great North Road, near Stevenage, by Whomerley Wood, are the Six Hills of old Hertfordshire. A rare group of Roman barrows, or burial mounds, they are popularly said to be the work of the Devil himself. One night, he visited Whomerley Wood, where he dug seven great holes with the intention of throwing the earth so obtained at Stevenage. The earth that he hurled over his shoulder fell short, however, to form the Six Hills. The seventh spadeful Old Nick spitefully aimed at Graveley church and knocked the spire off it. The remains of an Anglo-Saxon moat and earthworks can also be seen in the wood.

▶ *1 mile from Junctions 7 and 8 of A1(M). Whomerley Wood is part of Fairlands Valley Park, SE of town centre.*

❺ Burnham Green

The White Horse pub on the village green dates back three centuries – its name a reference to the legends of phantom white horses said to appear in the area. A sunken lane leading to Welwyn Village is a particular haunt of these fearsome creatures. Local people are said to avoid the lane after dark, while horses are shy of it at any time. The legend may represent a local memory of the white horse emblem on ancient Danish battle flags. The beasts are usually described as being headless, which is probably an allegory of the slaughter inflicted upon the Danes when the local Saxons rose against them in AD 1002.

▶ *On minor roads 3 miles N of Welwyn Garden City.*

❻ St Albans

Parishioners still Beat the Bounds on the first Sunday in May in the ancient city of St Albans, named in the 790s after the first Christian martyr in England. When, some time in the 3rd century, the good Christian was led out to his place of execution – the old Roman amphitheatre – a stream in his path miraculously dried up. At the top of the hill, he begged for water, and the stream immediately reappeared at his feet.

During the 15th century, St Albans was the home of the most famous of Hertfordshire witches, Mother Haggy, who is still spoken of with awe. Late in life, she changed from a 'white' to a 'black' witch, rode full tilt round the town at midday on a broomstick, and crossed the River Ver on a kettle.

St Albans also has its share of ghostly legends, perhaps unsurprisingly, since two bloody battles were fought there during the Wars of the Roses, in 1455 and 1461. The Abbey Green in particular, where Henry VI was defeated and captured in the first Battle of St Albans, and also Chequer Street, are said to be haunted.

▶ *3 miles N of Junctions 21A and 22 of M25.*

KENT

Throughout this most English of counties, stories of miracles and curses feature in equal part. Carvings of the pagan green man deck the churches, and local customs uphold historic events.

❶ Otford

Becket's Well in the village of Otford may have miraculous origins, if legend is to be believed. Apparently, when Archbishop Thomas Becket (1118-70) was in Otford, he was unhappy with the quality of the local water. To remedy the matter, he struck the ground with his crozier and two springs of clear water bubbled up from the spot.

Becket's Well is on land belonging to Castle House, a handsome residence of noble origins. This large gatehouse is all that remains of Otford Palace, a magnificent house built by Archbishop Warham of Canterbury in 1514, a rival to Hampton Court in its splendour. Today the well's spring feeds fishponds that were originally created in the Middle Ages and stocked with trout.

Becket has another connection with Otford. When a nightingale's singing disturbed his devotions, he commanded that none should sing there again. Apparently none has.

▶ *2 miles N of Sevenoaks on A225.*

❷ Ightham

An anonymous letter that hinted mysteriously at 'a terrible blow' soon to fall on parliament led to the discovery of the Gunpowder Plot in 1605. According to legend, James I showed the letter to Dame Dorothy Selby, who understood at once its dreadful implications and urged the king, who usually dismissed such letters as the work of cranks, to treat it with the utmost seriousness. A mural in Ightham church is dedicated to Dame Dorothy.

▶ *3 miles SE of Sevenoaks, close to junction of A25 and A227.*

❸ Combwell

In a yew alcove in the garden of the old manor of Combwell, near Goudhurst, stands the statue of a woman carrying a pestle and mortar. This commemorates a cook who worked in the house at the time of the Civil War. The story goes that one Sunday, when the family had gone to church, she admitted a beggar woman to her kitchen. But as the woman bent down by the fire, the cook noticed that she wore boots and spurs beneath her ragged dress. Dealing the

'woman' a blow with the poker, the cook rushed upstairs and rang the alarm bell. Her master returned just in time to save the house from being sacked by a band of deserters. The cook's statue stood in the house for many years, but because it was considered 'uncanny' by later generations of servants, it was moved to the garden.

▶ *8 miles SE of Royal Tunbridge Wells, close to A21.*

❹ Maidstone

Henry VIII is said to have first set eyes on Anne Boleyn at nearby Allington Castle. In Maidstone Museum is a chair from the castle, with a faded inscription on the back giving substance to the legend that it was King Henry's privilege to kiss any woman who sat in it. The inscription reads:

'... of this (chay)re iss entytled too one salute from everie ladie thott settes downe in itt Castell Alynton 1530 Hen. 8 Rex'

▶ *32 miles SE of London. 2 miles from Junctions 5, 6 and 7 of M20.*

❺ Boxley

A monument in the church records the gratitude of Sir Henry Wyatt for a cat. Imprisoned in the Tower of London in 1483 for denying Richard III's right to the Crown, Sir Henry was left to die of starvation in a cold, damp cell. However, 'God sent a cat to both feed and warm him' – by sleeping on his chest at night, and bringing him pigeons to eat.

▶ *On minor roads 2 miles N of Maidstone.*

❻ Aylesford

Kit's Coty House, a megalithic burial chamber on Blue Bell Hill, is reputed to be the tomb of a British chieftain who was killed in personal combat with the Jutish leader Horsa in AD 455. Phantom combatants are alleged to re-enact the battle occasionally, 'in silence'. Other megaliths on the hill are called the Countless Stones. Once, a baker tried to count them by placing a numbered loaf on each stone, but when he came to collect them, there was one extra; the Devil had added one, foiling the baker's plan.

▶ *Close to Junction 6 of M20. Kit's Coty House 1 mile N of village.*

SOUTHERN ENGLAND

❼ Rochester

The ancient cathedral city of Rochester hosts the Sweeps festival on May Day weekend. This celebration dates from the time when May 1 was an annual holiday for chimney sweeps.

Until the 1960s, Rochester stood at the lowest crossing of the Medway. Traditionally, the river, which flows from West Sussex in the south to the Thames Estuary, is generally considered to be the dividing line between East Kent and West Kent. Men of Kent and Maids of Kent were the names given to those who lived east of the divide, while those who lived west of it were known as Kentish Men and Kentish Maids. The line is disputed, and may originally have been set farther east, running through the town of Gillingham.

▶ *30 miles SE of London on A2.*

❽ Newington

St Mary the Virgin, set amid the Kent cherry orchards at Newington, bears the footprint of the Devil on a stone near the entrance. According to legend, Satan, unable to endure the ringing of the church bells, collected them in a sack and leapt down from the church tower in order to bear them away. Overbalancing as he landed, he left his footprint on a stone near the church gate, and the bells rolled out of the sack and disappeared in a nearby stream. The bells must have been either recast or found and reinstated, since today Newington has a fine peal, rung by a regular team of ringers.

The stone itself is a sarsen – the same hard, sedimentary rock used to build the huge trilithons at Stonehenge.

▶ *7 miles E of Rochester on A2.*

KENT CELEBRATES THE OLD SWEEPS HOLIDAY

❾ Faversham

A plaque on the wall of the Swan in Market Street records the place where two Roman saints, Crispin and Crispinian, are supposed to have lived in the 3rd century. Their story, first recorded in 1598, takes place during the Roman occupation of Britain. It tells of two young sons of a native prince, who was executed by the Roman emperor Carausius. The boys were sent away from their home in Canterbury by their mother, who feared for their lives. On the road, the well-disguised young princelings paused outside a shoemakers in the town of Faversham, impressed by the joyful sounds coming from the company within, and both boys immediately agreed to seven-year apprenticeships.

The boys mastered their craft, and Crispin began to make shoes for the princess Ursula. The two fell in love and were married in secret. Meantime Crispinian was pressed into fighting the barbarians in France. After many adventures the brothers revealed their noble origins and lived happily, one as the princely son-in-law to the local king, and the other as a triumphant warrior. Crispin and Crispinian are the patron saints of bootmakers, leatherworkers and cordwainers, and Faversham's parish church keeps an altar in their honour.
▶ *10 miles NW of Canterbury on A2.*

❿ Minster-in-Sheppey

Minster Abbey, founded in 664, houses the magnificent stone effigy of Sir Roger de Shurland, whose death was said to be the result of a curse. The author R.H. Barham, in his 1840s book of myths, *The Ingoldsby Legends*, tells how the tempestuous Sir Roger de Shurland, Lord of Sheppey in 1300, killed a monk who defied him. Hunted by the county sheriff, Sir Roger obtained Edward I's pardon by swimming out to the king's ship on horseback as it was passing by in the Thames estuary. Returning to shore, he was met by a mysterious hag who prophesied that his horse, having saved his life, would also cause his death. The fiery knight at once drew his sword and beheaded the horse. Some years later, walking on the beach, he came upon its skull. Enraged, he kicked it, but one of its teeth penetrated his boot, causing an injury from which he died soon afterwards.
▶ *On N coast of Isle of Sheppey, 3 miles E of Sheerness.*

⓫ Harbledown

The village was the last halting place for pilgrims going to Canterbury. It contains the Black Prince's Well, which is so-called because Edward, Prince of Wales – known as the Black Prince because of the black armour he wore – set such store by the healing properties of its waters that he drank a flask of it every day. The prince died in 1376, probably of syphilis contracted in Spain.
▶ *1 mile NW of Canterbury city centre.*

⓬ Canterbury

The magnificent cathedral at Canterbury abounds with extraordinary carvings of fabulous lions, mythical creatures and strange, foliate-faced green men. There are more than 70 in all, on bosses, bench ends, capitals and tombs. Medieval masons and woodcarvers created all manner of extraordinary figures and faces, which peer from on high or out from darkened corners, their symbolism and meaning now lost.

Canterbury is also one of the popular centres for Hoodening, an ancient alms-collecting ceremony still practised in East (but not West) Kent, and especially in Thanet. The tradition derives its name from the Hooden Horse – a mock horse's head with a flapping lower jaw into which money is dropped. The head is operated by a man concealed beneath a white sheet. In summer the horse appears with morris men, and at Christmas with carol singers, calling at houses and farms. It rewards generosity with high-spirited cavortings. The custom may be linked with the local 5th-century Jutish worship of the god Woden, who rode an eight-footed white stallion.
▶ *55 miles SE of London.*

SOUTHERN ENGLAND

⑬ Reculver

The remains of a Saxon church with ruined towers, known as the Twin Sisters, stand right at the edge of the sea. Once, each tower had a spire, added in the 16th century at the request of the abbess of the Benedictine nunnery at Davington, Frances St Clare. The spires were to serve as a memorial to her twin sister, Isabel, and as a landmark for shipping in the Thames Estuary. The two nuns were on a pilgrimage to the shrine of the virgin at Bradstow when their ship was wrecked off Reculver. Isabel died from her injuries and was buried in the churchyard. When Frances died some years later, she was buried beside her sister under the twin towers, which can still be seen for miles around.

Another old legend in Reculver tells of babies who can be heard crying on the wind on stormy nights. The tale may have its foundation in ancient folk memory since in the late 1960s archaeologists excavating at the Roman fort found a number of babies' skeletons buried beneath the barrack area.

▶ *On minor road N of A299, 3 miles E of Herne Bay.*

⑭ Margate

In 1835, a Margate gentleman, Mr James Newlove, discovered a strange underground passage while digging a pond in his garden. He lowered his son into the hole, and was amazed to discover 21m (70ft) of snaking passages and an oblong chamber entirely covered with mosaics made of shells. The discovery was a complete surprise, both to Newlove and to the people of Margate. No one had ever heard of such a grotto, there were no records of its existence and no myths associated with its presence in the town. Seeing its potential as a visitor attraction, Newlove installed gas lamps and opened the grotto to the public.

The chamber had 4.6 million shells formed into 185sq m (2,000sq ft) of mosaic in floral and sun-style patterns. Nothing existed anywhere else with which to compare it, which added to the great mystery of its origins. Some favoured recent construction. In the 18th century, shell grottoes and follies were popular additions to country estates, but the Margate grotto lay on farmland with no country house nearby. Some believed it

RUINED TOWERS KNOWN AS THE TWIN SISTERS DOMINATE THE SHORE
RECULVER

to be a pagan temple, its origins dating back to pre-Roman times, some thought the Phoenicians built it, while others thought it had the hallmarks of a secret meeting place for a covert sect. The most straightforward means of dating the grotto – radiocarbon dating the shells – has been attempted, but the carbon residue from the gas lamps made the results wholy unreliable.

A recent suggestion is that the grotto was a temple based on the alignment of the sun, which shines down into the chamber's dome from a small circular window at ground level. A comprehensive study undertaken on behalf of Kent Archaeological Society suggests that the grotto is an enlargement of a medieval Dene hole – a chalk mine – decorated with shells from the 17th century onwards. But with no historical records, all theories remain conjecture.

▶ *On N coast of Kent, 16 miles NE of Canterbury. Shell Grotto E of town centre.*

⑮ Minster-in-Thanet

Thunor, a Kentish thane, secured the throne of Kent for Egbert I by murdering the young princes Ethelbert and Ethelred, and secretly burying their bodies within the royal palace. Shortly afterwards, the graves were revealed by two mysterious columns of light, and penitent Egbert ordered that a deer should be set to run free and all land to the east of its course should be given to the dead princes' sister, Ermenburga, so that she could build an abbey. Ever devious, Thunor tried to divert the animal, but 'the wrath of heaven came upon him, the earth opened and swallowed him up'. In 670 Minster Abbey was duly founded by Ermenburga, and today it is occupied by Benedictine nuns. At the top of Minster Hill an enormous pit is still known as 'Thunor's Leap'.

▶ *On minor roads just S of A253, 12 miles NE of Canterbury.*

GHOST SHIPS OF GOODWIN SANDS

AS MANY AS 50,000 MEN, women and children are thought to have died in shipwrecks on the Goodwin Sands, a treacherous sandbank that lies some 4 miles offshore, stretching for 9 miles from Kingsdown to Pegwell Bay, just south of Ramsgate. At high tide, the sands are submerged; at low tide, they become dry enough to walk on, until the tide rises again and the sands transform into deadly quicksand, swallowing stranded ships and their fated passengers and crew.

Local legends tell of phantom ships. The most famous is the *Lady Lovibond*, a three-masted schooner that was lost with all hands in 1748 on February 13. She was bound for Oporto, and on board was the captain's bride Anetta. Sailors have always believed that it is unlucky to take a woman to sea, but especially in this case since the mate had been a rival for Anetta's love.

Exactly 50 years later, the master of the coaster *Edenbridge* entered in his log that he had almost collided with a three-masted schooner sailing straight for the sands; another ship reported seeing the schooner run aground. In 1848 the schooner was seen again, but the Deal lifeboatmen who went to her rescue could find no trace of her. She was next seen in 1898, and then in 1948. There was no reported sighting in 1998.

The ghost of the SS *Violet* has also been seen; the cross-channel paddle steamer was driven aground in 1857 during a snowstorm, with the loss of 18 crew and one passenger. At the beginning of the Second World War, Mr George Carter, on the look-out on the East Goodwin lightship, saw an old paddle steamer run on to the sands and called out the Ramsgate lifeboat. An hour-long search revealed nothing, and no paddle steamer was reported missing.

⑯ Sandwich

Every night at 8pm, the curfew bell is tolled in the church of St Peter's in the medieval town of Sandwich. Once known as the pigbell, it sounded the time for the townspeople to cover their fires and let out their animals. The morning bell, the goosebell, was once rung at 5am – a tradition the locals were happy to relinquish.

The naval Battle of Sandwich was fought on St Bartholomew's Day, August 24, 1217, when the French fleet crossed the channel, heading for London. Sailing with them was an English pirate, Eustace the Monk. Eustace, reputedly, made his ship invisible, but his wizardry was defeated by Stephen Crabbe – also versed in the black arts – who boarded the ship and cut off Eustace's head; immediately the ship became visible.

In fact, the French were defeated by the Cinque Ports' fleet on this day, and the head of the treacherous monk was carried through the streets of Dover and Canterbury. The Sandwich hospital where the wounded were cared for still exists; it was renamed St Bartholomew's Hospital in commemoration of the victory.

Today, children gather on August 24 to run around St Bartholomew's Church, after which they are given a specially baked bun.

▶ *12 miles E of Canterbury at junction of A257 and A256.*

⑰ Folkestone

The old fishing town marks its association with the sea at the Blessing of the Sea and Fisheries ceremony. On the nearest Sunday to St Peter's Day, June 29, a musical procession wends its way through the town to the old fishing harbour.

▶ *15 miles E of Ashford on M20.*

⑱ Hythe

St Leonard's Church in Hythe dominates the old town. Traces of its Saxon origins can still be seen, including a green man carving on the chevroned arch, but its most unusual feature is its ossuary, or bone house, in a vaulted underground passage. Around 8,000 thigh bones and 2,000 skulls from the 14th and 15th centuries are stored there. It was once common practice for old graves to be cleared, and the bones stored, to allow for new burials, but few such ossuaries survive. Today the bones attract the curious, and are a fruitful subject of study for archaeologists looking into past populations of the area.

▶ *4 miles W of Folkestone on A259.*

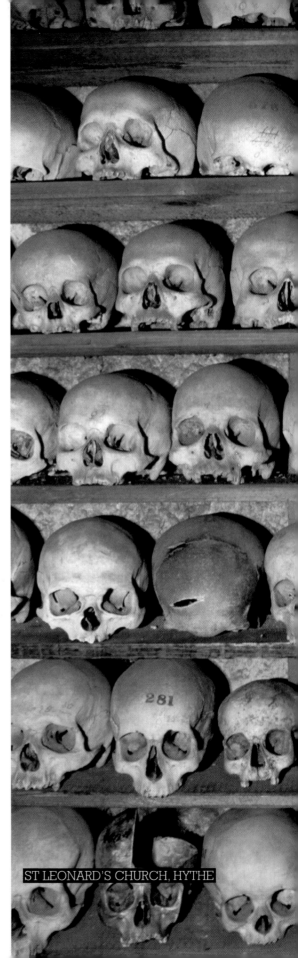

ST LEONARD'S CHURCH, HYTHE

⑲ Aldington

The ruined chapel at Court-at-Street is associated with the tragic story of the Holy Maid of Kent. In 1525, Elizabeth Barton, a local serving girl, claimed direct communication with the Mother of God. Her pronouncements made her famous, and money-seeking clergy persuaded her to enter a convent in Canterbury. In 1533, she made the mistake of prophesying death for Henry VIII if he should divorce Queen Catherine and marry Anne Boleyn. Together with the clerics who supported her, she was hanged at Tyburn in 1534.

▶ *5 miles SE of Ashford on minor roads.*

⑳ Eastwell

According to a local tale, when Sir Thomas Moyle was building his new mansion in Eastwell Park in 1545, he was astonished to find his foreman bricklayer reading a book in Latin. On being questioned, the bricklayer told Sir Thomas that he had been well educated as a boy. Then in 1485, he had been summoned to the royal camp at Bosworth Field to be told that he was the illegitimate son of Richard III, who had overseen his education and acknowledged him as his heir. The next day, Richard was killed in battle by the forces of Henry Tudor, and the king's son fled. To avoid recognition by Tudor agents, he became a bricklayer, and had worked at the trade ever since. Sir Thomas gave him a home at Eastwell, and there he died. The entry in the burial register reads 'December 22, 1550: Richard Plantagenet'. So it may be that an unmarked grave near the north side of the church contains the remains of the last member of the royal house of York.

▶ *W of A251, close to Boughton Lees. 4 miles N of Ashford.*

㉑ Biddenden

Anyone who visits the Old Workhouse on Easter Monday morning may apply for, and receive, a hard wheaten cake shaped like two women joined together at the hips and shoulders. These are given in memory of the Siamese twins, Elisa and Mary Chulkhurst, who were born in the village in 1100 and lived, joined together, for 34 years. They left their lands in trust to the poor of the village, and the rents are still spent on the sick and needy, as well as on the Easter dole of bread and cheese.

▶ *At junction of A262 and A274, 12 miles W of Ashford.*

SOUTHERN ENGLAND

The old and the new

Whether recently created or revived with a modern slant, southern festivals have an irresistible allure.

As the night of the midwinter solstice closes in, a dark-clothed cavalcade makes its way to the shore. Strange objects move above and around the procession – translucent stars, spiky crowns, faery figures, dragons that twist and float – each one a giant lantern made of willow wands and paper, intended to carry its maker's hopes and fears. On the beach the lanterns are set on fire, and with firework bursts and chants of 'Hail, bright herald, Hail!' the sun's return in ever-growing strength is invoked.

The ceremony is no Bronze or Stone Age ritual, and few of the celebrants are sun-worshipping pagans. They are car salesmen, teachers, unemployed youngsters, shop assistants, IT specialists and other inhabitants of modern-day Brighton in East Sussex. Each person wears a costume carrying the representation of a clock. This is the night of Burning The Clocks, one of Britain's numerous 'new traditions'. Burning The Clocks enjoys no ancient pedigree – it was created from scratch in 1993 by Brighton-based arts charity Same Sky, whose stated aim is creating 'new urban rituals to replace those traditional festivals that were lost in the dash to be new and non-superstitious.'

Ancient power base

Same Sky's manifesto speaks reassuringly of secularity, of celebration and of the sharing of thoughts and wishes – a nebulous yet all-embracing embodiment of New Age aspirations that find a ready response in the hip haven of modern Brighton. Others of the 'new traditions' are less warm and woolly, more flavoured with the spit and sawdust of old celebrations, decayed or altogether vanished, revived for a modern world. The May Day Jack-in-the-Green celebrations at Hastings, just along the south coast from Brighton, have a bucolic, timeless feel to them. What could be more atavistic, more traditional, than the figure of Jack himself? As tall as two tall men, Jack is a rustling, walking bush of leaves. His green face peers out from under a regal crown, his fixed expression, half jovial, half sinister. Surrounded by a capering, 600-strong crew of beer-ignited musicians, morris dancers and fools, he plugs us straight into the ancient terror and power of the primeval forest.

The Romans knew that power – they went to the greenwood in the springtime to gather boughs and blooms in honour of the goddess Flora. Citizens of old London acknowledged it in their May Day garland

parades, especially the chimney sweeps and their wretched little climbing boys. Released for one magical day from the black hell of the chimney flues they had to climb and clean, the boys would make greenery headdresses so exuberant they covered their entire bodies. So Jack-in-the-Green was born, according to some stories.

But Hastings Jack is a youngster in the tradition game. Climbing boys were abolished in 1868; polite Victorian society's disapproval did away with the drunken and randy Jacks. Hastings Jack slid quietly into oblivion, until Mad Jack's Morris Dancers

revived him in 1983 – two years after the Rochester Sweeps Festival enjoyed a rebirth of its own up on the North Kent coast. Now Hastings Jack-in-the-Green and the Rochester Sweeps go from strength to strength.

Ancient power base

The attraction of pagan festivals is stronger today than it has been for centuries – witness the druidical summer solstice celebrations at Stonehenge on the Wiltshire plain, for decades dismissed as a bunch of harmless cranks behaving oddly, but now attracting ever-increasing numbers of latter-day druids, neo-pagans and secular revellers. Church festivals used to link us to that pagan part of the collective psyche that is instinctively in tune with the seasonal cycle – Christmas and Epiphany around New Year,

Easter and Pentecost around May Day, Harvest Festival for the Celtic summer festival of Lughnasa, All Souls and All Saints for the autumn Samhain festival of the dead. But church festivals are not celebrated communally any more – at least not in significant numbers. Perhaps part of the magnetic attraction of outdoor celebration, especially if teamed with plenty of fire and pyrotechnics, has to do with filling the spiritual vacuum created by a secular society.

For ancient peoples, traditional ceremonies offered fixed points in the chaos of the world, times when at least some of the essentials – fire, food, fun – could be relied upon. Shut out the dark, set fears aside, let's have some light and some life! For the ceremonies' modern counterparts, nothing has really changed.

Each giant lantern made of willow wands and paper carries its maker's hopes and fears for the year

BURNING THE CLOCKS, BRIGHTON

OXFORDSHIRE

Deeply embedded amid the dreaming spires and verdant country, murmurs of an ancient past surface in seasonal celebrations. Traditions from medieval times and later are followed with equal gusto.

❶ Uffington Castle

Although fretted by the rains and frosts of 2,000 winters, the great chalk ramparts of Uffington Castle still loom protectively over the Vale of the White Horse. More important to the Celtic tribe who carved its battlements out of the hillside shortly before the Roman invasion was the fact that it commanded the Ridgeway, the prehistoric track that runs across England from the coast near Dover to Ilchester in Somerset. So obvious is its dominance that some people believe that Uffington was Mount Badon, the place where King Arthur finally defeated the Saxons, in about AD 518. There is little doubt that in the days when the valleys were thickly forested, whoever held the high Ridgeway route would control the West of England.

About a mile west along the Ridgeway from the White Horse is an empty Stone Age burial chamber which is at least 5,000 years old, and has been known as Wayland's Smithy since before the Norman Conquest. The story goes that after the coming of Christianity, Wayland, smith of the Norse gods, was forced to shoe mortals' horses for a living. So if you leave your horse and a coin beside the smithy, when you return, the horse will be shod, and the coin gone.

▶ *S of B4507, 6 miles W of Wantage.*

❷ Bampton

For nearly 500 years the Bampton Morris Men celebrated Whit Monday by dancing in the town; they now perform on Spring Bank Holiday. Based at the Horseshoe Inn, they are accompanied everywhere by the traditional Fiddler, the Fool with a bladder on a stick, and a Swordbearer. Impaled on his sword is a large plum cake, pieces of which he distributes for luck. One legendary member of the team, 'Jingy' Wells, was with the Bampton men for more than 60 years.

▶ *5 miles SW of Witney on A4095.*

❸ Finstock

To the northwest of Finstock lies the old Royal Hunting Forest of Wychwood, which once covered much of West Oxfordshire. The forest is now on private land, but access is granted on Spanish Liquor Day, the anniversary of an old tradition in which local people used forest water to make a special potion. This cure-all was based on Spanish liquorish, purchased and placed in bottles. The bottles were hung overnight, then taken to the 'Iron Well' where they were filled, shaken and used as medicine or drunk on the procession to the Lady's Well at Wilcote, on Palm Sunday. Girls picked flowers while walking to fill their new straw hats. The tradition is believed to be a relic of ancient well-worship, originally forbidden by the Church in AD 963.

▶ *5 miles N of Witney on B4022.*

❹ The Rollright Stones

The 77 weathered stones believed to be from the Middle Bronze Age have, for centuries, been known as the King's Men. Together with the King Stone, a solitary megalith, and the Whispering Knights, a 5,000-year-old burial chamber, they make up the Rollright Stones, one of the most legendary prehistoric sites in England.

The Rollright myth was first published in the 16th century, and told about a king – a would-be conqueror – and his army, all of whom were turned to stone by a witch. The spell is sometimes broken at midnight, when the stones go down to a spring to drink.

It is said that the stones can never be counted, and that those who try never arrive at the same number twice. Fairies are reputed to live beneath the stones, and good luck will come to those who leave the tiny spirits a small gift. Touching the King Stone was once believed to bestow fertility – today the King is protected behind bars because of the once-popular habit of chipping flakes from his majesty to ward off the Devil. Girls who want to know the names of their future husbands should ask the Whispering Knights, who will 'whisper' the reply.

▶ *1 mile S of Long Compton on A3400, 21 miles NW of Oxford.*

THE WHITE HORSE
– OR DRAGON –
IS ETCHED INTO
THE HILLSIDE
UFFINGTON CASTLE

❺ Chastleton

One of the bedrooms in the National Trust-run Chastleton House has a secret chamber. On the night of September 3, 1651, Arthur Jones, the owner of the house, rode home from the Battle of Worcester, where he had fought by the side of Charles II. Minutes later, a group of Cromwell's soldiers arrived. Jones hid in the secret room as the Roundheads began to search the house. Finding nothing, they settled for the night in the bedroom next to his hiding-place, and demanded a meal from Mrs Jones. She gave them well-drugged wine and they were soon unconscious, enabling Jones to escape. It was two years before he returned to Chastleton again. The bedroom has since been known as 'The Cavalier Room'.

▶ *Just off A44, 5 miles NW of Chipping Norton.*

❻ Otmoor

This bleak expanse of flat, swampy land covers some 6 sq miles just east of Oxford; it has been described in the past as 'bewitched' and 'cast under a spell of ancient magic'. Seven towns on its fringes share the rights to the common. According to legend, a lady from Otmoor once rode round the area while an oat sheaf was burning, saying that all the land within the circuit she covered while the sheaf still burnt should become common land for the citizens of the seven towns.

Many ancient customs are still continued in the Otmoor towns. At Charlton, for instance, there is a May Day procession, and at Oddington the crops are blessed on Rogation Sunday. There are also several medicinal wells on the moor. Those at Oddington cure 'Moor Evil', a disease that once affected many cattle in the area; and the black, peaty water in many of the others is said to heal various skin and eye complaints.

Since 1920, parts of the moor have been owned by the Ministry of Defence, and there is still an active rifle range. The RSPB have a reserve on Otmoor and are returning arable land to wetland meadows.

▶ *6 miles NE of Oxford.*

❼ Oxford

On May Day morning the choristers of Magdalen College re-enact a Christian ceremony that might well have its roots in some long-forgotten spring ritual. At 6am the choir gathers on top of the college tower and sings the 'Hymnus Eucharisticus', after which the chapel bells are rung and morris men begin dancing in the streets. Local pubs open their doors at sunrise to accommodate the huge crowd, but the recent tradition of leaping off Magdalen Bridge into the river, quite shallow at that point, has been halted, owing to the huge number of injuries sustained by participants. It may be that the choral custom developed out of a requiem mass said on the tower for Henry VII; after the reformation in 1534 the service was changed to suit the rites of the new Anglican Church.

At Queen's College, the ceremony of the Boar's Head is observed every Christmas Day. This is probably a relic of pagan custom, for boars were sacred animals to the Celts, and boar's flesh was the food of the Norse heroes who feasted with the god Odin in his paradise, Valhalla. When the Provost and fellows of the college have taken their places at the High Table, and grace has been said, a boar's head on a silver dish is carried into the Hall, followed by the college choir.

The procession stops three times to allow a soloist to sing a verse of the Boar's Head Carol, and, when the head is finally placed on the table, the singer is rewarded with the orange from the boar's mouth. Sprigs of bay and rosemary with which the head is decorated are distributed among the guests.

Local spells, charms and many curious artefacts fill the cabinets of the Pitt Rivers Museum, which is attached to Oxford's Museum of Natural History. Displays include items such as elf bolts (prehistoric stone arrowheads), thunder stones (stone axes), shrivelled potatoes to guard against rheumatism, and witches' ladders made of cock feathers on a string. Most of the museum's collection is devoted to archaeological and ethnographic artefacts from all over the world, including many of magical significance.

▶ *8 miles W of Junction 8 of M40.*

❽ Little Wittenham

Sinodun Hill and Harp Hill near Little Wittenham are collectively known as the Wittenham Clumps, since both are crowned with a clump of beech trees. The copse on Sinodun Hill is called 'The Cuckoo Pen', which comes from an old country story that if a cuckoo could be penned up in an enclosure of trees or hedges and prevented from flying away, summer would never end. Although cuckoos invariably flew out of such traps, it was hoped that when the hedges or trees grew higher, the birds would finally be unable to escape. Similar stories of rustics trying to pen the cuckoo occur all over Britain.

Sinodun Hill was once a Roman fort and treasure is believed to be buried in a hollow known as the 'Money Pit'. A local story relates how one day a villager dug a deep hole there. Just as he found an iron chest, a raven alighted on it and cried, 'He is not born yet!' Taking this to mean that he was not the one fated to have the treasure, the man immediately filled in the hole and went away.

▶ *On minor roads 2 miles S of A415, 8 miles S of Oxford.*

❾ Abingdon

Every year on the Saturday nearest to June 19, the Mayor of Ock Street is elected by those who live there. The candidates are often morris dancers, and the winner also becomes squire of the local morris men, who celebrate his victory by dancing outside the town's pubs. The tradition began in 1700 at Abingdon's annual St Edmund's Day Fair when, as was the custom, an ox was roasted and its meat distributed to the poor. An argument arose over the ox horns, and a wild struggle ensued for possession of them. An Ock Street resident, who was also squire of the morris dancers, emerged victorious and was declared the Mayor of Ock Street. The same horns and skull, set on a decorated pole, are now part of the Mayor's regalia and are brought out whenever the dancers perform. Another item of the Mayor's regalia, a wooden chalice, is said to be made from a cudgel used in the original fight.

The election of mock mayors was once a widespread tradition, their purpose being to make sure the civic mayor did the job properly without becoming too pompous. In Old Woodstock, where the tradition also continues, at the end of election-day festivities, the mock mayor is dropped in the river.

At Christmas time, the Abingdon Mummers tour the village, following a centuries-old tradition by acting out a morality tale – good versus evil wrapped up in the story of the seasons.

▶ *6 miles S of Oxford.*

ABINGDON

SURREY

The roar of ghostly engines, a stone that moves of its own accord and a tale of drowning and revenge all find their place among the old myths and modern legends of Surrey.

❶ Weybridge

The old motor-racing circuit at Brooklands, near Weybridge, was abandoned before the Second World War. Weeds and bushes have broken through the cracked concrete of the great sweeping embankments where Bentleys and Alfa-Romeos battled for supremacy, and the whole track has fallen into decay. Yet often at night, it is said, the roar of great engines and the scream of tyres can still be heard. At the end of the Railway Straight, the sheds of an aircraft factory were built over the track, covering the place where racing driver Percy Lambert was killed in October 1913. On several occasions, night-workers challenged an overalled, helmeted figure, and even chased it – until it disappeared through a solid wall. The figure is believed to be the ghost of Lambert.

Visitors with more earthly interests can visit the Brooklands Museum on the site. Check opening times before visiting.

▶ *2 miles E of Junction 11 of M25 on A317. Brooklands is 2 miles S of town centre.*

❷ Pyrford

The Pyrford Stone was probably used as a boundary mark before the Norman Conquest. It was shifted during road-widening operations but local people moved it again to a position as close as possible to its original site at the entrance to Pyrford Court. The stone is said to turn when it hears the cock crow at dawn – and when the clock on nearby St Nicholas's Church strikes midnight. The reference to the church is a Pyrford leg-pull – St Nicholas's has never had a clock.

▶ *2 miles E of Woking.*

❸ Guildford

An old charter says that 'whenever the King comes to Lothesley Manor near Guildford, the lord is to present His Majesty with Three Whores'. No one knows when the custom fell into abeyance.

Bull-baiting is said to have been introduced to England from the Continent by a 14th-century Earl of Surrey. The first contest took place in Guildford, and thereafter, each member of the Corporation, on appointment, was obliged to provide a breakfast for his colleagues and a bull for baiting. The custom lapsed as bull-baiting died out in the 19th century.

Under the terms of John How's will, ratified in 1674, 'two poor servant maids of good report' selected by the mayor and magistrates of Guildford, provided they 'do not live in any inn or alehouse', may throw dice for the interest on £400. Early in the 20th century, the legacy was added to under the terms of John Parson's will, and now 'Maid's Money' is contested each May at the Guildhall. The winner receives £62.

▶ *On A3, 9 miles from Junction 10 of M25.*

❹ Shere

The Silent Pool is a picturesque blue-green lake surrounded by trees, situated a mile west of Shere in Surrey, at the foot of the North Downs. This tranquil spot was the subject of a story written in 1858 by Martin Tupper, a gentleman from Albury, that has since passed into the realm of legend. The story concerned a local woodman with two teenaged children, a beautiful daughter and a handsome son. One day, a wealthy stranger rode past the pool near the woodman's hut and, seeing the woodman's daughter bathing, he stood his horse on her clothes and called for her to come out of the lake. She waded to the pool's deeper reaches and cried out in terror for her brother, who was working nearby. When he appeared the stranger rode off, but the girl was already struggling in the water as she could not swim. The boy rushed to help her, but he too was unable to swim and, tragically, the pair drowned.

Later, the woodman came by and found their bodies. In his grief he also noticed a feather caught in a tree, which had come from the stranger's hat. He took the feather to town and discovered that the stranger was none other than Prince John, who was ruling the country as Regent in place of Richard the Lionheart, while the king was away fighting in the Crusades. The woodman enlisted the sympathy of the local barons, and exacted a kind of revenge when the lords banded together, forcing John to sign Magna Carta in 1215.

The ghost of the unfortunate girl is said to haunt the pool to this day.

▶ *Just S of A25, 5 miles E of Guildford.*

SUSSEX

From playing marbles to carrying lucky stones, games and superstitions are deeply rooted in the traditions of Sussex, while pagan customs and festivals have been given a modern slant.

❶ Tinsley Green

Since 1932 the British and World Marbles championship has taken place on Good Friday at the Greyhound Pub in Tinsley Green, although the history of the event is thought to go back at least two centuries. Club, international and individual matches are overseen by the British Marbles Board of Control, and are played on permanent outdoor rings. For decades, the event has been treated as an excuse to sport team colours and fancy dress, by spectators as well as teams.
▶ *Close to A23, 3 miles N of Crawley.*

❷ East Grinstead

Snakes are considered unlucky in Sussex, and in 1936 the erection of a statue depicting the serpent and staff of Aesculapius, Greek god of medicine, outside the Queen Victoria Hospital caused a public outcry. Protesters were told it would cost £63 to remove the 'brazen serpent', and so there it remains.

The small town has a high number of different religious organisations, including the Full Gospel church, Methodist church, Baptist church and Jehovah's Witness church, the Opus Dei sect and the headquarters of the Church of Scientology. The mormons' striking London England Temple is just over the border in Surrey. A 1994 Channel 4 documentary failed to reach a conclusion about why East Grinstead has attracted so many faiths.
▶ *At junction of A22 and A264, 8 miles E of Crawley.*

TINSLEY GREEN IN THE 1970S

❸ Chanctonbury Ring

If a man or woman were to run around the Iron Age hillfort of Chanctonbury Ring at midnight on Midsummer Eve, the Devil may appear with the offer of a bowl of porridge. On no account should the food be accepted, because the Devil will take that person's soul in exchange – or, in another telling of the tale, his or her dearest wish will be granted.

The ring is fenced off and surrounded by a tangle of trees and scrub. It is an eerie place, even on a bright summer's day. The trees are said to be uncountable, and several visitors have reported seeing ghosts, strange lights and even little people nearby. Within the hillfort lie the remains of a Romano-British temple – a building, complete with a courtyard, that is estimated to have been in use for 300 years. The Ring has its own morris dancing side based in Woodmancote near Henfield.
▶ *On South Downs Way 3 miles W of Steyning, 11 miles NW of Brighton.*

❹ Worthing

From beneath a hollow oak tree at the end of Broadwater Green, skeletons were said to rise on Midsummer Eve and dance hand in hand around the trunk until the first cock crowed. Today, the ancient oak still stands proud, but on a triangle of land in the middle of a road intersection.
▶ *11 miles W of Brighton.*

❺ Highdown Hill

A windmill that once stood on the hill to the northwest of Worthing was inherited in 1750 by the miller, John Olliver. Prosperous and well regarded, the miller was nevertheless considered eccentric, because in 1764 he began work on the construction of a stone tomb on a nearby hilltop, on land owned by a neighbour, William Westbrooke Richardson. Olliver built a small wooden house beside the tomb and spent most of his time there; he also made a wooden coffin for himself and kept it under his bed.

Smuggling was big business all along the Sussex coast and it was suggested that the miller acted as a lookout for the gangs. But hilltop life must have suited him, since he lived happily to the age of 84. His funeral was a spectacular affair, with mourners dressed in bright colours as per Olliver's request. More than 2,000 people came, and it was reported that rioting broke out among the mourners, who had come to see his white coffin, drawn to his tomb by eight maidens clad in white. One of them, Ann Street, aged 12, read the sermon that Olliver himself had composed.

Modern legend has it that if you run seven times forward round the tomb you will summon Olliver's ghost. Most visitors prefer to look at the wealth of flora, the ancient remains of the Iron Age hillfort nearby and the magnificent views.

▶ *Off A259, 3 miles W of Worthing.*

❻ Steyning

The buildings of Steyning Grammar School stand on Penfolds Field, which was cursed by St Cuthman in the 8th century. When he was a boy, St Cuthman spread the gospel through Sussex, pulling his invalid mother along with him in a cart. As they passed Penfolds Field, the cart broke and the old lady fell to the ground. The haymakers laughed and jeered, so St Cuthman cursed the field; rain poured down and spoilt the hay, and to this day, it is always supposed to rain when Penfolds Field is being mown. Christopher Fry made St Cuthman the hero of his play *Boy with a Cart* and a stone in Steyning church is believed to have covered the saint's grave.

▶ *10 miles NW of Brighton on A283.*

❼ Henfield

A row of iron cats attached to the wall of a 16th-century timber-framed cottage near the church is said to recall a feud between a villager and the vicar. The church cat ate the villager's canary and, in retaliation, the local man

made models of cats out of sheet iron, attached them to a wire, and jangled them whenever the vicar walked by. The model cats were later cemented to the wall.

▶ *12 miles S of Horsham on A281.*

❽ Brighton

Brightonians still carry holed stones picked up on the beach for luck – a belief going back at least 5,000 years, to judge by similar stones found in the grave of a Stone Age woman at Whitehawk Neolithic Camp, east of the town.

Bat-and-trap, a traditional ball game related to cricket, is played on The Level – Brighton's central park – on Good Friday morning. The trap

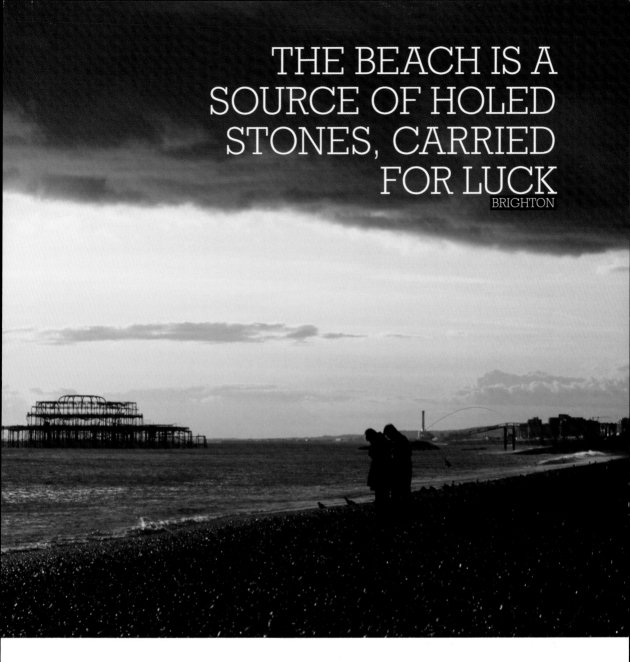

THE BEACH IS A SOURCE OF HOLED STONES, CARRIED FOR LUCK

BRIGHTON

is a seesaw-like catapult, which throws a hard rubber ball in the air when the batsman hits the trap's raised end with his bat. The game is also played in Kent, and may have its origins in ancient fertility rites.

In the grounds of the Pavilion stands an ancient oak; like several similar trees scattered throughout the country, it is said to be the one in which Charles II hid after the Battle of Worcester. A Sussex location seems unlikely, but the story is vouched for by the descendants of the captain of the ship that took the king to France from nearby Shoreham in 1651.

Built into the wall surrounding Rudyard Kipling's old house, the Elms at Rottingdean, is a lucky flint 'head'. Anyone who strokes the nose

gently in a clockwise motion with the forefinger of the right hand, then turns round three times, will be granted his or her dearest wish – or so local legend maintains.

The most spectacular of Brighton's 'traditions' is one of its newest. Burning the Clocks first took place in 1993 and is a lantern parade – an urban ritual that draws on elements of ancient fire festivals to create a winter solstice antidote to Christmas excess. Lantern makers imbue their white paper and willow creations with their fears, hopes and wishes, then walk with them through Brighton's streets to the sea front, where the paper clocks are cast into a gigantic bonfire while fireworks blaze overhead.

▶ *30 miles S of Junction 11 of M23 on A23.*

❾ Lewes

The town is famous for its November 5 celebration, a spectacular fire festival of individual bonfire societies culminating in the tossing of a flaming tar barrel into the River Ouse. The event dates from the time when the mostly Protestant townspeople were persecuted and many were burnt as heretics by the Catholic Mary Tudor. Lack of parking and public transport make it difficult for outsiders to attend, and for comfort and safety, it is recommended that the general public do not attempt to do so.

▶ *8 miles NE of Brighton on A27.*

❿ Alfriston

The site of St Andrew's church was chosen, according to legend, by four white oxen that were observed to lay rump to rump in the shape of a cross. As late as 1932, a shepherd was buried in the churchyard with a tuft of wool in his hand. Shepherds were often buried in this way so that they could prove to St Peter that their irregular attendances at church were due to the demands of their trade.

▶ *1 mile S of A27, 8 miles NW of Eastbourne.*

⓫ Wilmington

The origins of the famous 'Long Man', cut in chalk on Windover Hill and given its present form in 1874, are a matter for debate and have been ascribed to every period from the Neolithic to the Middle Ages. One theory is that it is a Saxon warrior-god, originally a spear-wielding figure in a horned helmet, identical to that engraved on a buckle found in a 7th-century grave at Finglesham in Kent. If so, the helmet and spear points must have been turfed over, leaving only the vague outline of a 'cap', mentioned in some early accounts, and two staffs. The 69m (227ft) figure may well date from the 16th century, following investigations in the 1990s, as there are no earlier historical notes of the figure.

▶ *7 miles NW of Eastbourne on A27.*

⓬ Friston

The churchyards of Friston and East Dean both have Tapsell gates, named after the 18th-century carpenter who built them. Balanced on a central pivot, they open at the lightest touch; at weddings, however, the gates are tied shut with white ribbon, and the bride is lifted over them by the groom.

▶ *4 miles W of Eastbourne on A259.*

⓭ Heathfield

April 14 is 'Hefful' – the old name for Heathfield – Fair Day. According to legend, an old woman at the fair lets the first cuckoo of the year out of a basket. It said to be lucky to hear the first cuckoo on that day.

▶ *Close to junction of A267 and A265. 14 miles S of Royal Tunbridge Wells.*

⓮ Brightling

'Mad' Jack Fuller was buried under a 7.6m (25ft) stone pyramid in the churchyard of St Thomas Becket in Brightling in 1811, wearing a top hat and seated at a table laid with roast chicken and a bottle of wine, according to local myth. Fuller was far from mad – heir to a fortune and a hardworking politician, he supported the Royal Institution, mentored Michael Faraday in his development of the electric motor and financed the Belle Tout lighthouse at Beachy Head. Renovations of the tomb in 1982 put an end to the rumour of his eccentric burial. He lies beneath the impressive pyramid in a conventional manner.

▶ *On minor roads off B2096, 6 miles NW of Battle.*

⓯ Rye

Inside a gibbet cage in Rye Town Hall is the skull of John Breeds, a local butcher who was hanged in 1742 for a crime that misfired. Instead of murdering the mayor, against whom he bore a grudge, he killed the mayor's brother-in-law. The rest of Breeds' bones may have been stolen to make medicine. It was a popular belief that a cure for rheumatism could be made from the bones of a person hung on a gibbet.

▶ *At junction of A259 and A268, 11 miles NE of Hastings.*

JACK-IN-THE-GREEN IS THE SPIRIT OF THE FOREST
HASTINGS

⑯ Hastings

A cock crowing is said to have woken a force of Danes occupying Hastings in the 9th century and foiled a local uprising against their tyranny. In revenge, the townspeople instituted the game of cock-in-the-pot. Sticks were thrown at an earthen pot containing a cock; whoever broke it won the bird. The game was held on Shrove Tuesday until the 19th century.

Today, Hastings is famous for another old tradition: the exuberant, rainbow-coloured Jack-in-the-Green festival, held in the town over the early May bank holiday. These 19th-century revels were revived in 1979 by Mad Jack's Morris Dancers, and celebrate the pagan character of 'Jack', a spirit of the forest and the winter form of the green man. Jack is accompanied by the bogies, of which there are several distinctive groups, all richly clothed and painted green. Drummers drum, musicians play and painters dab the noses of spectators with green-soaked sponges. There is also a contingent of giants and Hannah, a local Hastings witch based on a 16th-century character who lived in the Stag public house in the old town. She was a good witch, and was said to protect Hastings against Napoleonic invaders.

The town also celebrates the Blessing of the Sea in early June.

▶ *35 miles E of Brighton.*

WILTSHIRE

Folklore prevails where facts have faded, and Wiltshire's ancient monuments inspire tales of golden kings, thieving devils, Druid sacrifice and the healing power of stones.

❶ Avebury Stone Circle

Avebury World Heritage site is a henge monument enclosing one of the most impressive stone circles in Europe. This mighty ditch, bank and standing-stone structure was built and remodelled from around 2850 to 2200 BC. Its true function is unknown. An avenue runs from the circle to a place known as the Sanctuary on Overton Down 1½ miles away to the east. A second avenue leading to Beckhampton in the west was uncovered after an excavation in the 1990s. Certainly, whatever took place at Avebury was important to the people of Britain; it has been estimated that the monument took 1.5 million man hours to build.

In the Middle Ages, the Church gave orders for the pagan megaliths to be buried. It seems that the folk memory of their origins was buried with them, as there are no tales of wizards, devils or even Druids to explain their presence. In the 15th and 16th centuries many more of the stones were broken up and used for local building purposes, and the monument was all but forgotten by the outside world until its discovery by the antiquarian John Aubrey in the 17th century. Excavations carried out in 1938 revealed a man's skeleton beneath one of the buried stones. Several coins and surgical tools identified him as a tradesman – a barber surgeon – who died around 1320. He was undoubtedly killed when the stone he was helping to bury fell and crushed him. Today, concrete markers indicate the positions where the lost megaliths were once set.
▶ *12 miles S of Swindon near junction of A4361 and A4.*

❷ Silbury Hill

When, in 1967, archaeologists began excavating the massive man-made mound of Silbury Hill, part of their wish was to discover the remains of the legendary King Sil (or Zel), said to be buried in magnificent golden armour and possibly even mounted on a horse. They were unsuccessful, and further excavations in 2009 uncovered no such remains. The builders' intention in creating this phenomenal mound around 2400 BC remains a mystery. King Sil was said to gallop around the mound on his horse on moonlit nights. Alternative folktales involve the Devil using the hill to hide a golden statue, or dumping earth intended for the town of Marlborough by the roadside.
▶ *Just N of A4, 7 miles W of Marlborough.*

❸ Stonehenge

The 12th-century chronicler Geoffrey of Monmouth wrote that the massive stones standing proud on Salisbury Plain were originally brought from Africa to Ireland by a

THE LARGEST STONE CIRCLE IN BRITAIN
AVEBURY

race of giants. There they were known as the Giant's Dance, and were moved to Wiltshire in the 6th century by Merlin at the request of Ambrosius Aurelianus, King of the Britons. In another version of the story, the Devil stole the stones from an old Irishwoman and built Stonehenge according to Merlin's plans. Even serious speculation about its origins involved flights of fancy. The 17th-century antiquary John Aubrey claimed that it had been a Druidic centre of sun-worship and human sacrifice, a view that was echoed by William Stukeley over a century later. Inigo Jones, the architect, suggested it may have been a shrine to the Roman god Uranus.

Although much of the mystery remains, archaeology has revealed that the monument was constructed and constantly remodelled over a period of around 1,000 years, beginning about 3000 BC. Its builders were the same Late Stone Age farmer-shepherds and warriors who had previously buried their dead on the Plain.

To start with, a bank and ditch were built around a circle of small pits, known as the Aubrey Holes after their discoverer. It has been suggested that these were symbolic doors leading to the underworld, and that the blood of slaughtered beasts was poured into them as offerings to the gods. The Heel Stone, which lies outside the embankment, also belongs to this period. An old

legend says that the Devil caught a monk prying on his antics among the stones. Before the monk could escape, the Devil hurled the great boulder at him, pinning the unfortunate churchman by the heel. Many years later, huge bluestones were brought 200 miles from the Preseli mountains in South Wales and erected in two circles at the centre of the site, and many years after that, 40–50 tonne sarsen stones (hard sandstone) were transported 20 miles from Marlborough Downs. These were erected as outer and inner circles of trilithons (two stones with a third set crossways on top of them).

Geoffery of Monmouth wrote of the stones having healing properties and today that is exactly what some researchers believe, especially of the bluestones, since the Preseli mountains are known for healing springs. Perhaps the chronicler was reporting the fragments of a folk memory.

In 2001, English Heritage declared Stonehenge open and free to the public from the hours of 8pm on June 20 to 9am on June 21 to enable solstice celebrations to take place. This managed open access enables people to get close to the stones, and each year an exuberant mix of morris sides, Druids, witches, samba bands and musicians mingle with the general public in a night-long vigil to watch the sun rise above the Heel Stone.

▶ *8 miles N of Salisbury close to A303.*

London

Below the surface of the modern metropolis lies a city built on myth, where the beliefs of past generations have given rise to today's traditions. Latter-day lore tells of strange things, from a lucky hotel cat to an entombed Victorian train.

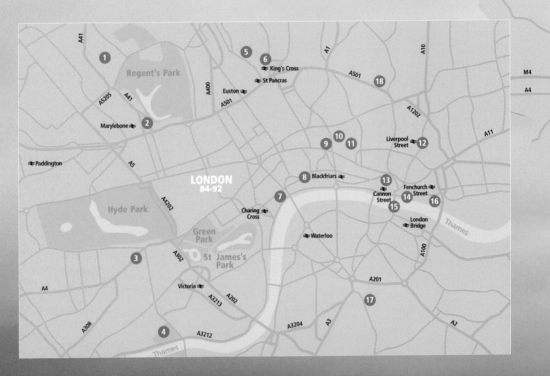

LONDON
84-92

LONDON

A long and eventful history has made London a hotbed of quirky tales and eccentric practices, where colourful, pomp-filled ceremonies rub shoulders with local traditions.

❶ St John's Wood

Travellers on the Bakerloo Line between Baker Street and St John's Wood stations often feel a 'popping' in their ears. The story goes that this is caused by the tunnel making a sudden dip to avoid the plague burial pit now covered by the Marylebone War Memorial. The same tale was told of the Piccadilly Line east of South Kensington and the Central Line between Liverpool Street and Bank. While there were undoubtedly plague pits in London, the tube story is an urban myth. There is no known pit in the Marylebone area and the particular section of the Bakerloo Line from Baker Street to Finchley Road was bored much deeper than a plague pit would ever have been dug in past centuries, and – had there even been such a pit – would simply have passed right underneath it.

▶ *W of Regent's Park. St John's Wood tube.*

❷ Baker Street

The most famous address that never existed is 221b Baker Street, London. It was here that Sherlock Holmes, the famous fictional detective, lived with his companion, Dr Watson, in Sir Arthur Conan Doyle's immortal stories. From 1932, letters addressed to Sherlock Holmes were answered by the Abbey National Building Society, occupiers of Abbey House on the supposed location in Baker Street. In 1990, the number – 221b – was assigned to the Sherlock Holmes Museum.

▶ *Museum at N end of Baker St close to Regent's Park. Baker Street tube.*

❸ Knightsbridge

In September 2005, Harrods owner Mohammed Al Fayed unveiled a statue of Diana, Princess of Wales and his son Dodi to commemorate their lives, tragically lost in 1997 in a road accident in a Paris underpass. The bronze sculpture by door three was created by Bill Mitchell, the store's artistic design adviser, and shows the pair dancing, together with an albatross. The decorative waters that comprise part of a second memorial at the foot of the Egyptian escalator on the lower ground floor have acquired something of the status of a holy well. People have been known to gather water surreptitiously in plastic bottles, presumably for its hoped-for healing properties.

▶ *S of Hyde Park. Knightsbridge tube. Sloane Square tube.*

LONDON'S DARK RIVER

LONDON OWES ITS EXISTENCE to a ford that apparently still exists beneath the Thames mud opposite the Houses of Parliament. Caesar's legions took this route in the 1st century AD before going on to storm the heights to the north – Primrose Hill, Hampstead and Highgate. As well as being the lowest fording point, London was the highest reach of the Thames where sea-going vessels could unload their cargoes, and a convenient place to build a bridge. The river became London's highway. In Tudor times boatmen plied for hire near the watergates of great houses, using a traditional cry of 'Eastward Ho!' or 'Westward Ho!' to attract passengers.

The name Thames is an evolution of the Roman 'Tamesis', which is derived from the pre-Roman 'Tems'. Etymologists believe this comes from the Sanskrit word 'Tamasa', meaning dark river or dark water, and may have been part of the language of proto-Indo European-speaking people who settled in southern Britain after the retreat of the ice.

During the 19th century, Thames dredgers often sifted swords, helmets and shields from the mud, thought to have been offerings to the gods. Similar finds of weaponry across Europe suggested that these were more than chance losses. Human skulls were also found, dating from around 4500 to 1300 BC. More than 300 survive in archaeological collections today. These skulls, rarely found with other human bones, were predominantly male. No conclusive studies have been undertaken, but various theories suggest they might be victims of human sacrifice, or subjects of excarnation, whereby corpses are exposed on platforms or in trees to divest their bones of flesh.

④ Royal Hospital

On May 29, the anniversary of the Restoration of the monarchy, the old soldiers – pensioners of the Royal Hospital, Chelsea – parade in their scarlet uniforms, which are adapted from those worn by the Duke of Marlborough's forces in the 18th century. They sport oak leaves to acknowledge the fact that, more than 350 years ago, May 29 was also designated Oak Apple Day or Royal Oak Day, to commemorate the future king's escape after his defeat at the Battle of Worcester in 1651. Charles evaded capture by hiding in an oak tree, and then made his way to France where he lived in exile until invited to return in 1660. He arrived on his birthday, May 29, and the day was celebrated as a public holiday until 1859. Statues of the king are traditionally wreathed in oak branches on this day, and at the end of the Chelsea pensioners' parade, they raise three cheers for 'King Charles II, our pious founder'.

▶ *On N bank of Thames close to Chelsea Bridge.*

ROYAL HOSPITAL, CHELSEA

❺ St Pancras Old Church

When the magnificent station was built in the 1860s, an old cemetery had to be dug up and destroyed. A young architecture student named Thomas Hardy was put in charge of the exhumation and was horrified at the lack of respect with which the dead had been treated before his arrival. The bodies were reinterred in a mass grave and many of the tombstones were crowded into St Pancras churchyard, set one behind another like sliced bread. These later became entwined in the roots and trunk of an ash tree. The tree is known as the Hardy Tree after the student, who changed career and later became the great English novelist and poet. His poem 'The Levelled Churchyard' recalls the event:

'We late-lamented, resting here, Are mixed to human jam, And each to each exclaims in fear, I know not which I am!'

▶ *On Pancras Rd N of St Pancras International Station. King's Cross St Pancras tube.*

❻ King's Cross Station

Boudicca, queen of the Iceni of eastern Britain, led a revolt against the occupying Roman army, but was finally defeated and allegedly took poison to avoid capture. No one knows where the last battle was fought, although some say it was on the site of King's Cross station, and that she is buried under Platform 10.

▶ *At junction of Euston Rd and York Rd. King's Cross St Pancras tube.*

TOMBSTONES ARE SET ONE BEHIND ANOTHER LIKE SLICED BREAD
ST PANCRAS OLD CHURCH

⑦ Savoy Hotel, Strand

At the Savoy Hotel, precautions were taken to avoid having 13 people at a table. In 1898 South African diamond millionaire Woolf Joel hosted a dinner party at the hotel, and a sudden cancellation meant guests numbered 13. When he returned home, Joel was murdered in his office by a blackmailer. To counter the possibility of people avoiding the hotel out of superstition, the management insisted that a member of staff dine with any party of 13. This was not always popular with guests, so in 1926, British architect Basil Ionides (1884-1950) was asked to create a sculpture of a cat, which he did out of a single piece of London plane. So if a party of 13 arrives, a 14th place is laid for the cat, Kaspar.

During the Second World War, Kaspar was kidnapped by RAF pilots, as a prank, but was eventually returned to his place in the Pinafore Room. In 2009 Kaspar was immortalised in a children's novel by Michael Morpurgo, illustrated by Michael Foreman.

▶ *S off The Strand, E of Charing Cross Station. Charing Cross tube.*

⑧ St Clement Danes, Strand

The oranges and lemons motif on a footstool in St Clement Danes church, recalls a time when in the Inns of Court, staff of St Clement's Inn gave fruit to residents. Another church, in Eastcheap, lays claim to be the St Clement's of the nursery rhyme – the church was once close to a wharf on the Thames where citrus fruit from the Mediterranean was docked, and would peal its bells when the cargo came in.

▶ *At junction of The Strand and Fleet St outside the Royal Courts of Justice. Temple tube.*

⑨ Ely Place

On his way to execution, the 4th-century Christian martyr St Blaise touched the throat of a boy choking on a fishbone, and saved his life. The miracle is commemorated in the Blessing of the Throats service held at St Etheldreda's Church on February 3, St Blaise's Day. People suffering from throat troubles kneel at the altar rail, and the priest touches their throats with two candles tied together to form a cross.

Ely Place was once the town residence of the bishops of Ely, and it is one of only two places in the City (the other is the Temple) over which the Lord Mayor has no jurisdiction. To proclaim its separate identity, a liveried beadle ritually locks its gates at 10pm each night.

▶ *N off Holborn Circus. Farringdon tube.*

⑩ Cowcross Street

The Castle is the only public house in Britain to have a pawnbroker's licence. The story goes that in the early 19th century, George IV, wearing a long cloak and large hat to conceal his identity, borrowed £1 from the landlord after gambling away all his ready cash at a cockfight in Clerkenwell. He left his watch as security, and went back to the ringside. Next day, a messenger redeemed the watch, and the king rewarded the publican by granting The Castle a pawnbroker's licence for as long as it remained standing.

▶ *E off Farringdon Rd, N of junction with Charterhouse St. Farringdon tube.*

⑪ St Bartholomew-the-Great

On Good Friday each year, sixpences are placed on a tomb in the churchyard and are collected by the poor widows of the parish. The women then step across the tomb and each is presented with a hot cross bun. Both money and buns are provided by the church. The origin of the custom is obscure, but it is probably connected with 'sin-eating', in which the living ritually assumed the sins of the dead by eating a morsel of bread over the corpse.
▶ *SE of Smithfield Central Market. Barbican tube.*

⑫ Bishopsgate

Dirty Dick's, a pub in Bishopsgate, takes its name from a well-known City eccentric of the 18th century, Nathaniel Bentley. He was a Leadenhall Street merchant who in his youth was noted as a scholar and a man of fashion, and was nicknamed 'the Beau of Leadenhall Street'. But the shock of his fiancée's death on their wedding eve drove him to retreat into slovenly isolation. 'Dirty Dick', as he became known, never washed, saying that if he did so, he would only be dirty again the next day. On his death, according to legend, the room in which the wedding breakfast had been laid was found as it had been left on the tragic day of his loved one's death 50 years before.
▶ *E of Liverpool St Station. Liverpool St tube.*

⑬ Cannon Street

A remnant of the London Stone was once set in the wall of St Swithin's Church, opposite Cannon Street Station. When the church was demolished, the stone was set into the wall of the building that replaced it, number 111 Cannon Street. The stone's origin is obscure. Archaeologists have suggested that the Romans measured distances from it along their road network, but legend insists that Brutus the Trojan, mythical founder of the city, laid the stone as a temple altar, and that 'so long as Brutus's stone is safe, so long shall London flourish'.
▶ *Opposite front of Cannon St Station. Cannon St tube.*

⑭ Billingsgate

According to a medieval tale, Billingsgate takes its name from Belin, a legendary king of the Britons who 'built a tower of prodigious height and a safe harbour for ships'. For 1,000 years Billingsgate market stood near London Bridge on the site of the old river gate to the City, selling all kinds of goods including coal, iron, wine and salt until the 16th century, when it became exclusively devoted to the selling of fish. Eels were the only exception – rights to sell eels were granted to the Dutch fishermen who moored their boats in the Thames in gratitude to the men who had fed Londoners after the Great Fire in 1666.

Today the old Thamesfront market is a corporate events and exhibition venue, only its fish-shaped weathervanes indicating its former use. The fish market moved to Poplar in east London in 1982. Spanning more than 5ha (13 acres), it is Britain's largest inland fish market. The porters' white sailcloth smocks have been retained, but the leather flat-topped hats, designed for bearing crates of fish and said to be modelled on those worn by the English archers at the Battle of Agincourt, are worn only on special occasions.
▶ *Original market site off Lower Thames St, E of London Bridge. Monument tube.*

⑮ London Bridge

Spanning the Thames between Southwark on the south bank and the City of London in the north, the present London Bridge was opened in 1973, although a bridge has existed here since the time of the Roman occupation. The historic 'old' London Bridge was considered a great wonder – a stone structure completed in 1209 with a gatehouse and drawbridge, and crowded with shops and dwellings projecting on jetties far out over the Thames. The London Bridge Experience and Museum, situated by today's bridge, are dedicated to its history.

The children's nursery rhyme 'London Bridge is falling down' is known in a number of versions, and it can be traced back as far as the mid 17th century. Its origins are obscure, though, and it is probably much older. There are several theories about its meaning, including that it is based on the bridge's destruction in the early 11th century by the Viking invader Olaf II of Norway, despite that invasion being the stuff of myth.

More sinister is the theory of child sacrifice, put forward by Alice Bertha Gomme, a Victorian folklorist. Gomme suggested that children were buried in the foundations as a form of offering, in the same way that ancient cultures interred babies and children in the foundations of buildings. There is no archaeological evidence to support this theory.

By the late 13th century, the first stone bridge was falling into serious disrepair, and it may be that the rhyme simply commemorates the disintegration of this famous landmark. The 'fair

lady' may be the spendthrift Queen Eleanor, who was given the tolls from the bridge by her husband, Henry III, as a gift.

The bridge was rebuilt several times over the following centuries, and in 1831 a five-arched stone bridge designed by the celebrated dock, bridge and lighthouse builder Sir John Rennie (1761-1821) was completed. When, in the 1960s this bridge was found to be sinking, a member of the Common Council of the City of London, Ivan Luckin, hit upon the idea of putting the bridge up for sale. It was purchased by an American oil magnate and entrepreneur, Robert P. McCulloch, in 1968 and today spans the Bridgewater Channel Canal at Lake Havasu City, Arizona. It forms a central part of an English theme park, London Bridge Resort.

The popular myth that McCulloch believed he was buying Tower Bridge is a modern fabrication. The £1,029,000 McCulloch paid still earns money for Bridge House Estates, the organisation that has maintained the City's bridges since 1282.

▶ *Lies between Southwark Bridge (W) and Tower Bridge (E). London Bridge and Monument tubes.*

⓰ The Tower of London

The most potent tourist attractions in the Tower of London are the Crown Jewels, and they have a dark side to their story. The Koh-i-Noor diamond, originally mined in India, was presented to Queen Victoria by the East India Company in 1850. Legend – derived from a medieval Hindu text – says that the owner will be ruler of the world, but if the owner is a man, he will die a violent death. Many male owners of the diamond have died in this way – some on the battlefield and some murdered. The diamond was last worn by the late Queen Mother as she lay in state in her coffin in 2002.

But it is the six ravens that are the subject of the Tower's most chilling legend: it is said that if they leave the Tower, a terrible disaster will befall England. The ravens are believed to have been at the Tower since the 13th century and to be protected by Royal order of Charles II, who decreed there would always be six ravens to protect the kingdom. However, 21st-century research suggests that the myth of the ravens is itself a myth. Dr Geoff Parnell, official Tower of London historian, found no evidence of the ravens before 1895, when he suspects they were kept as pets by the Tower's Yeomen.

Today's ravens are cared for by an official Ravenmaster, who feeds them with meat from Smithfield market and blood-soaked biscuits. They are not considered pets, but military personnel, enlisted for service. Just as they are enlisted, they can equally be dismissed. George, a raven enlisted in 1975 was dismissed in 1986 for conduct unsatisfactory, and ended his days in a zoo in Colwyn Bay. His crime? Biting through the cables of the Tower's television aerials.

▶ *On N bank of Thames, W of Tower Bridge. Tower Hill tube.*

Traditions of a city

A constantly shifting and enriching mix of people has given London a unique character and rich traditional life.

London traditions are many and varied. How could it not be so, with a large permanent population and a pre-eminent status since the Romans founded it? Strongest have been those traditions that have established a grip on the imaginations of Londoners, reinforcing particular cultures and personal myths – such as the Pearly Kings and Queens. Nowadays there are some 30 of them, one for every London borough and one each for the Cities of London and Westminster. The tradition began in the 1870s, when young Henry Croft, an orphaned roadsweeper, was inspired by the costermongers' habit of sewing buttons along worn-out trouser seams. He collected pearly buttons and sewed them on his clothes in words and patterns in order to raise money for charity. The idea spiralled and has wormed its way deep into the affections of Londoners. The ceremonial figure dressed in a showy costume decorated with pearl buttons represents working-class London, especially the East End, in party mood. Those suits are serious business – the most elaborate 'smother suit' can hold upwards of 20,000 pearl buttons and weigh as much as its wearer.

The Pearlies themselves have changed since Victorian times, of course. Few of the current incumbents are resident in their 'subject' boroughs, yet the tradition lives on. Folk still like to see a Pearly King and Queen put in an appearance at important occasions to lend a focal point and a sense of 'old London' to proceedings – and they continue to raise huge amounts of money for charity.

Ever-changing customs

Many once-famous London traditions have disappeared entirely, street cries for example. A master of performing dogs would call: 'See my pretty puppies dance/Just arrived here from France', and itinerant dentists had a less-than-reassuring: 'Worthies of the British nation/Attend to my new operation/Let babes' teeth go, decay'd ones come/My pinchers quick shall ease your gum!'

Why does an event or idea catch on? The more spectacular, and the stranger, the better chance of survival, it seems, especially if there is a frisson of the exotic. Take the tradition of Horseman's Sunday, for example, when on the third Sunday of September the Vicar of St John's Church in Hyde Park rides to his church in a magnificent cloak, at the head of a cavalcade of more than 100 horses, before the animals are paraded, blessed and decorated with rosettes. The first cavalcade took place in 1968 as a reminder to the authorities that Hyde Park's stables, under threat at the time, needed to be maintained. It has evolved into a tradition possibly because it is somewhat bizarre, and the riders enjoy the rare thrill of riding in a large company; also, people love the sight of massed horses in central London, a reminder of a now vanished feature of city life.

Very many of London's best-loved public festivals were originated by the city's ethnic minorities. When the Italian community around the Church of Our Lady of Mt Carmel in Clerkenwell began an annual religious procession in the 1880s, it was the first such public profession of the Roman Catholic faith in England since the Reformation. It could all have ended in a welter of bigotry. Instead, the mid-July festival gradually morphed into a celebration of Italian culture until nowadays it has the atmosphere of full-blown carnival.

The West Indian community's Notting Hill Carnival on August Bank Holiday was a simple street parade when it first saw the light in 1966. These days it's the biggest street carnival in Europe. For the Chinese New Year festivities, up to 25,000 people are drawn to Trafalgar Square to enjoy the traditional Lion and Dragon dances, firecrackers and Chinese snacks. Hindu festivals have become part of the warp and weft of London life, too – Diwali, the November feast of light and goodness, and Annakut, the Hindu New Year's Day, celebrated at Neasden's huge temple with flower-bedecked deities.

Street celebration seems to be a London tradition in excellent health, thoroughly established, impossible to extinguish, always being adapted or reinvented in vigorous new ways.

PEARLY KINGS AND QUEENS, LONDON

THE LIVERYMEN AND THE LORD MAYOR

FOR MORE THAN 500 YEARS, London's City life has been underpinned by the City Livery Companies, which were founded as charitable guilds of master craftsmen (the word livery referred to the guildsman's right to wear the distinctive dress of his company).

There are currently 107 Livery companies, of which the 'Great Twelve' are traditionally paramount – Cloth-workers, Drapers, Fishmongers, Goldsmiths, Grocers, Haberdashers, Ironmongers, Mercers, Merchant Taylors, Salters, Skinners and Vintners. Some crafts, such as bow-making or fletching (the making of arrows), are hardly more than memories, but Liverymen continue to banquet, dispense charity and manage schools, and play a major role in London's commerce and trade. Prominent even among the 'Great Twelve' are the Vintners, who together with the Dyers, share ownership of all Thames swans that do not belong to the Queen.

On the Thursday after July 4, the Vintners enact one of the few ancient Livery customs that does not take place in private. After the installation of their new Master, they walk in procession from Vintners' Hall in Upper Thames Street to the Church of St James, Garlickhythe on Garlick Hill. They are led by two white-smocked Wine Porters sweeping the road with brooms, and some of them carry bouquets of herbs. These customs were started in the reign of Edward III (1327–77), lest the Vintners 'do slip in mire or their nostrils be offended by mal odor' (a bad smell).

The most famous Livery ceremonies take place at the Guildhall. (The present building is mostly 15th century.) On Midsummer Day, the Liverymen elect two Sheriffs for the City, and on September 29 they elect the Lord Mayor (so titled since 1546). The Lord Mayor's Show takes place on the second Saturday in November, beginning and ending at the Guildhall.

⑰ Old Walworth Town Hall

The Cuming museum features the fruits of more than 100 years of careful purchase by gentlemen collectors, father and son Richard and Henry Cuming. The most curious display is the collection of Edward Lovett (1852-1933), a city banker and founder of the Folklore Society. His bequest comprises charm bracelets and amulets purchased from 19th-century Londoners together with folk remedies and cures: a piece of cat skin used to cure rheumatism and chest complaints; dried bread containing the hair of a person with whooping cough – if a dog could be persuaded to eat it, the malady would pass to the dog; and a necklace of acorns worn to cure diarrhoea.
▶ *On Walworth Rd, S of Elephant and Castle. Elephant and Castle tube.*

⑱ Shepherdess Walk

The Eagle pub is immortalised in the song 'Pop goes the Weasel'. One verse reads:
'Up and down the City Road,
In and out of the Eagle;
That's the way the money goes,
Pop goes the weasel.'
The weasel was a tool used by saddlers to bore holes in leather. Apparently, a saddler who lived in nearby Nile Street sometimes 'popped' or pawned his weasel to obtain drinking money.
▶ *Eagle at junction of Shepherdess Walk and City Rd. Old St tube.*

⑲ Crystal Palace

The park at Crystal Palace is popular for its dinosaur statues, farm and green spaces. It is also the supposed location of the 'entombed train', one of London's greatest urban myths. The area was named after the huge glass buildings made for the Great Exhibition of 1851 and afterwards re-erected here. The Crystal Palace & South London Junction Railway (opened in 1854) offered access from Victoria or Moorgate. The branch was closed for several years during both world wars; the Palace burnt down in 1936 and the line was finally closed in 1954.

A second, experimental line operated for one year. The Crystal Palace Pneumatic Railway was designed by Thomas Webster Rammell based on a Post Office mail propulsion system. A train was propelled by a fan along an airtight tunnel. His ultimate aim was to create a train to run under the Thames. Nothing remains of his Crystal Palace forerunner save a few engravings and contemporary accounts. According to legend, dating from at least the 1930s, a train remains sealed in a now defunct tunnel. The BBC TV programme 'Nationwide' sponsored a dig for it in the 1970s, but nothing was found. Two more extraordinary versions of the legend describe how people were sealed up in a train after a tunnel collapse, and how a woman accidentally broke into a tunnel and found a carriage full of seated skeletons all in Victorian dress.
▶ *S London. Crystal Palace Station on S side of park.*

⑳ Devons Road

Some 200 hot cross buns, said to have been baked on successive Good Fridays, hang in a net from the ceiling at the Widow's Son public house. It is a condition of tenancy that a sailor must add a bun every year and be paid a pint of beer for his trouble. The story goes that a widow once lived in a cottage on the site. Her son went to sea, promising to be back by Easter, so she baked a hot cross bun for him but he never arrived. She baked a bun for him every year in the hope that he would one day return, but he never did. Some time after she died, the cottage was replaced by a pub and given its present name, and the custom has never flagged.

In fact, the custom probably derives from a once widespread belief that bread or buns baked on Good Friday would never go stale, had remarkable curative powers and would protect the houses where they were kept from fire.

▶ *Widow's Son at junction of Devons Rd and Campbell Rd. Bromley-by-Bow tube.*

㉑ Hayes Common

The second Saturday in May is the date of the May Queen Festival, the last surviving event of the old Merrie England Festival. Today's celebrations are relatively genteel – an announcement for the fair in 1804, entitled 'Rural Amusements or Rustic Gambols', lists: A match at grinning through a horse collar A match at cricket, to be played on Hayes Common A gingling match A race for boys or men in sacks A race for ladies in a Holland chemise A match at eating hot tasty pudding, by boys A match at drinking hot tea by elderly ladies An ass race – with various other amusements The different prizes to be adjusted and settled by proper persons appointed for that purpose. NB No ladies permitted to enter the prize lots who may appear to have drunk too freely of Strong Waters.

▶ *S London. 2 miles S of centre of Bromley. N of A232 Croydon Rd.*

93

East Anglia

The landscape figures strongly in the legends of the eastern counties, where the devil and his familiars lurk in estuaries and fens. Magnificent medieval churches bear their Christian relics proudly, but some still whisper of an older, pagan past.

Hunstanton

A149 Cromer

A148 Fakenham

③

② A148

① King's Lynn

A47 East Dereham ⑤

⑤ Wisbech

A122 Downham Market

Swaffham ④

NORFOLK
106-107

A134

A1065

A11

Norwich

The Broads

A140

A149

⑥

A47 Great Yarmouth

⑦

Lowestoft

A47

A146

A1

A47 Peterborough ⑫

A141

A1101

A10

Thetford

A1066

A143

Southwold ⑥

④

⑮

A10(M)

A14 Huntingdon

CAMBRIDGESHIRE
96-99 ⑭

⑧

Ely ⑨

A10 A142

A11

⑦

Bury St Edmunds
A14

② ⑧

A134

SUFFOLK
108-109

A12

Aldeburgh

A1 ⑩

St Neots A428

⑬

⑥ Cambridge

⑪ ③

A11 ④ ①

Newmarket ①

A14

Stowmarket ③

Ipswich ⑤

A505

A10

② ⑦ Saffron
Walden

Sudbury

A14 Felixstowe

Harwich

M11

ESSEX
100-103

④

A131

A12

A120 Colchester

A133

Clacton-on-Sea

③ Braintree A120 ⑨ ⑫ ⑪

⑥

Harlow

Chelmsford ⑧ Maldon

② A414

M25 A12 A130

① Brentwood ⑬ ⑩

A127 Southend-on-Sea

Basildon ⑭

A13

CAMBRIDGESHIRE

Folk festivals are alive and well among these rich fenlands, from Stilton cheese rolling to dicing for Bibles. Demon dogs prowl the lanes, while a straw bear leads a parade of mummers.

❶ Horseheath

The hamlet of Horseheath was renowned for its witches until well into the 20th century. One of the most famous was Daddy Witch who lived in a hut by the sheep pond in Garret's Close, and was said to have gained all her knowledge from a book called *The Devil's Plantation*. Local tradition has it that, when she died in 1860, she was buried in the middle of the road that leads to Horseheath Green, and that her grave remains dry when it rains because of the heat given off by her body. Villagers long believed that it was necessary to nod nine times before passing over the grave in order to avoid bad luck.

Mother Redcap, who died in 1926, was the last of the well-known Horseheath witches. She inherited imps from her predecessor and named them Bonnie, Red Cap, Blue Cap, Jupiter and Venus. In 1928 a villager claimed that Mother Redcap was often seen with a rat, toad, cat, mouse and ferret. By custom, no witch can die until she has given her imps to her successor.
▶ *4 miles W of Haverhill on A1307.*

❷ Whittlesford

On St Mark's Eve (April 25) the wraiths of Whittlesford folk destined to be buried in the churchyard in the following year come out to inspect their graves. They seek their plots, lie down and vanish underground. More cheerfully, the shades of those destined to be married walk arm in arm around the Church of St Mary and St Michael. A carving on the church tower features a Sheela na gig (female) and ithyphallic (male) figure from the 12th or 13th century.
▶ *6 miles S of Cambridge, on minor roads N of A505.*

❸ The Gog Magog Hills

The curiously named Gog Magog hills, south of Cambridge, rise from the flat expanse of the fens to a height of 71m (234ft). Gog and Magog were either one giant or two. The names feature in the myths of many countries, from Russia to Israel and were recorded (as one giant) in the chronicles of Geoffrey of Monmouth in the 12th century. According to one story, the hills are said to be the petrified form of the giant, who metamorphosed when he was spurned by the nymph Granta. In 1955 the director of excavations for the Cambridge Antiquarian Society, Thomas Charles Lethbridge, discovered chalk carvings of three figures on the hill. A year later the Council for British Archaeology declared two to be natural hollows consistent with the local geology. The one figure that was deemed real was thought to have been cut into the turf by medieval scholars from Cambridge.

The giants are not the only myth associated with the hills. Local children were told tales of gods sleeping beneath the rising folds, a golden chariot buried beneath Wandlebury or Fleam Dyke, and a fearsome night rider defeated by a Norman knight.

The hillfort, below the crest on the south-facing slope, was once an impressive stronghold, occupied from around 400 BC. Evidence suggests that it was used extensively by the Romans.
▶ *4 miles SE of Cambridge, just off A1307.*

❹ West Wratting

The Shug Monkey – a jet-black, shaggy-haired creature with a monkey's face and staring eyes – haunts the countryside between West Wratting and Balsham. The myth may be Norse in origin, derived from stories of Viking settlers to the area. The Shug Monkey is similar to the Black Shuck or Bargest of Norfolk, Essex and Suffolk, and the black dogs of wider folklore.
▶ *8 miles SW of Newmarket on B1052.*

❺ Wisbech

In a small graveyard behind the Friends Meeting House, a headstone marks the last resting place of Jane Stuart, alleged to be the illegitimate daughter of James II. Most of the other graves in this peaceful place are of Peckovers, the local Quaker family, who lived in nearby Peckover House, now run by the National Trust. The rose garden has more than 60 varieties, the reclaimed fenland soil being ideal for rose cultivation. Each year in late June the town celebrates its horticultural heritage with the Wisbech Rose Fair, centred on the Norman church of St Peter and St Paul. The fair was started in 1963 to raise funds for the church.
▶ *12 miles SW of King's Lynn close to junction of A47 and A1101.*

⑥ Cambridge

The Mathematical Bridge of Queens' College, Cambridge is the subject of a myth involving Sir Isaac Newton, who is said to have designed the bridge in such a way that it needed no nuts and bolts. When students took it apart, they were unable to assemble it again without bolting it together. The bridge was in fact designed by William Etheridge and built by James Essex, the younger in 1749, some 22 years after Newton's death.

Generations of Cambridge children have been told the story of the stone lions that flank the entrance to the Fitzwilliam Museum. According to different versions of the tale, when the clock of the Catholic Church strikes midnight, the lions roar, come down to drink from the Trumpington Street gutters, or leave their plinths and go inside the museum.

Evidence for a plethora of Cambridge traditions and beliefs can be found at the Cambridge and County Folk Museum, which has a room devoted to 'Fens and Folklore'. Exhibits include items such as witches bottles, a booklet on old folk remedies, moles paws – a traditional cure for fever – and various bones once hidden in the walls and chimneys of old Cambridge buildings as a safeguard against witches and the evil eye.

▶ *2 miles E of Junction 12 of M11.*

THE MATHEMATICAL BRIDGE, CAMBRIDGE

❼ Wicken

In the lounge bar of The Maid's Head there is an arrow cut into the wall above the fireplace. Once, this symbol appeared in many Fenland homes, indicating that visitors were welcome to food, drink and warmth, but that they should not expect to stay the night.

The Wicken arrow is different. This was the emblem cut by Richard Fielder, an undergraduate at Jesus College, Cambridge, in the mid 19th century. He spent an Easter vacation in Upware, staying at the Lord Nelson Inn (later renamed The Five Miles from Anywhere – No Hurry), which burnt down in 1956. With him were members of two undergraduate societies – the Idiots and the Beersoakers – and they spent time drinking and playing games with the locals. Fielder was elected King of Upware, and put in charge of the revels.

Some ten years later, Fielder returned to his former kingdom and set about consolidating his image as a folk hero. He spent his days fighting and drinking, treating the Fenmen to rum punch from a huge earthenware jug called His Majesty's Pint, and scrawling doggerel verses on the walls of the public houses. Everywhere, he cut arrows into the wall, often initialling them with his name and royal title. In The Maid's Head, there is a list of the places where his rhymes could once be read. After many years of roistering, Fielder retired and lived respectably in Folkestone.

A more sinister legend is that of Black Shuck, a large shaggy dog that roams between Wicken and Spinney Abbey. A foreteller of death, he has much in common with the Shug Monkey of West Wratting.

▶ *7 miles NW of Newmarket on A1123.*

❽ Littleport

Well into the 20th century it was the custom in the Littleport fens for a young man courting a girl to pin three stalks of corn woven together in a lover's knot on to the front of his Sunday smock. Without speaking, he gave a similar token to the girl, which she took home. If her parents approved of the match, she wore the corn pinned over her heart the following Sunday; if they disapproved, she wore it on the right-hand side of her dress. The lovers continued wearing the knots until they were married, and the ceremony was supposed to take place before the ears of corn shelled out.

If a girl wanted to inflame a young man with love for her, she wore a bunch of yarrow on her dress – the smell was supposed to make her irresistible. If, as occasionally happened, the boy remained unmoved, she waited for a night when the moon was full and then walked bare-footed among yarrow plants at midnight. With her eyes closed she picked a bunch, took it home and put it under her bed. If there was dew on the plant at dawn, the boy was just being shy, and would soon overcome his reticence; if the yarrow was dry, she was out of luck, but she could always try again at the next full moon.

▶ *On minor roads off A10, 5 miles N of Ely.*

❾ St Ives

During the 13th century, St Ives was famous for its Easter cloth fair. The cheaper kinds of cloth were sold in St Audrey's Lane, corrupted to Tawdry Lane. In this way, the word 'tawdry' entered the English language.

Each year on Whit Tuesday, six boys and six girls meet in the parish church to throw dice. The winners are each presented with a Bible. This curious custom has its origin in the will of Dr Robert Wilde, who died in 1675, and left £50 to buy land and endow the gift with the rent obtained from its letting. The plot is still known as Bible Orchard.

▶ *6 miles E of Huntingdon on A1123.*

❿ Hilton

The village of Hilton has one of the finest surviving turf mazes in England. It is about 15m (50ft) across, with ridges almost a 30cm (12in) high and well-defined pathways. According to an inscription on the stone pillar at its centre, the maze was laid out by 19-year-old William Sparrow in 1660. The origin of turf mazes, or miz-mazes, is obscure (see page 56). Country people used them for games and races during festivals, but they are thought to have been first constructed by monks, who would do penance by crawling round them on their knees.

▶ *5 miles SE of Huntingdon on B1040.*

⓫ Grantchester

Legend has it that a disused tunnel leads from the cellars under the old Manor House, now blocked by centuries of fallen rubble. According to one tale, a fiddler once entered the tunnel, playing as he went, to try to find where it ended. The music grew fainter until it could be heard no more, and the fiddler never returned.

The local pub is called The Green Man, and a sign depicting a foliate being – half-man half-tree – stands in front of the 500-year-old building.

▶ *2 miles SW of Cambridge.*

STRAW BEAR DAY PARADE
WHITTLESEA

⑫ Whittlesea

Straw Bear Day is an old tradition that was revived in 1980, and takes place on the first Tuesday after Twelfth Night. Originally, the bear – a man covered in straw – was led from house to house and made to dance in return for money. Today, the Straw Bear is the lead character in a procession that includes morris and molly dancers, mummers and groups of local musicians.
▶ *6 miles E of Peterborough on A605.*

⑬ Eynesbury

Two giants, one mythical and the other real, have figured in Eynesbury's past. The legendary giant is said to have stood on Coneygear Field near the river, which is the site of a small Roman fort, and hurled spears at a second giant, who was located half a mile upstream on the earthworks in the neighbouring village of Eaton Socon. The story may spring from folk memory of a Roman ballista, a weapon very like a catapult.

Eynesbury's real giant, James Toller, was born in 1798, and was alleged to have been 1.6m (5ft 5in) tall when he was ten years old. By the time he was 18, he had grown to 2.6m (8ft 6in). He died in 1818, and his huge body was buried inside the church to prevent it being stolen by body snatchers for anatomical research.
▶ *Just S of St Neots town centre.*

⑭ Oldhurst

At the side of the boundary road between the parishes of Oldhurst and Woodhurst was where the Abbot's Chair, or Hurstingstone, once stood. This was the base of a stone cross that marked the meeting place of the Hurstingstone Hundred. Administrative divisions of counties were known as Hundreds, dating back to Saxon times, because each division contained 100 families.

The Abbot's Chair is now in the garden of the Norris Museum, St Ives, Cambridgeshire.
▶ *5 miles NE of Huntingdon on A141.*

⑮ Stilton

Each May Day Bank Holiday, the villagers of Stilton gather on the main street to watch teams roll the world-famous blue-veined cheese (actually a length of wooden telegraph pole) in competition. The tradition began in the mid-20th century and the prize is a whole Stilton cheese.
▶ *At Junction 16 of A1(M), 6 miles S of Peterborough.*

EAST ANGLIA

ESSEX

Forest and seashore govern a county of contrasts. Legendary characters from Epping's shady past live on in tales of magicians and witches; and time-honoured rituals safeguard the oyster beds.

❶ Buckhurst Hill

At a local inn, The Bald Faced Stag, a hunting ritual took place every Easter Monday from the 12th century to the 1880s. A tame stag, decorated with ribbons, was released in Epping Forest and hunted by up to 500 riders of all classes from 'dandies and dustmen' to the 'nobocracy and snobocracy', all dressed in gay and motley clothing. After the unfortunate beast had been hunted to death, handfuls of hair were snatched from its face as trophies of the chase.
▶ *1 mile W of Chigwell.*

❷ Epping Forest

The great Forest of Essex, later known as the Forest of Waltham, and finally Epping Forest, once stretched from Bow in London almost to Cambridge and Colchester. Its dark glades of oak, elm and beech sheltered hermits, vagrants and gipsies, outlaws and highwaymen.

After the Norman Conquest, the 26,000ha (66,000 acre) forest was declared a royal hunting preserve where poachers were punished with branding, mutilation and death. Some parts of the forest, however, were common land on which adjacent parishes had the right to graze cattle, lop wood and collect fuel. Some parishes retain pasture rights, although most tree-lopping rights lapsed long ago. To keep them, the villagers had to be in the forest on November 11 and the oldest inhabitant had to embed his axe in one of the trees. One story tells of an unscrupulous lord of the manor who, having made his commoners drunk, locked the door on them, hoping to stop them exercising their rights. But he forgot that they had their axes with them and, chopping down the door, they ran to the forest to ensure the ancient ceremony was carried out.

Old Dido, a forest hermit who prescribed herbal remedies, lived in a tent near Hainault in the 1900s. Another character who lived about the same time was a white witch known as Old Mother Jenkins, the Goose Charmer. She could often be seen waving her stick and muttering incantations over a flock of geese at the roadside. Many farmers paid her to do this, believing that their geese would not fatten without her blessing.
▶ *Between Epping and Chingford, access from Junction 26 of M25 or Junction 5 of M11.*

❸ Great Dunmow

One of the oldest Essex ceremonies, the Dunmow Flitch Trial, is held about once every four years on Whit Monday. A flitch of bacon – a whole side – is awarded to married couples who can prove to a mock court that 'they have not repented of their marriage for a year and a day'. The 'trial' originated under Baron Robert Fitzwalter in the reign of Henry III, when it was held at Dunmow Priory. After the Dissolution in the 16th century, the lord of the manor presided. Successful claimants were borne aloft on a chair said to be made from church pews. The chair can still be seen in Little Dunmow Priory Church.
▶ *8 miles W of Braintree on A120.*

❹ Henham

A pamphlet entitled 'The Flying Serpent or Strange News out of Essex', published in 1669, told of a winged dragon, 2.7m (9ft) long, that had been seen basking in the sun at Henham. The dragon had two rows of sharp teeth and eyes about 'the bigness of a sheep's eye'. It soon disappeared. Model dragons were once all the rage at Henham Fair, which is still held in July.
▶ *6 miles NE of Bishop's Stortford on B1051.*

❺ Thaxted

Since Conrad Noel, vicar of Thaxted, founded the Morris Ring in 1911, morris dancing has been thriving in this corner of Essex. The Thaxted Morris Men meet with many other sides annually in late May or early June for two days of music and spectacular dancing.
▶ *12 miles NW of Braintree, at junction of B184 and B1051.*

❻ White Notley

During the 18th century, the Cross Keys was an overnight stopping place for waggoners taking timber from Maldon to Braintree. First-timers had to pay a 'footing' by buying everyone in the bar a drink. They also had to nail a coin to the wall with a nail specially forged by the village blacksmith. Many of these coins can still be seen beside the front windows of the pub.
▶ *On minor roads, 3 miles SE of Braintree.*

SAFFRON WALDEN

❼ Saffron Walden

The gable of the 14th-century Old Sun Inn
features a large plastered relief of Tom
Hickathrift and the Wisbech giant, figures from
East Anglian legend, although it has also been
suggested that they represent the mythical giants
Gog and Magog. The plaster technique is known
as pargetting and is a local decorative tradition.
▶ *14 miles SE of Cambridge, access from Junction 9
of M11.*

❽ Little Baddow

Set in the north wall of Little Baddow's
14th-century church is an unadorned
entrance known as a 'Devil Door'. To
medieval Christians, the north side of the church
was the province of Satan, because it was on the
left facing the altar, and Christ had said that he
would 'set the sheep on His right hand and the
goats on His left'. Baptisms were performed in
the south porch of the church. If an infant cried
after being christened, it was traditionally thought
to be a sign that the Devil had been driven from
the child's soul. The north door was left open
during the ceremony to allow Satan to escape 'to
his own place'.
▶ *On minor roads, 5 miles E of Chelmsford.*

❾ Colchester

The town derives its name from an
encampment built by the Romans on the
River Colne. Local tradition, however,
associates the name with the legendary British
King Cole, the 'merry old soul' of popular rhyme.
Geoffrey of Monmouth, the 12th-century
historian, relates that King Cole was the father of
the Roman emperor Constantine, and gave his
name to the town of Colchester, meaning Cole's
Castle. The site of a Roman gravel pit that has
been unearthed in the town is known as King
Cole's Kitchen.

The town has long been famous for its oysters,
and the season is opened by a traditional festival
in early September. The Mayor, civic dignitaries
and members of the Fishing Board go by boat to
Pyfleet Creek, where the oyster-fattening beds lie.
Here the loyal toast is drunk, gingerbread and gin
are consumed, and the Mayor makes the first
ceremonial oyster dredge of the season. The
gingerbread is traditional and may once have
been an offering to the local sea god.

Following this, on or about October 20, the
400-year-old Oyster Feast takes place. This
commemorates the granting by Richard I of the
River Colne oyster-fishing rights to the town.
▶ *60 miles NE of London on A12.*

EAST ANGLIA

THE MARSHY ISLE IS SAID TO BE THE HAUNT OF A HORNED DEMON

WALLASEA ISLAND

⑩ Wallasea Island

A Second World War bomb and a 1953 tidal flood combined to wipe out the haunt of Wallasea Island's most evil inhabitant. The Devil's House, or Tyle Barn, was said to shelter a horned demon that tormented anyone who moved in. The creature was rumoured to have driven a farm labourer to suicide by perpetually repeating in his ear 'Do it! Do it! Do it!'. Many people believed the demon to be the familiar of Old Mother Redcap, the legendary witch of nearby Foulness Island, unable to return to hell. Whatever the truth, Tyle Barn, according to one brave man who did manage to live there, was always 'ice-cold, unhappy and miserably evil'.
▶ *Access from minor roads 10 miles NE of Southend-on-Sea.*

⑪ St Osyth

In 1921, two female human skeletons were discovered buried in a back garden in the village. In both cases, the elbows and knees had been riveted through with iron prior to burial, possibly in an attempt to prevent 'walking' after death. The skeletons may be those of two witches hanged by Witchfinder General Matthew Hopkins in 1645, or those of Ursula Kemp and Elizabeth Bennet, executed in an earlier purge in 1582. One of the skeletons is now in the museum of witchcraft at Boscastle, Cornwall (page 23).
▶ *3 miles W of Clacton-on-Sea on B1027.*

⑫ Brightlingsea

This is the only town outside Kent and Sussex that is a member of the Cinque Ports – ports on the southeast coast with ancient privileges. Brightlingsea is described in an Elizabethan charter as being 'a Limb of the Cinque Port of Sandwich', and on the first Monday in December, a Deputy of the Cinque Port Liberty is elected from among the Freemen of the town. At a ceremony that takes place in the belfry of All Saints Church, the Deputy swears allegiance to the Mayor of Sandwich. He then visits the Mayor and presents him with 50p for Ship Money. This is probably a relic of an ancient tax on southern ports to provide ships for the defence of the realm.
▶ *9 miles SE of Colchester on B1029.*

⑬ Ashingdon

St Andrew's Church was founded by King Canute to commemorate his victory in battle on the hill where the church now stands. Although lawns surround the church today, legend says that after the battle no grass would grow on the 'bloodstained' hill. In medieval times, a shrine in the church was said to bestow fertility upon women. The shrine was lost at the Dissolution in the 16th century, but the church retained its reputation as a lucky place in which to marry.

▶ *On minor roads, 5 miles N of Southend-on-Sea.*

⑭ Hadleigh

From 1812 to 1860, the town of Hadleigh was the home of James Murrell, the last and most famous witch doctor in Essex – although his house has now gone. Born the seventh son of a seventh son, he was known as 'Cunning Murrell', and enjoyed a lucrative career as a white magician. His equipment included a magic mirror for discovering lost or stolen property, a telescope for looking through walls and a copper charm that enabled him to distinguish between honest and dishonest clients.

Murrell often said he was 'the Devil's Master', claiming that he had the power to exorcise spirits and overcome witchcraft by counter-spells. He was well known for his iron witch bottles, into which he put samples of the blood, urine, nails and hair of clients whom he had diagnosed as bewitched. At midnight, the mixture would be heated to boiling point in absolute silence, the object being to create a burning sensation in the witch's body that would force her to remove the spell. One story relates how a girl was brought to him, barking like a dog after being cursed by a gipsy woman. When Murrell heated up his witch bottle that night, it exploded, and the next day the charred body of a woman was found lying in a nearby country lane.

A secretive man, Murrell travelled only at night, and always carried an umbrella with him regardless of the weather. On December 15, 1860, the day before he died, Murrell accurately predicted the time of his death to the minute. He is buried in an unmarked grave in Hadleigh churchyard.

▶ *5 miles W of Southend-on-Sea on A13.*

Thaxted Morris Men's first public performance was to celebrate the coronation of George V in 1911

THE GUILDHALL, THAXTED

The madness of the morris

Today the unmistakable jingle of the dancers' bells enlivens fetes and festivals as it has done, on and off, for centuries.

East Anglia, that rural corner of Britain, has always retained links with the 'ancient madness of the Morris', even when it was dying out elsewhere. The madness began with a Spanish court dance in the 15th century, after which it spread like wildfire throughout Europe. May Day and all other outdoor celebrations would be graced by the morris men. The Puritans put a stop to it during the days of the Commonwealth, but it made a joyous return along with the monarchy, and morris dancing became virtually synonymous with various religious festivals, such the Whitsun ale, when 'ale' was used to mean a 'celebration' for which churches would brew specially, the ale being sold to raise money. Through the peaks and troughs of the following centuries distinct regional styles emerged and are now keenly preserved.

Molly dancing

One particular form of the morris, referred to as molly dancing – possibly because one dancer was invariably a man dressed as a woman – evolved in East Anglia. On Plough Monday, the first Monday after Twelfth Night, the farmboys would decorate a plough and dance with it round the villages, begging for money. Almost unbelievably, knowledge of the dance steps has survived, and nowadays molly dancing is performed all year round.

One reason traditional dances can still be performed is that, at the beginning of the 20th century, after a long period of decline, morris dancing was discovered by one Cecil Sharp, who set about travelling the country, noting down the dances and the music. Thaxted in Essex was one of the first places to be re-enthused and the local morris men gave their first public performance to celebrate the coronation of George V in 1911. Now sides congregate in Thaxted every year in early summer for a three-day meeting, and Thaxted Morris is one of the best-known sides in the country.

The madness of Will Kempe

Surely the strangest morris dancing story is that of Will Kempe's 'Nine Daies Wonder'. What possessed this well-respected actor and colleague of William Shakespeare's to morris dance from London to Norwich – a distance of well over 100 miles – on rough, filthy roads in February 1600, no one really knows. But Kempe did it – and did it in style, with bells on. Setting off early from the Lord Mayor's residence, he danced away through Whitechapel and Mile End to the sound of fife and tabor played by faithful musician,

Tom Slye. Crowds flocked, as they did throughout the journey. He got as far as Romford, narrowly missing death on the way by dancing between the upraised forefeet of two fighting horses, before stopping for two days 'to giue rest to my well labour'd limbes'. At Brentwood, a pair of cutpurses, who'd followed him from London hoping for easy pickings in the crowds, were arrested and thrown in jail.

Rest and recreation

He rested at Chelmsford, but found the strength to accept an invitation from a teenaged girl to dance the morris with her 'in a great large roome. I was soon wonne; to fit her with bels, besides she would haue the olde fashion with napking on her armes; and to our iumps we fell. A whole houre she held out: but then being ready to lye downe I left her off: but thus much in her praise, I would haue challenged the strongest man in Chelmsford, and amongst many I thinke few would haue done so much.' A nice pen picture.

On dancing Day 4 Kempe made for Braintree over very muddy and foul roads. A pair of silly youths tried to emulate Kempe's leap across a puddle, fell in and got stuck in the mud, where Kempe left them wallowing 'like two frogges'. On Day 5 a Sudbury butcher lasted just half a mile, dancing alongside, but a plump young girl in the crowd took his place and to Kempe's admiration did rather better.

He reached Bury St Edmunds on Day 6, where he was snowed in for the best part of a week. Free to go at last, he almost flew to Thetford on the Suffolk/ Essex border. 'I far'd like one that had escaped the stockes, and tride the vse of his legs to out-run the Constable: so light was my heeles, that I counted the ten mile no better than a leape.' At Rockland the innkeeper wanted to join him, but was too out of condition to keep up. 'Good true fat belly he had not followed mee two fields, but he lyes all along.'

On the last day, such a crowd turned out to greet Kempe at Norwich that they blocked the roads and he had to ride into the city to his civic reception. But he went back and danced the final mile – much to the embarrassment of a young woman, whose petticoat he inadvertently ripped off as he was dancing past. Urchins grabbed it and she had to run after them in her smock (luckily a clean one), with 'her cheekes all coloured with scarlet', to snatch it back.

What a tale! What a bawdy, brilliant escapade! And what an advertisement for the magic, and the madness, of the morris!

NORFOLK

Visions of the past shimmer fleetingly among inland waterways and gentle hills. Saintly exploits are commemorated by pilgrims, while churches bear reminders of the dark days of the Black Death.

❶ King's Lynn

A diamond-shaped brick, with a heart carved in its centre, is set above the window of a house on the northwest corner of Tuesday Market in King's Lynn. The market was once a place of execution, and according to local legend, the brick marks the spot where a witch's heart smashed against the wall, having exploded from her body as she burnt on a pyre. Margaret Read, one of England's few witches to suffer death by fire, was burnt here in 1590. In another version, her evil heart, refusing to submit, bounded away and jumped into the River Ouse.

▶ *A17 from W, A10 from S (Ely), A47 from E (Norwich).*

❷ Castle Rising

Queen Isabella was supposedly confined to the Norman keep – which still stands – for having taken part in the murder of her husband, Edward II. The story goes that she went mad with loneliness, and her insane screams are said to ring out over the surrounding countryside.

In 1614, the Earl of Northampton established a charity home at Bede House for elderly women 'of honest life and conversation' who were 'not haunters of alehouses'. The women who live there still go to church wearing Jacobean dress of tall hat and red cloak embroidered with the Northampton Howard's arms.

▶ *Just W of A149, 4 miles NE of King's Lynn.*

CASTLE RISING

❸ Walsingham

The ruins of an Augustinian priory church in Walsingham recall pre-Reformation days, when the village was one of Europe's great centres of pilgrimage. According to legend, Lady Richeldis, wife of a Norman lord, had a vision here in 1061 in which the Virgin Mary appeared to her. The Virgin took her in spirit to Christ's home in Nazareth, and commanded her to build an exact replica of it in Walsingham. With heavenly aid, Lady Richeldis built a shrine, which soon became so famous that pilgrims journeyed to it from all over Europe – Edward the Confessor, Richard the Lionheart and Erasmus among them. Miraculous healing powers were attributed to Our Lady's Well, and even the Milky Way became known as Walsingham Way, because it pointed across the heavens to England's Nazareth.

At the Reformation in the 16th century, the shrine and all the buildings that, by that time, clustered around it were destroyed. It was not until 1931 that sufficient funds were gathered to rebuild it. Today, Walsingham has rekindled some of its former glory. Throughout the year, especially at Whitsun and on other Church festivals, pilgrims once more flock into the village, as they did centuries ago in Medieval England.
▶ *On minor roads 6 miles N of Fakenham.*

❹ Swaffham

A long time ago, a Swaffham pedlar named John Chapman dreamt that if he stood on London Bridge, a man would tell him how he might become rich. Chapman walked to London and stood on the bridge for hours, but no rich man came by. At last, he fell into conversation with a shopkeeper and told him how he had been led on a fool's errand by a dream. The shopkeeper replied that he, too, had had a curious dream, in which he saw treasure being buried in the garden of a John Chapman in far-off Swaffham. Chapman returned home and began digging. Sure enough, he found two enormous pots of gold buried beneath a tree, and as a thanksgiving offering, the pedlar built the north aisle and tower of Swaffham church.

Similar tales are told all over Britain, Europe and even Persia; but in Swaffham the story has been recorded with a modern wooden effigy of the pedlar that stands by the market cross. His figure, together with his dog, also appears in the choir of the church. According to church records, a certain John Chapman paid for the north aisle to be rebuilt in the 15th century.
▶ *14 miles SE of King's Lynn on A47.*

❺ East Dereham

The name Dereham is said to derive from a miracle associated with St Withburga, who founded a nunnery there in AD 654. During a severe shortage of food at the nunnery, the saint prayed for help, and in response, two milch deer appeared and gave their milk for the nuns each day. A huntsman who set his dogs on the deer apparently met with divine wrath, for he fell from his horse and was killed.

St Withburga was buried in the churchyard at the nunnery. Her body – still perfectly preserved – was later exhumed and taken within the church, where her shrine attracted pilgrims for centuries. In AD 974, her remains were reburied in Ely. Her shrine and well lie near St Nicholas's Church, East Dereham.
▶ *12 miles E of Swaffham on A47.*

❻ Horning

At the Dissolution, in 1537, St Benet's abbot was also the Bishop of Norwich. Since he surrendered the estates of the bishopric to Henry VIII, he was allowed to keep all of the monastery's lands. Ever since then the Bishop of Norwich has continued to draw his revenues from the old abbey estates, and every year on the first Sunday in August he visits the ruined abbey by water to hold a service during which he blesses the Norfolk Broads.
▶ *On A1062, 8 miles SE of North Walsham.*

❼ Wickhampton

In the chancel of the parish church of St Andrew are the defaced effigies of a medieval knight and his wife – Sir William and Lady Gerbygge. Originally, each clasped a small stone heart. According to local tradition, they were not a knight and his wife at all, but two brothers named Hampton, who tore out one another's hearts after a dispute over the parish boundaries. God turned their bodies to stone, and they were placed in the church as a warning against quarrelling. That, at least, is what Wickhampton parents told their children in the 19th century.

The church has some magnificent 14th-century wall paintings, including depictions of the three living and the three dead – three fine figures and three skeletons – which were a popular decorative theme after the Black Death. The text reads: 'Traveller, gaze, as you pass by, as you are, so once was I. As I am, so you must be, Therefore prepare to follow me.'
▶ *On minor roads 12 miles E of Norwich.*

EAST ANGLIA

SUFFOLK

Old tales reflect strange local beliefs, while the customary opening of an ancient fair could be symbolic of life; but a colourful way of picking a winner may be more to do with wishful thinking.

❶ Kentford

About 1½ miles beyond Kentford, at a crossroads on the main road to Bury St Edmunds, is a roadside grave maintained by unknown hands. Known as 'The Boy's Grave', it is the burial place of a young shepherd or gipsy boy who hanged himself after either losing sheep or being accused of sheep stealing long ago. It was an age-old custom for suicides to be buried at a crossroads, sometimes even with a wooden stake through their heart, to prevent the unhappy spirit from wandering. Possibly, it was once believed that crossroads confused ghosts, and prevented them from returning home. The last known such burial took place at St John's Wood, London in 1823.

Outside Kentford, several cyclists have reported feeling an uncanny force when passing the Boy's Grave, which compelled them to dismount.

Fresh flowers still appear on the grave and a piece of modern folklore states that on any racing day, the colour of the flowers on the grave will be the colour of the winning horse.
▶ *Just S of A14, 4 miles NE of Newmarket.*

❷ Bury St Edmunds

Somewhere in the abbey lie the remains of Suffolk's martyr-king St Edmund. He was born in Nuremberg in AD 841, and became king of the East Angles in AD 855. Despite his youth, he was remarkable both as a soldier and a Christian; his reign, however, was brief. He was captured by Danes at the Battle of Hoxne (AD 870), and although he could have saved his life by denying his faith, he refused. He was tied to a tree, shot full of arrows and beheaded.

His own army recovered his body, but the head remained lost. His soldiers searched for 40 days, until coming to a thick wood, they became separated. They were crying out to one another, 'Where are you?', when another voice answered, 'Here, over here!' The voice was the king's, and so they found his head, perfectly preserved, resting between the paws of a grey wolf. When the head was placed with the body, the two were miraculously joined.

Until the Reformation in the 16th century, St Edmund's tomb in the abbey was a shrine second only to Canterbury in importance. Over the centuries, the monks built up an amazing collection of relics, including 'the coals that St Lawrence was toasted withal; the parings of St Edmund's nails; St Thomas's boots and pieces of Holy Cross able to make a whole cross'.
▶ *25 miles NW of Ipswich on A14.*

❸ Woolpit

The striking wrought-iron sign of this historic Suffolk village depicts the church of St Mary, a wolf (the village name is often said to derive from 'wolf pit') and two children, painted green. The children are reminders of an event said to have occurred in the 12th century, when a boy and a girl appeared from a hole in the ground, fearful of sunlight, their skin a strange shade of green. They spoke no language that the villagers could understand and so could give no clue to their identity or where they had come from. The boy soon died, but the girl lived on, learned to speak English and later married a local man. The story was first published by Ralph of Coggeshall in his 13th-century book *The Chronicle of England*. There has been considerable speculation about the children's origins, including reports of a twilit underground kingdom beyond a river. Their green colour also led to suggestions of a fairy connection, although the clue may lie in the original account. Ralph of Coggeshall reports that the children were 'green tinged', as opposed to 'green', which can be a symptom of severe anaemia, caused by lack of iron in the diet.

Mythical creatures of a different kind inhabit the tall-spired church of St Mary's. Hundreds of angels roost in the hammerbeam roof, looking down on the fantastical animals on the bench ends below. To the northeast of the church, Our Lady's Well is reputed to be good for ailments of the eyes.
▶ *Just S of A14, 8 miles E of Bury St Edmunds.*

ANOTHER VOICE ANSWERED,

BURY ST EDMUNDS

ANGEL, BLYTHBURGH

❹ Blythburgh

The church of the Holy Trinity in Blythburgh is disproportionately large for a small village – and it was once visited by the Devil. In August 1577, according to an old pamphlet, 'a strange and terrible tempest' struck the village, sending the church's spire crashing through the roof so that it shattered the font, killed three of the congregation and injured others, while lightning 'cleft the door'. The Devil's scorched fingerprints can still be seen on the door today.

When the 12 magnificent angels in the roof were restored in the 1970s, they were found to be filled with lead shot. The story goes that this was on the orders of William Dowsing, a 17th-century Anglican Reformer who had been charged with ridding Suffolk's and Cambridgeshire's churches and university colleges of statues, images, idols and stained glass. The angels, it is said, were fired upon so they would fall, but the shot is 18th century and dates from a time when men were employed to shoot jackdaws that had taken up residence in the roof.
▶ *5 miles W of Southwold on A12.*

❺ Blaxhall

The 5-tonne sandstone boulder that sits outside Stone Farm in Blaxhall was said to have been the size of a small loaf when it was first noticed two centuries ago. This stems from the common East Anglian belief that pebbles grow in the soil and develop into large stones. The boulder is a glacial erratic – a stone deposited by glacial action around 150,000 years ago and as such is an unusual feature in the relatively stoneless county of Suffolk.
▶ *On minor roads 2 miles E of A12, 4 miles S of Saxmundham.*

❻ Southwold

In late May or early June, Southwold's three-day Trinity Fair is opened by the Mayor from the steps of a merry-go-round. He then mounts the machine, attended by his Corporation, and takes the first ride. The fair's charter, one of the oldest in England, dates back to the reign of Henry IV.
▶ *12 miles S of Lowestoft.*

'HERE, OVER HERE!'

EAST ANGLIA

Grimsby

A16

The Wolds

A1028

Skegness

A52

Boston
9 11

A16 A17

Spalding

Central England

England's green heartland is a country of Briton kings and Saxon warlords, whose bygone battles and enmities mark its landscape even today. But there are other legends too, myths of water, rock-cut passages and carved stones that hint of older times.

KEY

① Main entry

— County boundary

Motorway

Principal A road

DERBYSHIRE

Among the county's rocky peaks, green dales and deep caverns, the power of water reigns supreme, flowing through the heart of many long-established customs and magical tales.

❶ Earl Sterndale

The local pub in this small village, The Quiet Woman, is said to be more than 400 years old, and the inn sign is unusual. It shows a woman without a head and above the headless body is the motto: 'Soft words turneth away wrath.'

The woman is said to be 'Chattering Charteris', who made her husband's life a misery by her endless scolding. When she began to talk in her sleep as well, he could stand it no more and cut off her head. According to tradition, the villagers were so grateful that they made a collection to buy a headstone for her grave, inscribed with a warning to chatterboxes, and gave what was left over to her husband.
▶ *4 miles SE of Buxton on B5053.*

❷ Treak Cliff

Two caverns in the Castleton Caves, Treak Cliff and Blue John, are the only places in the world where the mineral Blue John – a fluorspar banded in red, blue, purple and yellow – is mined. Alongside these beautiful natural deposits, Treak Cliff has spectacular stalactites and stalagmites, and has been designated a Site of Special Scientific Interest. Blue John vases were highly prized by the Romans. One of them is said to have cost the Roman author and dandy Petronius the equivalent of £30,000. He smashed it, to prevent the ornament from falling into the hands of the Emperor Nero.
▶ *1 mile W of Castleton.*

❸ Hathersage

The 3m (10ft) long grave of Robin Hood's henchman, Little John, said to have been born in Hathersage, is marked by an inscribed headstone in the churchyard. His cap of Lincoln green and his mighty yew bow, 1.8m (6ft) long, hung in the church for many decades, but they were later moved to Cannon Hall, near Barnsley. The cap vanished at some point in history but the bow remains. Antiquarians opened the grave in the late 18th century and discovered a thigh bone 81cm (32in) long. The bone was, allegedly, re-interred after the man who had ordered the exhumation suffered a series of accidents.
▶ *10 miles SW of Sheffield.*

❹ Castleton

Until the 17th century, several cottages stood in the mouth of Peak Cavern, and the rope makers who lived there did so rent and rate free. Some say they specialised in hangman's ropes, and that the Devil sometimes visited the cave. When water poured out after rain in the hills, he was said to be relieving himself.

On Oak Apple Day, May 29, a Garland King and Queen ride through Castleton accompanied by a band, and morris men dance in the streets.
▶ *15 miles W of Sheffield at end of A6187.*

❺ Kinder Scout

From the flat-topped plateau of Kinder Scout, the Mermaid's Pool can be clearly seen, near Kinder reservoir, some way below. Anyone who stares intently into the pool's dark waters just as Easter Sunday begins may see a mermaid swimming.
▶ *Hayfield is on the A624, 5 miles S of Glossop. Kinder Scout lies 3 miles E of Hayfield.*

❻ Beeley

A Bronze Age burial mound on Harland Edge, near Chatsworth House, is called Hob Hurst's House. Hob Hurst is a goblin who frequents lonely and remote woods. The mound is a cist, built with stones now covered with grass and vegetation and is notable for its square shape.
▶ *On B6012, 3 miles E of Bakewell.*

❼ Bakewell

A milliner, Mrs Stafford, and her maid were hanged at Derby in 1608 on the flimsy evidence of a destitute Scottish tramp. In London, he said he had been whisked there from Mrs Stafford's home in Bakewell 'like the wind' after the two women had called upon the Devil. He seems to have made up the story in revenge for Mrs Stafford seizing his gear in lieu of rent.

In the churchyard, there is a 2.4m (8ft) high cross that dates back 1,200 years to a time when Christianity and the ancient myths went hand in hand. On one side, carvings show the crucifixion; on the other are the Norse gods Odin and Loki.
▶ *12 miles W of Chesterfield.*

SHROVETIDE FOOTBALL, ASHBOURNE

⑧ Ashbourne

Shrovetide football goes on for two days at Ashbourne, starting on Shrove Tuesday afternoon. The game is played between Up'ards, who live north of the River Henmore, which divides the town, and Down'ards, from south of the river. The mill wheels at Clifton and Sturston, which are 3 miles apart, are the goals, but these are rare. The ball is filled with cork dust to make it heavy and to limit the action. Any number can join in, and most of the game is played in the river.

▶ *15 miles NW of Derby on A52.*

⑨ Winster

On Shrove Tuesday, for more than 100 years, a pancake race has been run between the Crown Inn and the ancient Market House – a course of about 100m (110yd). Men, women and children can all take part, and small frying pans are provided. Special pancakes are issued, too, designed to wear well rather than to eat.

On June 24, visiting teams of morris men dance outside the Market House as part of the Winster Wakes celebrations, a week-long carnival at which, according to an old song, 'there's ale and cakes.'

▶ *4 miles W of Matlock.*

⑩ Deepdale

A tiny elf, or hob, once lived below Topley Pike, in a cave still known as Thirst House. The hob guarded a nearby spring, and the water was said to cure all kinds of disease, if drunk on Good Friday. Once, the hob was caught by a farmer, but it shrieked so loudly that he let it go. Thirst House is an abbreviation of Hob o' the Hurst's House, 'hurst' meaning a wooded place.

▶ *Access Deepdale on footpaths from A6, 4 miles W of Bakewell.*

⑪ Swarkestone

Legend tells that the original Swarkestone Bridge, part of which survives, was built in the 13th century by two daughters of the Harpur family. They were celebrating their joint betrothal at a party when their fiancés were summoned to a meeting of barons across the River Trent. While they were absent, a torrential rainstorm caused the river to flood, and both men were drowned as they tried to ford the waters on their return. The two sisters built the bridge as a memorial to their lovers, and both women died impoverished and unwed. The bridge, still in use today by modern traffic, is the longest stone bridge in England.

▶ *5 miles S of Derby at junction of A5132 and A514.*

GLOUCESTERSHIRE

Every year, processions, games and races draw huge crowds, as they have done for centuries. Winter festivals are enlivened by the antics of mummers, and summer heralded with cheese rolling and welly wanging.

❶ St Briavels

For nearly eight centuries, a Bread and Cheese Dole has been distributed on Whit Sunday at the village church of St Briavels (pronounced Brevels) in the Forest of Dean. After the evening service, a local forester stands on top of a wall outside the church and throws pieces of bread and cheese to the assembled churchgoers. The custom allegedly began during King John's reign, in 1206, to help the local poor.
▶ *6 miles W of Lydney.*

❷ Avening

Pig Face Day, a village feast said to date back almost 1,000 years, takes place every other September, and has its foundations in a tragic story of love and remorse.

The local lord, Brittic, was ambassador to the Flanders court, where he met Matilda, daughter of the count. She fell in love with him but he spurned her. Later, when she married William of Normandy – who became William the Conqueror – she had Brittic imprisoned and he died. She was so upset that she had the village church rebuilt to attone for her sins, and when she came to inspect progress, she was given a great feast, including a boar's head. The Church of the Holy Cross remains the only church in England built by a queen.
▶ *6 miles SE of Stroud on B4014.*

❸ Tetbury

The steeply undulating streets of Tetbury between two public houses are transformed into a racetrack on the late May Bank Holiday in an event that has taken place since 1972. The village was once famous for its wool and yarn markets, and locals believe that the races had their origins in the feats of prowess shown when young men of the 17th century carried heavy woolsacks to impress the girls. Today they run with the woolsacks on their shoulders – the winner is the first to reach the finish line.
▶ *10 miles SW of Cirencester on A433.*

❹ Randwick

On the second Saturday in May an exuberant procession, called the Randwick Wap, is led by the Mop Man, who brandishes a wet mop towards the crowd. The assembly, which includes the mayor, a queen and attendants, marches from the war memorial to the Mayor's Pool, where the mayor receives a dunking. This is followed by a cheese-rolling event. According to local legend, the procession dates back seven centuries to a specific occasion when a church builder was dunked in the pool in an effort to sober him up.
▶ *On minor roads 2 miles NW of Stroud.*

ONLY 99 YEWS CAN SURVIVE AMONG THE GRAVES

ST MARY'S, PAINSWICK

⑤ Painswick

Ninety-nine clipped yew trees stand among the gravestones of St Mary's churchyard, by tradition. A local belief states that only this number can grow there; whenever a hundredth tree is planted, it never survives. Records at the Victoria & Albert Museum in London show that there are, in fact, 103 trees; the church itself claims 100, but verifying the number is a challenge for all but the most dedicated visitor.

Every year, on the Sunday nearest to September 19, the children of Painswick perform an ancient ritual called 'Clipping the Church'. In the afternoon, the town band leads a procession around the boundary of the churchyard, after which all the children join hands to form a circle around the church. They dance back and forth towards the church several times while singing the traditional Clipping Hymn. The ceremony ends with a Clipping Sermon, which is read by the vicar. The custom is thought to have been adapted from an old pagan rite, in which a community shows its faith by symbolically embracing its place of worship. 'Clipping' may be derived from the Saxon cly-pan, or clasp.

Some of the inhabitants of Painswick make 'puppy-dog pie' on Clipping Sunday – the nose of a small china dog pokes through the crust of a fruit pie. A local story relates that some travellers once ordered a meal at the Falcon Inn. The landlord, who had no food at the time, is said to have served them a pie made of cooked puppies. Ever since then, Painswick people have been known as 'bow-wows'.

▶ *3 miles N of Stroud on A46.*

6 Cooper's Hill

The annual cheese-rolling competition on the precipitous Cooper's Hill near Brockworth has historic – possibly ancient – origins. Certainly it existed in the 18th century as part of a series of midsummer entertainments and may have been carried out in honour of a good harvest. The event traditionally takes place on the Spring Bank Holiday – the last Monday in May. Entrants must chase a round cheese down the hill, which in some places has an incline of 1:1. The winner is the first to reach the bottom. A hugely popular spectator sport, the entrants tumble and roll more than the cheese, finishing up in the straw bale safety barriers if they are not caught and slowed by a helper.

▶ *Brockworth is close to junction of A417 and A46, 4 miles SE of Gloucester. Cooper's Hill is just S of Brockworth.*

7 Gloucester

Gloucester is one of the most ancient cities in England. It is believed to have been founded around 2000 BC by Iberian settlers, and was later inhabited in turn by Britons, Romans, Saxons and Normans. The town is centred round the cathedral, in which Cromwell reputedly billeted his troops, who passed their leisure time throwing stones through the medieval stained-glass windows.

The cathedral – or its forecourt – is the venue for an annual event, dating back to 1969, that takes place on Boxing Day. Here, the City of Gloucester Mummers perform old local plays.

Many rural traditions of Gloucestershire are preserved in Gloucester Folk Museum, which is housed in the building where the Protestant bishop John Hooper was imprisoned. The bishop was burnt at the stake in the town in 1555 on the orders of Mary Tudor.

▶ *4 miles W of Junction 11 of M5.*

8 Deerhurst

In ancient times the people of Deerhurst were plagued by a terrible serpent. They lost both men and cattle to the beast, and eventually petitioned the king. The king promised land to the person who could vanquish the monster, and a labourer called Smith came forward with a plan. He approached the dragon's lair, and left a pail of milk in front of it to tempt the creature. Drinking the milk made the dragon drowsy and eventually it fell asleep in the midday sun with its scales fluffed up. Smith chose his

moment, swung his axe at the beast, making contact between the scales on its neck, and killed it outright. Smith was granted the land and his descendants lived there for centuries. Local myth told how an 18th-century gentleman, a Mr Lane, had married a widow of the Smith family and still had the axe, although no such axe survives today. The story has local resonance in the church, where fine Saxon carvings include dragon heads. In nearby Tredington, the church of John the Baptist also has a series of dragon carvings, and the fossil remains of an ichthyosaurus in the floor of the porch.

▶ *On minor road N of B4213, 3 miles S of Tewkesbury.*

9 Bisley

Each year, the people of the picturesque Cotswold village of Bisley turn out on Ascension Day, 40 days after Easter, to dress the wells with flowers to give thanks for the water. The wells, and their five spring outlets, were beautifully restored by the Reverend Thomas Keeble in 1863. This essentially pagan celebration, banned by the church for many centuries, was revived by Reverend Keeble and incorporated into the Ascension Day church ceremony.

▶ *On minor roads 4 miles E of Stroud.*

10 Chipping Campden

The curiously named Cotswold Olympiks and Skuttlebrook Wake takes place at the scenic location of Dovers Hill, above Chipping Campden in early June. The event dates back more than 400 years and was originally presided over by a Norfolk man, Robert Dover (1582-1652). Games are traditional, and include welly wanging, barrowing bales of hay and backsword fighting, followed by a torchlight procession and fireworks. The wake the next day includes the crowning of the Skuttlebrook queen and children's races.

▶ *18 miles NE of Cheltenham.*

11 Snowshill

The manor house, now owned by the National Trust, contains a room the door of which bears the inscription 'Amor et tussis non celantur' – 'You cannot conceal love or a cough'. In this room, Anthony Palmer secretly married heiress Ann Parsons in 1604. The adage was proved true, for their secret was discovered, and Anthony was tried before the Court of Star Chamber for marrying without the permission of Ann's relatives.

MUMMING IN MARSHFIELD

Today, the house contains the wonderfully eccentric collection of Charles Paget Wade (1883-1956) whose family motto was 'Let Nothing Perish'. Masterfully upholding this motto, he assembled more than 22,000 objects over his lifetime – ordinary and extraordinary – with the proviso that they were all works of beautiful craftsmanship. He also assembled a costume collection of 2,000 pieces.

A room at the top of the house, known as 'The Witch's Garret', was once filled with objects associated with witchcraft. These have now been loaned to the Museum of Witchcraft in Boscastle, Cornwall (page 23).

▶ *On minor roads 2 miles S of Broadway.*

⑫ Bourton-on-the-Water

The annual August Bank Holiday football match in Bourton-on-the-Water is a game with a difference – it is played in the normally quiet and picturesque River Windrush, which flows through the town. Two six-a-side teams battle for victory in the knee-high waters, soaking themselves and surrounding spectators. The event dates back more than a century, and lasts for 15 minutes per half.

▶ *15 miles E of Cheltenham at junction of A429 and A436.*

⑬ Marshfield

On Boxing Day, the Marshfield Mummers re-enact a traditional play through the village streets. The troupe's alternative name is the Paperboys, because their costumes are made from all sorts of paper streamers. Local lore has it that the paper was once leaves, symbolising the cyclical nature of life, and that mumming plays have been performed here since the 11th century.

▶ *9 miles W of Chippenham on A420.*

⑭ Fairford

St Mary's is the only church in Britain to retain all of its original medieval stained-glass windows. They were installed by John Tame, a merchant, whose monument is in the church. The story goes that Tame was a part-time pirate who looted the glass from a Flemish ship and gave it to the church for the good of his soul (the terrors of hell are vividly depicted) The truth is more prosaic. John Tame rebuilt the church in the last 30 years of the 15th century, and probably employed Flemish craftsmen to make the glass. Outside, the church has some odd stone carvings of animals and humans, including a boy climbing down from the parapet.

▶ *9 miles E of Cirencester on A417.*

HEREFORDSHIRE

Amid the unspoilt countryside and bustling market towns of this most rural of counties, vague memories of the distant past are reflected in local legends and fables.

❶ Hentland

The parish church is dedicated to 5th-century clergyman St Dubricius, who is depicted on a stained-glass window with a hedgehog (the county symbol of Herefordshire) at his feet. Dubricius's mother, Eurddil, was the daughter of Peibau, king of Archenfield, who was known as King Dribbler because of his uncontrollable foaming at the mouth. Legend states that one day King Dribbler returned to Madley, near Hereford, from a hunting expedition and noticed that Eurddil, although unmarried, was pregnant. He immediately ordered her to be drowned in the River Wye, so she was tied up in a sack and thrown into the water, but the current washed her ashore. Her executioners threw her back in several times, but each time the river saved her life. The king then sentenced her to be burnt alive, and she was thrown on to a blazing pyre. The next morning she was found unharmed among the ashes with the infant Dubricius in her lap. When mother and child were taken before the king, he had a change of heart and warmly embraced them. And when Dubricius touched his grandfather's face, the king's malady vanished at once, and he never again foamed at the mouth.

On Palm Sunday, after the service at Hentland church, small cakes stamped with the slogan 'Peace and good neighbourhood' are distributed among the congregation. They are called Pax Cakes, and the custom was begun in the 18th century by a local farmer. He hoped that it would stop the centuries-old feuding between local families of Celtic, Saxon and Norman descent.
▶ *On minor roads off A49, 10 miles S of Hereford.*

❷ Aconbury

At the stroke of midnight on Twelfth Night, the water in St Anne's Well is reputed to bubble furiously and rise into a blue haze. Until the First World War at least, there used to be great competition to draw the first bucket after Twelfth Night. The water was said to be useful for curing eye infections.
▶ *Just E of A49, 5 miles S of Hereford.*

❸ Much Marcle

The 13th-century St Bartholomew's church is an architectural treasure trove, featuring a rare wooden effigy of a man in 14th-century civilian dress. He is thought to represent Walter de Helyon, a local landowner. According to an old belief, the effigy was once carried at the head of all funerals in the parish.

A fine series of six green men is to be found amid the church's stonework; and the yew tree in the churchyard is believed to have been planted in the year 500.
▶ *9 miles E 7 miles NE of Ross-on-Wye on A449.*

MUCH MARCLE

❹ Hereford Beacon

An Iron Age hillfort on Hereford Beacon near Colwall is traditionally the place where Caratacus, king of the Britons, made his last stand against the invading Romans in AD 50. The Britons lost the battle, and their broken king was taken captive and shipped to Rome, where he died soon afterwards.

▶ *4 miles S of Great Malvern, just off A449.*

❺ Ashperton

Katherine Grandison, who died about 1360, was born here and christened in the ancient font, which now stands in the churchyard. Katherine is locally affirmed to be the lady who dropped her garter at a court ball in 1349, although this is more generally accepted to be the Countess of Salisbury. Whoever it was, the lady played her part in founding England's highest order of chivalry. Tradition says that to cover her embarrassment, Edward III picked up the garter, and with the words 'Honi soit qui mal y pense' (roughly: 'Shame on anyone who thinks evil of this'), buckled it on his own leg. It has been pointed out that it took more than a dropped garter to ruffle the modesty of a 14th-century court lady. The true significance may lie in the fact that the garter was the badge of a witch, and Edward's action saved Katherine (or the Countess) from certain death for sorcery.

▶ *8 miles E of Hereford.*

❻ Sutton St Nicholas

About a mile from the village, in the middle of a privately owned field, stands the Wergin's Stone, also known as the Devil's Stone. Apparently, there used to be at least two of them and it is said that one night in 1652 the stones were moved 240 paces by the Devil, and it took nine yoke of oxen to restore them to their proper place. The base of the stone is hollowed out and may once have been used for tributes or for the ceremonial collection of rents, but no one now remembers by or to whom the tributes were made or the rents paid.

▶ *On minor roads 4 miles N of Hereford.*

❼ Orleton

On Orleton Hill, near an opening in the rocks known as Palmer's Churn, is a 1.8m (6ft) deep hole in the ground. A narrow passage, 3.6m (12ft) long, leads from the hole to the surface, and in the 19th century local youths would try to crawl through it. According to popular belief at the time, those who got stuck in the middle, or turned back, would never marry. A local legend tells how a goose once entered the hole, found an underground passage and came out 4 miles away at Woofferton. When it emerged it said 'Goose out!' and as a result the spot was named Gauset.

Traditionally, St George's churchyard at Orleton was held to be the place where the Resurrection would begin on the Day of Judgment. People from all over England arranged to be buried there, believing that they would be the first to rise from their graves.

▶ *5 miles N of Leominster on B4361.*

❽ Leominster

Merewald, a 7th-century king of Mercia whose fierce behaviour earned him the nickname 'Lion', had a dream one night in which a Christian missionary brought him some important news. At the same time, a hermit from the neighbourhood, Ealfrid, dreamt that a lion was eating out of his hand. The king and the hermit met in the place now called Leominster – legend says named after the 'Lion' king – and in the course of their conversation, they described their dreams. Merewald was so impressed that he became a Christian, and founded a church and convent at Leominster in AD 658.

This story, which provides one explanation of how Leominster got its name, is carved in stone on the west door of the Norman church of St Peter and St Paul. According to another theory, the town is named after Earl Leofric, who was the husband of Lady Godiva. He died in 1057.

▶ *13 miles N of Hereford on A49.*

❾ Dorstone

Up on Merbach Hill, near Dorstone, Arthur's Stone is reputed to mark the grave of a king who was foolish enough to start a fight with King Arthur. Another story claims that it is Arthur himself who is buried there, and yet another that the grave is that of a giant whom Arthur killed. There is uncertainty, too, about the marks on the stones beside the grave, which were made either by the giant's elbows as he fell dying, or by King Arthur's knees as he knelt in prayer after the battle.

Not far from Merbach Hill, a town is supposed to have been buried beneath a field, engulfed by an earthquake many centuries ago. There is a pond in the field, and deep in the darkest part of it, so the story goes, the top of a church steeple is sometimes just visible.

▶ *6 miles E of Hay-on-Wye on B4348.*

LEICESTERSHIRE & RUTLAND

The statue of a mother goddess, thousands of years old, and the tale of a hag who devours wayward children, symbolise pagan ancestry in a land once preoccupied with witchcraft and the Devil's work.

❶ Belton

The church of St John the Baptist holds the tomb of Lady Roesia de Verdon, who founded the now ruined Gracedieu Priory. Originally buried in the priory grounds, she was later moved to the parish church when the priory was disbanded. The lady also inaugurated an annual fair, which was held in late May or early June, mainly for the sale of horses. The nuns of Gracedieu chose to wear white habits, rather than the usual black of the Augustinians, and the priory ruins are the site of a well-documented haunting by a white or grey-robed figure known as the 'white lady'. A number of witnesses are consistent in their description of a monk or a nun. Writer Stephen Neale Badcock has speculated that the apparition may be the result of a natural phenomenon caused by the Thringstone fault – the boundary of the coalfields of Leicestershire. Unexplained lights, or earthlights, have been recorded along fault lines in different locations around the world.

The village also has a permanent maypole, around which the children dance on the first Saturday in May.

▶ *6 miles W of Loughborough.*

❷ Newtown Linford

An 18th-century folly, shaped like a drinking mug and handle, stands in Bradgate Park. Known as Old John's Tower, it was built by Lord Stamford in memory of a local miller noted for his liking of ale. The miller died at Stamford's 21st birthday party, in 1780, when a log in the centre of a bonfire burnt through and fell on him.

▶ *Off A50, 6 miles NW of Leicester.*

❸ Sileby

Every year, on Whit Sunday, the vicar distributes oranges to local schoolchildren under an ancient elm tree in St Mary's churchyard. The earliest part of the church dates from the 12th century, but this custom is believed to have started in 1815 to commemorate the Duke of Wellington's victory at Waterloo. It lapsed for several years and was recently revived by the gift of an anonymous donor.

▶ *On minor roads between A6 and A46, 7 miles N of Leicester.*

❹ Braunstone

A Hay Sunday Service, in which fresh hay is spread over the church floors, is conducted in Braunstone church each year on the Sunday after St Peter's Day, June 29. A local legend maintains that, long ago, the daughter of the lord of nearby Glenfield Manor was lost in Leicester Forest when a gang of outlaws began to pursue her. She was saved by the clerk of Braunstone church and, in gratitude, her father dedicated an acre in one of his meadows to the clerk, to provide hay every year for the church floors.

▶ *2 miles SW of Leicester city centre.*

❺ Leicester

The Dane Hills are the old name for the high ground to the right of King Richard's Road and Glenfield Road on the way out of the town. Here, respectable suburban homes and a convent occupy what was a dreaded patch of wasteland and the home of a terrifying hag, Black Annis. Black Annis's bower was said to be a cave that she had clawed out of the hillside with her own talons. She had tattered hair and yellowed fangs, and in her cave she lay in wait for disobedient children who had strayed too far from home. Parents would warn their children of the dreadful fate that awaited them if they played late at night in the hills. Black Annis would seize them, skin them alive and eat them, scattering their bones and hanging their skins to dry on a nearby oak.

This tale was still being used to frighten local children into good behaviour well into the 20th century. It possibly goes back to the ancient Celtic myths, and Annis could be Anu, wife of the sky god, Ludd.

▶ *Access from Junctions 21 and 22 of M1.*

❻ Enderby

An annual Whit Monday ceremony is known as 'The Selling of the Keep of the Wether'. The hay crop, or keep, from a field called the Wether is auctioned at The Nag's Head. A silver coin is passed from hand to hand, and only the person holding it is allowed to bid. John of Gaunt is said to have started the custom around 1380. The money pays for a celebration dinner.

▶ *5 miles SW of Leicester city centre.*

⑦ Wigston

Although he brought pain to his respectable family, tall, handsome George Davenport endeared himself to the local people by his generosity and carefree ways. Even when he turned highwayman, no one would betray him, and everyone thought that his favourite trick of making recruiting sergeants drunk before stealing their horses was a huge joke. Then one day, he made the mistake of waylaying a butcher who promptly clubbed the unfortunate George over the head and dragged him off to Leicester Assizes, where he was condemned to death. Game to the last, George borrowed a chaise and pair from an innkeeper and to the cheers of the crowd drove himself to the gallows on Red Hill.

▶ *4 miles SE of Leicester city centre on A5199.*

⑧ Braunston-in-Rutland

The winds and rains of at least 2,000 English winters have battered the stone female figure that stands outside Braunston church in Rutland. She was discovered in about 1920 beneath the church doorstep, and may predate the original 14th-century church. The carving is quite unlike any grotesque, gargoyle or figure from any historical period and is popularly known as a goddess, although her origin and purpose are unknown.

▶ *On minor roads 2 miles SW of Oakham.*

⑨ Wistow

The old Hall and St Wistan's Church are all there is left of the original village of Wistow, in the meadows on the outskirts of the present village, between Arnesby on the A50 and Great Glen on the A6.

Wistan was a Saxon prince, heir to the throne of Mercia. On the death of his father, his kinsman and godfather, Britfardus, proposed marriage to his mother, Elfleda, who had been appointed regent. Britfardus wanted to strengthen his own claim to the throne, but the young prince Wistan opposed the match, saying that it was incestuous in the eyes of the Church.

On a pretext of discussing the matter, Britfardus lured the boy to a lonely spot and there clove his skull in two. The murderer's hope of secrecy was dashed, however, when a column of light appeared over Wistan's grave, and where his blood had been spilt, human hair sprouted from the ground. Vilified by the Church and people, and tortured by his own conscience, Britfardus went insane. Wistan was re-interred at Repton, where fragments of his bones attracted pilgrims until the Reformation, when they disappeared. It was rumoured that visitors to Wistow on June 1, the anniversary of the killing, might be fortunate enough to see hair springing from the ground.

▶ *On minor roads 6 miles SE of Leicester.*

⑩ Hallaton

On Easter Monday, villagers go 'Bottle-kicking' in a brawling spring festival rite that dates back to pre-Christian times, but now has the blessing of the Church. It starts with a short service, after which portions of hare-pie are distributed. Some of the pie is put into a sack and taken in procession to Hare Pie Hill, where it is scattered over the ground. On the way, three 'bottles' – wooden barrels, two containing 9 pints of beer each, and one empty – are cheered at certain points, then fought for, one by one. Youths from Hallaton and rival Medbourne struggle to carry them over a brook into their parishes. The first team to succeed shares the contents of the barrel, before fighting over the empty cask. When the second full 'bottle' has been won, one of the winning team is chaired back to Hallaton's ancient stone buttercross to drink the first pint, which is the signal for a village celebration.

The symbolism may represent the sacrificial beast scattered on the land to promote fertility, and a ritual battle between summer and winter.

▶ *On minor roads 14 miles SE of Leicester.*

⑪ Oakham

For centuries, every peer or member of the royal family visiting the former county of Rutland has had to give a horseshoe to the Lord of the Manor at Oakham. There are some 220 in the castle; the oldest, dated 1600, is said to have been given by Elizabeth I. The biggest, from George IV, cost £20 to make, and the king left his host to pay for it.

▶ *18 miles E of Leicester at junction of A606 and A6003.*

⑫ Edmondthorpe

St Michael's Church is the resting place of Sir Roger Smith, whose gloriously extravagant 17th-century alabaster tomb lies alongside those of his two wives. The lower effigy, Lady Ann, has a dark, rust-coloured stain on one of its wrists. According to popular legend, Lady Ann was a witch who, having taken the form of a cat, was wounded in the paw by her butler who struck her with a meat cleaver.

▶ *On minor roads 7 miles E of Melton Mowbray.*

CENTRAL ENGLAND

LINCOLNSHIRE

Events ascribed to abbeys, churches and a cathedral have all acquired legendary status in this land of fens and golden beaches. But hidden in the depths of one annual contest, vestiges of an ancient cult survive.

❶ Brigg

A roadside gallows, which stands 3 miles east of Brigg on the A18, was erected by James I early in the 17th century. At that time, bitter rivalry existed in the district between the Ross family of Melton Ross and the Tyrwhitts of Kettleby. One day, retainers from both families met while hunting in what is now Gallows Wood, and a savage fight broke out in which people from either side were killed. The king had the gallows erected as a reminder that any further bloodshed between the two families would be treated as murder.

▶ *8 miles E of Scunthorpe at junction of A18 and A1084.*

❷ Glentham

The stone effigy of 14th-century Lady Tourney, which lies in St Peter's Church, used to be washed by seven maids every Good Friday. Each was paid a shilling, from rent on a piece of land. The practice ended in 1832, when the land was sold. The habit of washing holy images was known in local dialect as 'malgraen', which became corrupted to Molly Grime. People in the area still call a child with a dirty face 'Molly Grime'.

A 15th-century stone statue of Mary holding the body of Christ adorns the porch. Known as a 'pieta', these are rare and it may be why the church was once called St Peter and Our Lady of Pity.

▶ *14 miles N of Lincoln on A631.*

❸ Caistor

A legend of this area features St Paulinus, a 7th-century missionary who joined St Augustine in Kent in AD 601. One day, the story goes, St Paulinus was riding an ass along the ancient trackway that runs near Caistor when he met a man sowing corn. He asked for some grain to feed the ass, but the man said he had none. Seeing a sack in the field, Paulinus asked what was in it. 'That is no sack,' the man lied, 'but only a stone.' 'Then stone it shall be,' Paulinus retorted. The Fonaby Stone stands there to this day on Fonaby Top, and dreadful misfortune allegedly follows any attempt to move or damage it.

▶ *22 miles NE of Lincoln on A46.*

❹ Haxey

An annual custom that retains a pagan flavour is the Hood Game at Haxey, held near the time of the winter solstice, on St John's Eve, January 6. The legend says that some 700 years ago on that day, the wife of Sir John de Mowbray, an ancestor of Thomas Mowbray, Duke of Norfolk, lost her big red hood in the wind as she was riding over Haxey Hill. A group of 13 'Boggans' – people from the boggy fenland – gave chase and finally rescued it. The country 'fool' who seized the hood was too shy to hand it over, so another man, less tongue-tied, gave it to Lady de Mowbray, who was so delighted with the pursuit that she gave each man half an acre of land, in return for a promise to re-enact the event each year.

So, every January, the Lord selects his 12 Boggans, and one of them, the Fool, makes an opening speech at the Mounting Stone, near the gates of church of St Nicholas. He tells the crowd they are to play 'hoose agin' hoose, toon agin' toon; if a man meet a man knock a man doon, but down't hurt 'im'. Then the Boggans, dressed as morris men, lead the crowd to a field near the hill.

The Boggans form a huge circle, and the crowd stand inside it. A number of Hoods made of rolled-up sacking are thrown into the air, and the players try to get these away, past the Boggans. Any who succeed are later rewarded with a shilling by the Lord. But the game starts in earnest when the main Hood – made of leather, and containing a coiled rope – is thrown up. Men from the five local hamlets struggle to win possession and 'sway' the Hood away to their local inn. First to succeed are the winners. Part of the concluding ritual is the Smoking of the Fool, who must stand on the Mounting Stone while damp straw is lit around it. This has replaced an earlier ritual of dragging a plough round the green.

Haxey is part of an area known as the Isle of Axholme, west of the River Trent – Axholme apparently means 'holme' or island of Haxey. This was once marshland and the villages were built on raised ground. The land was drained in the 17th century by Dutchman Cornelius Vermuyden on the orders of Charles I.

▶ *On A161, 8 miles N of Gainsborough.*

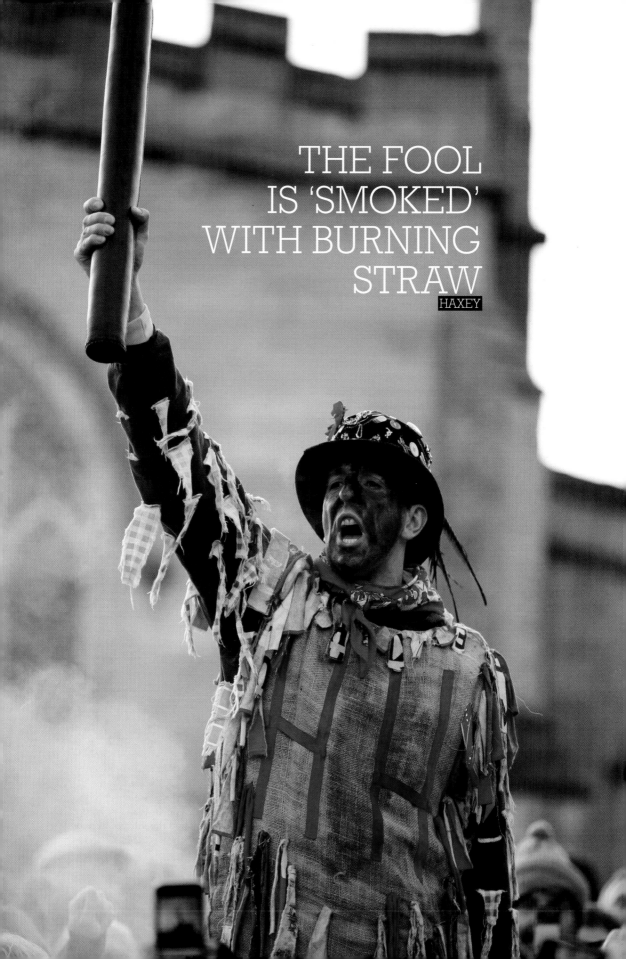

THE FOOL
IS 'SMOKED'
WITH BURNING
STRAW
HAXEY

❺ Lincoln

Sitting comfortably in the spandrel of two arches in Lincoln Cathedral's Angel Choir is one of the city's most famous characters – the Lincoln Imp. This 30cm (12in) monster grins toothily down at visitors, having been turned to stone by an angel. According to legend, this imp was the protégé of the Devil, who once released a pair of them to make mischief on earth. The two were blown in to Lincoln on the wind and they flew into the cathedral, where one caused havoc while the other hid in horror at his companion's antics. Eventually, the bad imp was petrified as he surveyed the mess, while the other escaped to fly on the wind. When a storm blows around the south side of the cathedral, it is said that this is the good imp crying for his companion's return.

The Angel Choir is also the home of the earliest surviving cadaver tomb in Britain – a curious form of memorial in which a lifesized effigy of the deceased is twinned with a skeletal sculpture of decay, to illustrate what the contents of the tomb will really contain. Lincoln's tomb is that of Richard Fleming, founder of Lincoln College, Oxford, who died in 1431. The tombs were intended as a memento mori, or 'reminder of death', to show how transient life – and any glory gained in life – may be.

▶ *A46 from SW, A15 from N and S.*

❻ Bardney

Monks at King Ethelred's great Bardney Abbey refused to accept the bones of St Oswald, out of envy of the Northumbrian saint. The bones were left outside the abbey's locked doors all night, whereupon a pillar of light shot up to the skies. Rebuked by this sign from heaven, the monks embraced the bones next day, and the people of Bardney vowed never again to close their doors. That was in the 7th century, and 'Do you come from Bardney?' is still a local saying, if a door is left open.

▶ *10 miles E of Lincoln at junction of B1190 and B1202.*

❼ Cranwell

Three sets of horseshoes in the turf where Ermine Street crosses the A17 just west of the RAF College, commemorate the wild leaps of a blind horse called Bayard, as it struggled to unseat Old Meg, a wicked local witch. Abner, the owner of the horse, was fighting Old Meg, too, and cut off one of the hag's breasts, but still she clung on, her long talons sunk deeply into Bayard's flanks. The dreadful battle ended when Abner plunged his sword through the witch, but he stabbed his horse as well, and Meg and Bayard died together.

▶ *5 miles NW of Sleaford.*

8 Bourne

Hereward the Wake, the Saxon nobleman who became a legendary outlaw, was born at Bourne around AD 1036. He is thought locally to have been the son of Lady Godiva and Leofric, Earl of Mercia. Hereward gained renown for his heroic exploits in leading Anglo-Saxon resistance against the Norman invaders. His manor house stood on the site of Bourne Castle, of which all that remains are the earthworks and moat, opposite Bourne church.

The lease of Whitebread Meadow, 1½ miles north of Bourne, is auctioned annually during a 183m (200yd) race between two boys, held on the Monday before Easter. The bid made just before the race ends is taken as the final one, and the rent money obtained is donated to a local charity established in 1742.

▶ *At junction of A15 and A151, 16 miles S of Sleaford.*

9 Swineshead

After King John lost the Crown Jewels in The Wash in October 1216, he dined at Swineshead Abbey, where over-indulgence in peaches and new ale is alleged to have killed him a few days later. Years afterwards, people said that he had been poisoned by a monk who gave his own life 'to save all England'. According to legend, the king told the monk that he intended forcing up the price of bread to increase his revenue. A true patriot, the monk poisoned the king's ale, and drank first from the cup to make the king believe it was safe.

▶ *7 miles SW of Boston.*

10 Anwick

The entrance to Anwick churchyard is marked by two large stones deposited by an ancient glacier. In the days before geological learning, they acquired their name, the Drake Stones, and a story to match. The legend told of a farmer who lost his plough horses in a bog. As they disappeared, a drake appeared in their place, and the next day an enormous drake-shaped stone appeared where the horses had sunk. The stone was broken in an attempted move in 1832 and in 1913 the two parts were set in their current position.

▶ *5 miles NE of Sleaford on A153.*

11 Fishtoft

A window in Fishtoft church shows the 7th-century hermit St Guthlac, to whom the church is dedicated, holding a whip reputedly given to him by St Bartholomew. As long as he held this whip, legend claimed, Fishtoft would be free of rats and mice.

▶ *On minor roads 3 miles SE of Boston.*

THE IMPS WERE BLOWN IN TO THE CITY ON THE WIND
LINCOLN CATHEDRAL

NORTHAMPTONSHIRE

Tales of saints and perpetrators of good deeds fill the annals of this landlocked county, where rivals were reconciled in a feast of love and a noisy midnight parade still thrives.

❶ Norton

There is nothing in the village or the nearby site of Bannaventa, a Roman settlement, to show that this was once the home of St Patrick, the patron saint of Ireland. Born in Wales in AD 389, he lived in Bannaventa with his parents, the Roman official Calpurnius and his British wife, until 405, when the town was plundered by Celts and the able-bodied population taken into slavery. The 16-year-old Patrick was sold to an Irish landowner.

Patrick, who had been brought up as a Christian by his father, led a miserable life as a cattleminder among the pagan Irish. Then one day, as he rested on a mountainside, a boulder that was falling towards him split into two pieces and passed on either side of him. Believing this to be a sign that God had work for him, he escaped to Gaul, and later returned to Bannaventa, where he became a farmer. But he became daily more convinced that God had singled him out to convert the Irish. In 432, he returned to the land of his captivity, where his miracles and piety convinced the people of the truth of his message. He died around 461.
▶ *2 miles NE of Daventry.*

❷ Wicken

The parish of Wicken was originally divided into two hamlets, Wyke Hamon and Wyke Dyke. Bitter rivalry existed between them and quarrels were commonplace, until in 1586 the two communities were united into a single parish. A Love Feast was instituted in that year both to commemorate the event and to promote future harmony, and the feast is still held every All Saints' Day, November 1. After a brief service in the church, parishioners sing hymns around the village's traditional Gospel Oak, where Gospel readings formerly took place. They then meet at a local hotel to partake of cakes and ale.
▶ *Just off A422, 15 miles S of Northampton.*

❸ Northampton

The Norman church of St Peter stands on the site of an earlier Saxon church. In the early 11th century, the parish priest of this old church was a man named Brunning, who had a Norwegian servant as devout as himself. Brunning felt it would benefit both their souls if his man made a pilgrimage to Rome, but before

THE VISARD MASK OF DAVENTRY

ACCORDING TO RESEARCHERS working on the Deliberately Concealed Garments Project at Glasgow University, there may be as many reasons for concealing articles of clothing and footwear in buildings as there are concealed articles of clothing and footwear. The project was set up by the Textile Conservation Centre in 1998 to study garments discovered hidden or buried in buildings – in chimneys, under floors, in roofs and behind plaster walls. Most are well worn or damaged before they are hidden (or cached – that is, stashed with other objects) and include boots, children's shoes, hats, corsets, shirts and petticoats.

One of the most unusual finds was made in Daventry in 2010, when an Elizabethan visard mask was found inside a niche in the wall of a 16th-century house. These oval masks, made of stiffened leather and black velvet and designed with nothing more than two eyeholes and a tiny slit for the mouth were worn to protect a lady from the damaging rays of the sun, and to shield her from unwelcome glances while in public. She held it in place with a single glass bead stitched to the inside near the mouth, which she held between her teeth. An excerpt from Phillip Stubbes Anatomie of Abuses, published in 1583, states:
When they use to ride abrod, they have invisories, or masks, visors made of velvet, wherwith they cover all their faces, having holes made in them against their eyes, whereout they look. So that if a man, that knew not their guise before, should chaunce to meet one of them, he would think hee met a monster or a devil; for face hee can see none, but two brode holes against her eyes with glasses in them.

The mask may have been placed in the niche to deflect evil or curses, to bring luck or even have been hidden by builders as a joke. They may be a reminder of a deceased loved one, anchoring their presence for the benefit of the inhabitants.

the servant's ship had sailed, he was commanded in a dream to return home. Sensing some divine purpose, Brunning asked his servant to keep a vigil in the church. Sure enough, the servant was rewarded by another dream in which he was told to search a certain part of the building, where he discovered an ancient tomb.

Convinced a great revelation would follow, Brunning and his servant sent for a local lame girl named Alfgiva in the hope that she might be cured. At sunset, the three knelt at the altar; then, as midnight struck, the church was suddenly filled with light. A snow-white dove appeared and sprinkled the watchers with holy water from the font. Alfgiva was immediately cured. They opened the tomb, and discovered from a document within that it contained the bones of St Ragener, a nephew of the martyr-king St Edmund. A stone coffin lid in the present church is believed to be that of St Ragener's reliquary.

▶ *Access from Junctions 15, 15A and 16 of M1.*

❹ Orlingbury

An effigy in Orlingbury church is supposed to commemorate the man who killed the last wild wolf in England. In legend, he is remembered as Jack of Batsaddle, and a farm and wood in the neighbourhood are named after him. However, the effigy is officially that of John de Withmayle, who was a generous donor of land to the Church.

The deed occurred in 1375 and, in fact, there is some dispute about whether the creature that Jack killed was really a wolf or a giant boar. One version of the legend even claims that he fought and slew two creatures – a wolf and a boar.

There is no doubt that Jack died as a result of his famous battle. When the creature, whatever it was, lay dead, Jack, tired and thirsty, took a drink from a nearby spring. And, apparently, the shock of the ice-cold water killed him.

▶ *On minor roads 4 miles S of Kettering.*

❺ Broughton

The annual parade of the Tin Can Band through the village is an ancient custom, which still persists as noisily as ever. It starts from the church gates just after midnight, when residents beat various instruments to make as much noise as possible.

The parade probably dates from the early 17th century, and is held on the first Sunday after November 12. The reason why the event takes place on this particular date, and at the midnight hour, is not clear. The original purpose, however, is thought to have been to make as much noise as

possible in the darkness in belief that superstitious gipsies would be deterred from camping nearby. The gipsies, who were feared as weavers of spells, traditionally favoured the area because of the many good camping sites available in the district.

▶ *Just off A43, 3 miles SW of Kettering.*

❻ Woodford

In about 1550, according to local legend, John Styles, the vicar of St Mary's Church at Woodford, lost his parish because of his Catholic beliefs. He fled to a monastery in Belgium, taking with him a costly chalice from the church, and soon afterwards died there. A new vicar, Andrew Powlet, brought the chalice, together with John's heart, back to Woodford several years later, but with the passage of time, both relics were mislaid and forgotten. In 1862, Powlet's ghost was seen in the hallway of Woodford Rectory by the young man who then had the living. It appeared twice, each time hovering near a certain panel in the wall. Examination revealed a secret cavity, which contained the missing chalice and a faded letter. The letter led to the discovery of John's heart, entombed in a pillar in the church. The heart is still there, and can be seen through a glass panel in the pillar.

The relic, wrapped in cloth, is also said to have belonged to a local lord, who died on a pilgrimage to the Holy Land, or Roger Maufe, a Knight of Peterborough.

▶ *Just S of A14, 7 miles E of Kettering.*

❼ Stanion

The church at Stanion houses a strange relic, an enormous bone nearly 2m (6ft) long. According to local legend, the bone belonged to a huge dun cow that appeared one day in the village and promised milk to all who needed it, in return for kindly care. The cow's fame spread far and wide and came to the ears of a witch. One morning the witch appeared and, producing a sieve from under her cloak, ordered the cow to fill it. The poor animal strained to keep her promise but in the end died exhausted. One rib was preserved as a memorial.

The whole legend of the dun cow and its rib was recorded in a poem by David Townsend, the village blacksmith at Geddington, 3 miles from Stanion, around the end of the 19th century. In fact, the bone is probably that of a whale, brought back by some adventurous mariner to his native village round about the beginning of the 17th century.

▶ *2 miles SE of Corby.*

Sports and merrymaking

Boisterous fun, these quirky old games remain seriously competitive. All but the faint-hearted are welcome to join in.

The splendid ceremony of Hocktide Revels used to take place in the second week after Easter on Waytyng Hill (otherwise known as Bonfirehill Knoll), overlooking the village of Hexton in the Barton Hills of the Bedfordshire/Hertfordshire border. The men and women of Hexton would climb the knoll together; then the men would raise a tall ash pole and try to keep it erect, while the women would endeavour to topple it and drag it downhill into Hexton. It's not tremendously hard to untangle the imagery behind that springtime ritual. But why did it die out? Almost certainly because of church and community disapproval, as social behaviour became less free and easy during the later Victorian era.

Puritan souls certainly disapproved of Kissing Friday, the first Friday in Lent, when boys could extract a 'free kiss' from girls, and couldn't be either punished or denied. The gentlemen of Sileby, a small village north of Leicester, knew Kissing Friday as Nippy Hug Day, and would pinch the bottom of any woman who turned down the offer of a kiss.

This bottom-pinching tradition migrated down the calendar to Oak Apple Day, the May 29 annual celebration of the Restoration of Charles II to the throne, which became known as Pinch-Bum Day. The 'pinch-bum' element might have attached itself to Oak Apple Day as an expression of support for the saucy freedoms frowned on by the recently ousted Puritan government, or perhaps in acknowledgement of Charles's own notorious lechery. Some say that a pinched bum was the penalty imposed by royalists on anyone who failed to wear a loyal sprig of leaves on that day. Pinch-Bum Day was also known as Nettle Day, because those who didn't show oak leaves could expect to be whipped with a bunch of nettles.

Simple pleasures

Rustic sports and merrymaking go from strength to strength these days. In some cases, men try to impress a watching crowd with shows of strength, endurance and virility. In the Staffordshire village of Abbots Bromley, on Wakes Monday in early September, six sets of huge reindeer horns are danced around the village by a team of men. The heavy horns are at least 1,000 years old – a long-standing link with Merrie England.

The Cotswolds are another stronghold of macho sporting display. On May Bank Holiday in Tetbury contestants, many in fancy dress, struggle up and down a 1:4 hill with a heavy woolsack draped across their shoulders – 27.2kg (60lb) for men, 15.9kg (35lb) for women.

At Chipping Campden, on the Friday after Spring Bank Holiday, an 'Olimpick Games' has been held since 1612 – predating the international Olympic games by some three centuries. Some of the sports are not exactly Corinthian in character; they include Back-sword, Tug-o'-war, Obstacle Race, Standing Jump and Shin-kicking. This last is open to all comers, and is the source of great hilarity and plenty of bruises. Nowadays participants have their legs bound with padding, but in former times men wore steel-tipped boots and laid into one another with such bone-breaking ferocity that players ended up with deeply corrugated shins.

Everybody welcome

Some traditional sports require mass participation, as with the famous May Bank Holiday cheese rolling at Cooper's Hill in Gloucestershire, in which anyone can have a go at breaking their necks chasing a rolling cheese down a precipitous grass bank. Others are very definitely for locals. The Shrovetide football match between the Up'ards and the Down'ards of Ashbourne in Derbyshire involves hundreds of players, with the whole town and surroundings for a playing field. On Easter Monday in east Leicestershire it's the Hare Pie Scramble and Bottle Kicking, a massed mud bath in which 'bottles' (wooden beer casks) are contested between the rival villages of Hallaton and Medbourne. Anyone can join in, but thumps and bruises may be more than bargained for.

All these sports have several characteristics in common. There's an element of rough-and-tumble, of boisterous ragging and misrule and generally being let off the leash. A few key figures are chosen for ceremonial roles, and large numbers of participants merge their individuality in general pack activity.

Survival fears

Sadly, some traditional sports may in the end become victims of their own success. In 2009 the Cooper's Hill cheese-rolling drew a crowd of 15,000, three times the capacity of the site. In 2010 and 2011 the event was cancelled, amid fears for the safety of these onlookers. Traditional sports have survived wars, weathers, changing fashions, religious intolerance and the march of the centuries. Whether they can survive the demands of health and safety remains to be seen.

Anyone can have a
go at breaking their
necks chasing a rolling
cheese down a
precipitous grass bank.
COOPER'S HILL, GLOUCESTERSHIRE

NOTTINGHAMSHIRE

Stories that hold sway in this ancient county are entwined with the good-hearted men in Lincoln green. Their medieval exploits may be reflections of much older tales from a pagan past.

❶ Mansfield

The ballad of the king and the miller tells how Henry II became lost while hunting in Sherwood Forest, and met John Cockle the miller, who failed to recognise him. The miller gave him a venison pasty but warned him never to let the king know they 'made free with his deer'. The king was so amused, and so delighted by the miller's forthright country ways, that he made him a forest overseer, and gave him £300 a year and a knighthood. Mansfield is one of the main centres from which to explore Sherwood Forest.

▶ *15 miles N of Nottingham.*

❷ Laxton

The village of Laxton has the last remaining open-field system in Britain. Commonly used across Europe from early medieval times, the system involved land being divided into narrow strips, and each one being farmed separately. This required a close working relationship between the farmers, and was administered by a Court Leet – a committee of farmers and local officials. Laxton's Court Leet meets in The Dovecote, the village pub, following an inspection of the fields by the Laxton Jury. They ensure that strict crop rotation is observed, adjudicate on grazing rights and boundary issues and check that common areas of fields are in good order.

▶ *3 miles SW of Tuxford on A1.*

❸ Newark-on-Trent

St Catherine's Well, by the river at Sconce Hill, in Devon Park, has a sad tale attached to it. In the 13th century, Sir Guy Saucimer killed Sir Everard Bevorcotes out of jealousy, for Sir Everard had won the affections of the fair Isabell de Caldwell, whom they both loved. A spring gushed forth on the spot and Sir Guy, plagued by guilt, fled abroad. Isabell died from grief and Sir Guy caught leprosy. One night, St Catherine appeared to him in a dream and told him he would be cured if he bathed in the spring. He returned to Newark, bathed in the waters and was healed. Sir Guy built a chapel around the spring and led a holy life ever after. When he died, he was canonised as St Guthred.

▶ *18 miles NE of Nottingham.*

❹ Nottingham

The 'oldest pub in England', The Trip to Jerusalem, is built on the site of a brewery where travellers to the Holy Land stopped to buy ale. The cellars are carved from rock, and a passageway from a nearby cave, Mortimer's Hole, leads up to the castle. Edward III's men may have crept down it to capture Roger Mortimer, who was later executed. His ghost haunts the cave.

The city is famous for its Goose Fair, first mentioned in a charter dated 1284 and still held from the first Thursday in October. The fair had its own Pie-powder Court – from the French *pied-poudre,* meaning 'dusty feet' – to deal summarily with wrongdoers.

▶ *6 miles E of Junctions 25 and 26 of M1.*

❺ Sherwood Forest

Robin Hood and his Merry Men are folk heroes, but the facts that underlie the legend are as shadowy as their supposed forest home. The earliest known ballad about the outlaws of Sherwood Forest, 'The Lytell Geste of Robyn Hode', dates from the 15th century, at least 200 years after the death of the hero. But from earlier references it is clear that the tales were well known long before this time. Some scholars believe that stories of real or fictitious outlaws were grafted on to a memory of a more sinister personality – the guardian god or spirit of the woods. 'Robin' was a name often given to fairies, and green, the colour worn by the outlaws for camouflage, was the fairies' colour too.

Nottinghamshire tradition still firmly asserts the existence of the county's most famous son. The gigantic, 1,000-year-old Major Oak in Birkland Wood, near Edwinstowe, is indicated as the outlaws' meeting place. Another great oak, the Centre Tree, halfway between Thoresby and Welbeck estates, is reputed to be the marker from which Robin's network of secret routes ran through the forest. Maid Marion, who married Robin in Edwinstowe church, was born in the village of Blidworth, 7 miles to the southwest. At Blidworth, too, the gang hid food in a cave; Friar Tuck lived nearby, and Will Scarlet is said to be buried in the churchyard.

▶ *The forest lies N and S of Edwinstowe on A6075, 20 miles N of Nottingham.*

THE TREES RETAIN
A SHADOWY MEMORY
OF THE SPIRIT OF THE WOODS
SHERWOOD FOREST

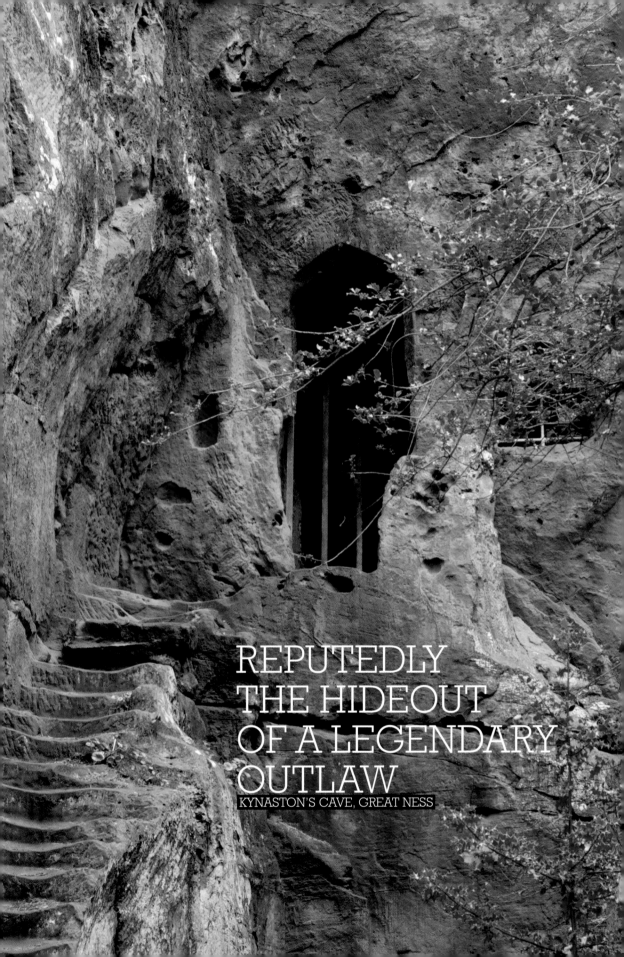

REPUTEDLY
THE HIDEOUT
OF A LEGENDARY
OUTLAW
KYNASTON'S CAVE, GREAT NESS

SHROPSHIRE

Natural features of the landscape lay behind many legends. In the Marches, a vast inland expanse of water had to be accounted for, and inventive Shropshire folk of old came up with two salutary tales.

❶ Ellesmere

This small market town is set among nine lakes, the largest of which is the 47ha (116 acre) Great Mere. Formal Victorian gardens and a lakeside walkway have recently been restored. Two local legends explain how this expanse of water appeared, both beginning with a well in a field near the town, from which all the inhabitants were permitted to draw water. In one legend, the farm to which the well belonged changed hands, and the new tenant refused to let anyone draw water. Retribution was swift, for one morning when the tenant's wife went to fetch water, she found that the whole field had become a lake. As a punishment for his churlish conduct, the tenant was forced to continue paying rent for the now useless land.

In the second story, the well was the only source of water for the townsfolk of Ellesmere, and a new landowner imposed a charge for every bucketful. The people prayed that God might redress their wrongs, and one night the water in the well rose until it flooded the land. From that day, everyone had free water in abundance.

▶ *8 miles NE of Oswestry.*

❷ Great Ness

Kynaston's Cave, in the side of Nesscliffe Hill near Great Ness, is reputed to have been the hideout of a legendary 15th-century outlaw, Wild Humphrey Kynaston. Like Robin Hood, he stole from the rich and gave to the poor, earning so much local goodwill that he never ran short of food, either for himself or for his remarkable horse. Not only was his horse shod backwards, to mislead anyone who pursued him, but it also once jumped 9 miles from Nesscliffe Hill to Ellesmere after one of the outlaw's daring robberies. On another occasion, his horse carried Kynaston to safety by leaping over the River Severn at a point now known as Kynaston's Leap, where the river is 12m (40ft) wide. It was rumoured by his enemies that Kynaston had sold his soul to the Devil, and some even said that his horse was the Devil himself. Having successfully evaded every attempt to capture him, Wild Humphrey Kynaston ended his life by dying peacefully in his cave.

▶ *Just off A5, 8 miles NW of Shrewsbury.*

❸ Norton in Hales

Until the beginning of this century, any man or boy in Norton in Hales who worked on Shrove Tuesday suffered a traditional punishment known as 'bradling'. The culprit was dragged over the rough surface of the 'Bradle Stone', a large boulder that stood on the village green, and was then beaten by the villagers. When the custom was discontinued, the Bradle Stone was moved and now stands near the front of the village church.

▶ *On minor roads 3 miles NE of Market Drayton.*

❹ Shrewsbury

This historic town, birthplace of Charles Darwin, has more than 600 listed buildings. One of them, St Alkmund's Church, is believed to have been founded around AD 912 by Aethelfleda, daughter of Kind Alfred. It was substantially rebuilt in 1795, but the medieval spire – dating from 1475 – remains. According to local legend, the Devil appeared in the church in 1553 during mass, his presence accompanied by a frightful storm. He flew up the steeple, destroyed the clock and clawed the fourth bell, knocking off the spire's pinnacle before leaving. The veracity of the story can never be proved: the five original bells became six in 1695, and these were replaced in 1812 with a ring of eight. The spire's fragility made ringing inadvisable and in 1972, to raise funds, the bells were put up for sale. In 1990 they were restored and sent to their new home, St Andrew's Cathedral, Honolulu.

▶ *15 miles W of Telford on A5.*

❺ Church Stretton

By tradition, while James II was travelling to Shrewsbury one day, the royal procession passed through the village of Stretton. The church was the first thing the king noticed and he christened the place Church Stretton. Two other nearby villages were also called Stretton. Of the first one, King James said, 'It's a very little Stretton,' and so Little Stretton it became. The second one the king named All Stretton because, as he remarked, 'They're all Strettons in this part of the country.'

▶ *12 miles S of Shrewsbury on A49.*

CENTRAL ENGLAND

STAFFORDSHIRE

Despite a rich industrial heritage, country pursuits loom large among this shire county's continuing traditions, and cherished annual events show few concessions to the present day.

❶ Endon

This is the only place in the county where the ritual of well-dressing survives. The ceremony takes place during the Spring Bank Holiday and has done so almost every year since the practice was revived in 1845. A Well-Dressing Queen is crowned twice on Saturday and twice on Monday, when a fete and fair are held with morris dancing and a tossing the sheaf competition. A heavy sheaf of corn was once used and heaved by pitchfork over a bar, which was gradually raised. Now a 6.8kg (15lb) sack of straw is used instead, pitched in the same way.

▶ *5 miles NE of Stoke-on-Trent on A53.*

❷ Leek

Black Mere Pool is reputed to be bottomless – and the home of Britain's only inland mermaid. She is said to swim to the surface at midnight and lure travelling bachelors to a watery grave. In the mid 19th century a nearby inn was named The Mermaid after the legend, and carries, many of the accounts on its walls. Several local reports mention strange lights at the pool after dark – will-o'-the-wisp type illuminations that may account for the mermaid myth.

▶ *10 miles NE of Stoke-on-Trent on A53.*

❸ Gradbach

Robin Hood himself is said to have sheltered in the huge, hidden natural cleft known as Lud's Church in the Black Forest. Dripping, mossy, fern-decked rocks rise steeply either side of the narrow, flat-based chamber, which is large enough to hold a 'congregation' of more than 100 people. The Lollards – followers of 14th-century religious reformer John Wycliffe – are known to have worshipped here, which is how the cleft got its name. Wycliffe was the first to translate the Bible into English, although his strict adherence to it tenets – and calls for church reform – meant that he was condemned as a heretic after his death and the Lollards outlawed.

The place is believed by Arthurian scholars to be the inspiration for the Green Chapel, where Sir Gawain faces the Green Knight and is spared in the 14th-century poem.

▶ *On minor roads 6 miles N of Leek.*

❹ Stafford

St Chad's church is the oldest building in Stafford. This late Norman marvel was built on an island in the marsh between 1100 and 1180, and has a Latin carving: 'The man who founded me is called Orm.' Inside, grotesque faces glare out from the carved capitals, men in skirts hold up their arms and weird, stylised creatures known as beakheads sit in rows beside the chancel arch. A small carved figure standing on a severed head is believed to be David with Goliath. According to local legend, the church was built by Moorish stonemasons brought back by Orm of Biddulph from the Crusades.

▶ *Access from Junctions 13 and 14 of M6.*

❺ Abbots Bromley

The Abbots Bromley Horn Dance, which takes place annually on Monday following the first Saturday after September 4, is unique in Europe. It starts at dawn by the church, makes a 20 mile circuit of local farms where the dancers are hailed as bearers of good luck and fertility, and finishes in the main street in the afternoon.

The dance, or 'running', is enacted by six deer men, carrying white or black wooden replicas of reindeer heads with real reindeer horns attached, accompanied by a Fool, a Hobby Horse, Maid Marion and a Bowman. Music is provided by a melodion player. The design of the costumes and the dance steps have been preserved for hundreds, perhaps thousands, of years, although the original purpose of the ritual has long been forgotten. One idea is that it may have started as a medieval pageant held to raise funds for the local church; now the money collected by the dancers is used for this purpose. Other authorities believe that the ritual is much older than Christianity. The presence of a man dressed as a woman (Maid Marion) suggests an ancient fertility rite, while the black and white deer men may have symbolised light and dark or winter and spring.

Scientific proof of the event's antiquity came in 1976, when a broken piece of antler was sent for radiocarbon dating. The horn was found to date from around 1050, suggesting the ceremony had Viking origins – the antlers may even be the most recent of a set of much older horns.

▶ *12 miles E of Stafford.*

THE HORN DANCE
MAY HAVE
VIKING ORIGINS
ABBOTS BROMLEY

WARWICKSHIRE

The woods and villages that inspired Shakespeare are the setting for many legendary tales. Customs have evolved through the ages, and one holy vigil has turned into a boisterous carnival.

❶ Bilston

During the Middle Ages, the Staffordshire town of Bilston, like many other towns and villages, held an annual Watch Service in honour of its patron saint, St Leonard. On the night before his feast day, November 6, the townspeople carried lighted candles into the local churchyard where they kept vigil. The custom was known as 'waking' or 'the Wakes'.

After the Reformation in the 16th century, the yearly Wakes were moved to the town's market place, and there the custom soon lost its religious meaning. The solemn ritual of guarding the dead by candlelight gave way to picnics, sporting contests and side-shows, and by the 19th century the observance of St Leonard's feast day, still known as a Wake, had become a holiday lasting several days. The festivities ranged from bull-baiting to plays put on by strolling players. Heavy drinking was commonplace, and a poster advertising the nearby Tipton Wake in 1869 proclaimed that 'Flaming Gin, Sparkling Wine, Muddy Porter and frothy Ale will be in active attendance', and each day would end 'in the usual way with Drunkenness, Brawling, Wife Beating, Empty Pockets and Aching Heads'.
▶ *3 miles SE of centre of Wolverhampton.*

❷ Walsall

In 1870, the mummified arm of an infant and a Cromwellian sword were discovered in the attic of the White Hart Inn at Caldmore Green, Walsall. The arm, thought to be a relic of witchcraft, became known, incorrectly, as a 'Hand of Glory'. In folklore, this is the hand of a hanged criminal pickled in various salts and dried in the sunlight, used as a holder for a candle made of a hanged man's fat, virgin wax and sesame. Its light was said to lull householders to sleep, and so such gruesome artefacts became the prized possessions of burglars.

The arm and the sword became associated in popular belief with a young girl who had killed herself in the inn about a century before. Various ghostly encounters were reported, including a handprint in the dust on an attic table.
In fact, the arm may not be such a sinister artefact at all. It is now believed to be a surgical specimen that had been injected with formalin in order to preserve it. It is now in the Walsall Museum, where it has the dubious honour of being one of the most popular exhibits.

The White Hart – a rural manor before it became a town inn – was restored in 1995 and today is a heritage centre and housing complex.
▶ *1 mile E of Junctions 9 and 10 of M6.*

❸ Atherstone

At 3pm on Shrove Tuesday, a large ball is thrown from the window of The Three Tuns inn in Long Street, and two Atherstone teams begin to fight for its possession in a free-for-all game of street football. It is permitted to deflate the ball and hide it any time after 4.30, and whichever team has the ball at 5 o'clock wins. Until about 1900, the game was played between Leicestershire and Warwickshire teams, and is said to have originated in King John's reign when men of the two counties fought for a bag of gold.
▶ *6 miles NW of Nuneaton.*

❹ Berkswell

The set of stocks on the village green has five holes for feet. The local explanation for this is that they were made for an old one-legged soldier and his two friends, whose drunken habits often landed them in the stocks.
▶ *On minor roads 6 miles W of Coventry.*

❺ Stretton-on-Dunsmore

The payment of Wroth Silver, which has continued since Saxon times, takes place on Knightlow Hill on November 11, St Martin's Day. Its purpose is to preserve the ancient right of villagers to drive cattle across the Duke of Buccleugh's land. Each year, representatives of the parishes that form the Knightlow Hundred assemble by a hollowed stone, which is all that remains of the Knightlow Cross. In answer to the summons of the Duke of Buccleugh's steward, each man puts his due, ranging from 1p to 22p, into the hollow. Anyone who fails to pay is fined £1 for each penny, or must present a white bull with red nose and ears to the duke. The ceremony is followed by breakfast – paid for by the duke – in the Old Dun Cow Inn.
▶ *Just S of A45, 7 miles SE of Coventry.*

❻ Bidford-on-Avon

In the 16th century, so the story goes, the village was famous for its beer drinkers, who used to challenge men from the neighbouring villages to drinking competitions. One day, Shakespeare came with a team from Stratford, but the Bidford men quickly out-drank them. The challengers fell asleep outside the village, and next morning, when his companions suggested renewing the contest, Shakespeare replied that he had had enough, having drunk at:

> Piping Pebworth, dancing Marston,
> Haunted Hillbro', hungry Grafton,
> dudging [ill-humoured] Exhall, papist
>   Wicksford,
> beggarly Broom and drunken Bidford.

These places have been known as the Shakespeare villages ever since.

▶ *7 miles W of Stratford-upon-Avon on B439.*

❼ Stratford-upon-Avon

In Shakespeare's world-famous birthplace, traditions and stories of its most illustrious citizen's youth are still remembered. The best known is that the young Shakespeare poached deer from Charlecote Park, and was afterwards prosecuted by the owner, Sir Thomas Lucy. Not so well known, however, are the lines that the poet allegedly wrote in revenge:

> A Parliament Member, a Justice of Peace,
> At home a poor scarecrow, at London an asse;
> If lowsie is Lucy, as some folks miscalle it,
> Then Lucy is lowsie whatever befall it.

Shakespeare is also said to have composed a satirical epitaph on a neighbour, John Combe, who died in 1614, and is buried in Stratford church. Despite the charitable bequests recorded on his tomb, he was locally unpopular as a usurer.

> Ten in the hundred lies here engraved
> Tis a hundred to ten his soul is not saved;
> If any man ask who lies in this tomb,
> Oh! Oh! quoth the Devil, 'tis my John-a-
>   Combe.

In the gardens behind the Memorial Theatre, there is a space marked out for playing nine men's morris. This game was common in Shakespeare's time, when it was played by Warwickshire shepherds and other country folk. A kind of imperfect chessboard was cut out of the turf on which the game, a mixture of chess, draughts and Chinese chequers, was played.

▶ *8 miles SW of Warwick.*

LADY GODIVA – MYTH AND REALITY

IT SEEMS UNLIKELY that anyone ever saw the real Lady Godiva riding naked through the streets of Coventry, with the possible (but historically unprovable) exception of Peeping Tom. But from about 100 years after her death in 1067, the truth of the story was taken for granted, and the thought of the pious beauty naked on her horse has haunted the English imagination ever since.

Unlike many characters of British myth, Lady Godiva is known to have existed: her real name was Godgifu and she was married to Earl Leofric of Mercia, one of the four all-powerful lords who ruled England under the Danish king, Canute. She was also a rich landowner in her own right, and the most valuable of her properties was Coventry.

Godgifu was wise, virtuous and charitable, but her husband tyrannised the Church, and mercilessly squeezed the heregeld – an oppressive tax that paid for Canute's bodyguard – from the people of Coventry. According to the legend, when Godgifu begged him to change his ways, the exasperated earl replied that first she would have to ride naked through Coventry on market day. That, he was certain, was something this modest woman would never do.

The earliest accounts of what happened were written in Latin by two monks at St Albans Abbey in Hertfordshire – Roger of Wendover in the 12th century and Matthew Paris in the early 13th century. The abbey stood on an important road junction, so it seems likely that the monks heard the story from travellers stopping there to rest.

Leofric's challenge is mentioned and it is possible that Godgifu performed public penance in Coventry for the misdeeds of her husband. She may have gone out stripped of her badges of rank, and the memory of this voluntary act of self-humiliation may have become mixed up with a Christian vision of Eve.

By the time the story reached Roger of Wendover it was beyond dispute that the beautiful Godiva had ridden naked through the marketplace, and her long hair had so thoroughly veiled her body that no one saw anything other than her face and 'her fair legs'. Leofric, so the story went, remitted the hated heregeld and stopped persecuting the Church.

It is true that Leofric underwent some sort of religious conversion during his life. After that, he and Godgifu founded a Benedictine monastery in Coventry, in which both were eventually buried. Not even the ruins of their joint creation remain.

CENTRAL ENGLAND

WORCESTERSHIRE

This historic, rural county provides the backdrop for many mythical tales of witches and devils, but the wraiths that frequent the Malvern Hills keep away from the happy occasions of well-dressing.

❶ Kidderminster

Becky Swan, a white witch, lived in Worcester Street in the mid 19th century. She is supposed to have had extraordinary healing powers and an uncanny ability to find lost property. However, the manner of her death cast some doubt on her goodness. One day, it is said, an enormous black cat appeared in the village, and local dogs fled howling as it stalked towards Becky's house. The cat clawed at her front door until Becky, who had suddenly turned as pale as a corpse, came to let it in.

From time to time during the next three days, the cat was seen around the cottage. But on the fourth day, the door had been barred and locked, no smoke came from the chimney, and Becky and her strange visitor seemed to have disappeared without trace. Eventually, her neighbours broke down the door and went inside. They were just in time to see the cat leap from the hearthrug ⋅ and vanish up the chimney. All that remained of Becky was a pile of ashes on the floor.
▶ *14 miles N of Worcester on A449.*

❷ Bromsgrove

A boar appears on the coat-of-arms of the Bromsgrove Town Council. A local legend connects it with the mythical Sir Ryalas, known as the Jovial Hunter, who is said to have been out riding one day when he came across a wild woman sitting in a tree. She told him that a huge wild boar had just killed her husband and 30 of his men, and begged Sir Ryalas to kill the creature. So he blew his hunting horn to all four points of the compass and the boar emerged from a dense thicket. After a fierce and bloody battle, the animal fell dead at the Jovial Hunter's feet. As he rode back to the place where he had met the wild woman, she ran to meet him, shrieking 'You wicked man, you have slain my pretty pig!' and began attacking him with razor-sharp claws. Instantly, Sir Ryalas recognised her as a sorceress, raised his battle-axe and split her head in two. He later discovered that she had changed her son into the boar, hoping that it would gore him to death.
▶ *12 miles NE of Worcester at junction of A448 and A38.*

❸ Little Comberton

A labourer was once employed on a local farm and his skills seemed to the farmer to be little short of miraculous. With one blow of his flail he could thresh a sheaf of corn – a job that usually took six blows at the very least. And he could throw down sheaves from the top of the stack so fast that the farmer found it impossible to keep up with him.

A local cunning man told the farmer that his employee was none other than the Devil, and advised him to get rid of the stranger at once by giving him a job that he was unable to do. But this was not easy. The stranger was able to count the threshed grains of corn, fill a water barrel with a sieve, and mow a field filled with iron spikes. In desperation, the farmer asked the advice of a passing gipsy, who told him to take a curly hair from his wife's head and to tell the Devil to hammer it straight on the local blacksmith's anvil. The more the Devil hammered, the curlier the hair became, and in the end he gave up, vanished from the farm and was never seen again.
▶ *On minor roads 5 miles W of Evesham.*

❹ Worcester

Worcester Cathedral was founded in AD 680 but the present building dates mainly from the 14th century. Inside, among the notable monuments, the colourful effigies of Sir John and Lady Joan Beauchamp stand out, their heads resting on a pair of sinuous black swans. Legend tells how Sir John, away so long at the Crusades, was feared dead, and his wife planned to remarry. Then one day, a ragged man was found sleeping in a field, his arms manacled. Sir John's dog was beside itself with excitement but Lady Joan would not believe this was her husband until he showed her a ring that matched her own. He had been captured and languished in a dungeon from which there was no escape until an angel came to him, and he had a dreamlike sensation of flying. Then he found himself in the field. Believing himself unworthy of being saved by angels, he was convinced that swans had carried him home, and so made them part of his family crest.
▶ *3 miles W of Junctions 6 and 7 of M5.*

⑤ Malvern Hills

An abundance of springs well forth from the Malvern Hills, from the centre of Great Malvern to the wall of Great Malvern station. The most famous is Holy Well, renowned for its curative properties from the days when monks began wrapping patients in water-soaked cloths. The water is said to be especially good for skin diseases and eye disorders. A bottling plant was put into operation in the early 17th century, making Malvern water the first bottled water in Britain. A rhyme of the time told of:

A Thousand Bottles there
Were filléd weekly,
And many Costrils rare
For stomachs sickly;
Some of them into Kent,
Some of them to London sent,
Others to Berwick went,
O Praise the Lord!
(A Costril was a flask used by pilgrims)

In the 18th century, physician John Wall, co-founder of Royal Worcester Porcelain, proved that Malvern water contained 'nothing', its virtue lying in its purity. He set up a treatment centre and published a best-selling book on water cures.

Holy Well – together with all the other wells of the Malvern Hills – is dressed in May and at other notable pre-Christian festivals.

Up in the hills, Mrs Dee's rock is the subject of legend. The story goes that the lady, mistreated by her husband, threatened to haunt him if he was violent to their young daughter, but it made no difference. The daughter attempted to drown herself in a nearby pond, but the ghost of her mother stopped her. Although the place has been exorcised, a spectral woman has been seen sitting on the rock, head in hands.

▶ *S and W of Great Malvern, 8 miles S of Worcester.*

THE SPRING WATER'S VIRTUE LIES IN ITS PURITY
MALVHINA WELL, GREAT MALVERN

CENTRAL ENGLAND

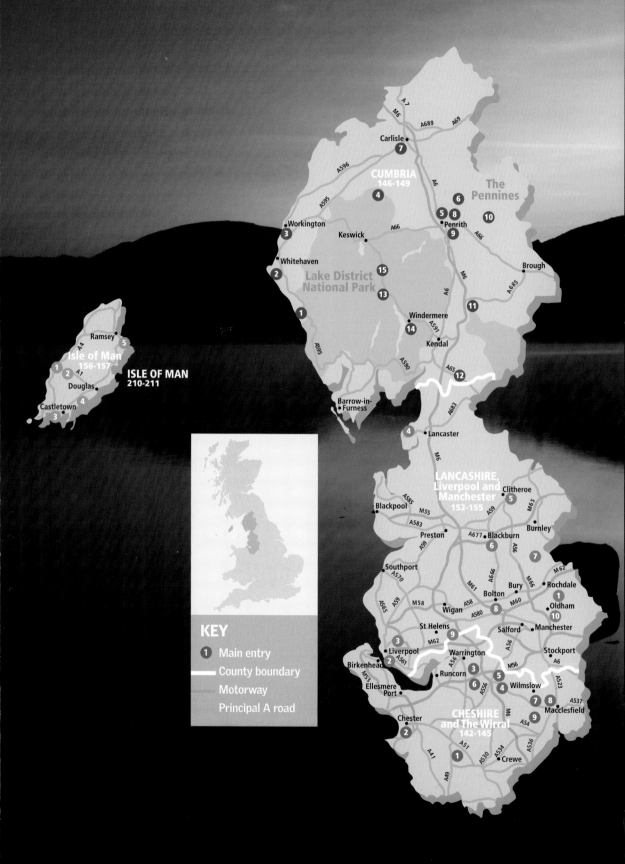

A 7
M6
A689
A69
Carlisle
7

A596

CUMBRIA
146–149
4
A6

The
Pennines

A595

5 **8**
6
10

Workington
3
Keswick
A66
Penrith
9

Whitehaven
2
Lake District
National Park
15
Brough

13

A6
M6
A685

11

1
Windermere
14
A591
Kendal

A595
A590
A65
12

A683

4 Lancaster

M6

LANCASHIRE,
Liverpool and
Manchester
152–155
Clitheroe
5

A585
Blackpool
M55
A59
M65
Burnley

A583
Preston
A677 Blackburn
6
A56
7

Southport
A6 66
M61
Bury
M66
Rochdale
1

A570
A58 Bolton
M60
Oldham
10

A665
M58
Wigan
A580
8
Manchester

St Helens
9
Salford

3
M62
Liverpool
Warrington
Stockport
A6

Birkenhead
2
A561
Runcorn
3
M56
5
Wilmslow
A523

M53
A56
6
A56
4
7 **8**
A537

Ellesmere
Port
9
Macclesfield

Chester
CHESHIRE
M6
A54

2
and The Wirral
142–145
A536

A41
A51
A530
A534

1
Crewe

A49

Isle of Man
Ramsey **5**
A4
156–157

1
A7
2

Douglas
4

Castletown
3

ISLE OF MAN
210–211

KEY
1 Main entry
County boundary
Motorway
Principal A road

Barrow-in-
Furness

Northwest England

There is magic in the northwest counties, where fairies, wizards and mermaids guard each glen, river and mere. In village streets, men and women celebrate old customs – bearing antlers, decked in flowers and dancing to the beat of a different drum.

CHESHIRE & THE WIRRAL

In historic market places and small villages across the region, from Macclesfield to Appleton Thorn, annual festivals and fairs attract increasing crowds, keen to keep old traditions and customs alive.

❶ Bunbury

On the Whitchurch road there is a cottage known as the Image House, from the number of carved stone figures that adorn the walls and garden. The cottage was built, probably in the 17th century, under an ancient dispensation that permitted squatters to build on common land provided the roof was raised in a single night and the chimney was smoking by dawn. The images are said to represent a sheriff and his men, and were apparently carved by a poacher who came to live at the cottage on his return from a term of transportation. As can be imagined, the figures were not carved out of admiration for the law, but simply in order that the poacher could sit in his house and daily curse the authors of his misfortune – presumably in the same spirit that led witches to make wax images.

▶ *7 miles NW of Nantwich.*

❷ Chester

The magnificent Chester Cathedral, built between 1092 and 1520, is believed to stand on the site of a Druid temple, which later became a Roman temple and was in turn reconsecrated as a Christian church. A church is known to have been founded on the spot in 660 by King Wulfhere, and in 875 a great edifice was erected to house the relics of St Werbugh.

Inside, on the clerestory windows of the nave, is a small carved imp in chains. It is said to represent the Devil, as seen by one of the monks peering through a window. The Abbot instructed a carving to be made of the imp in his fetters, so that the Devil would know what awaited him if he tried to come inside. There is also a rare picture – the only one in Britain – of the Virgin and Child painted on a cobweb made of caterpillar silk.

The city is famous for its Mystery plays, which originated in the 14th century. At this time, all church services were conducted in Latin, and to assist the congregation in their understanding of the Bible, monks re-enacted the stories for them. These popular plays were moved to the streets, where they were taken on by the guilds: wheelrights, slaters, tylers, daubers and thatchers performed the Nativity,

for example, while the cooks, tapsters, ostlers and innkeepers performed the Harrowing of Hell. Such plays were banned across the country in the 16th century, and Chester was the last city to comply in 1578. The plays were revived for the Festival of Britain in 1951, and have been staged ever since every five years.

▶ *2 miles SW of Junction 12 of M53.*

❸ Appleton Thorn

The custom of Bawming the Thorn is carried out in the village of Appleton in June, on the closest Saturday to Midsummer's Day. The 'thorn' is a tree, protected by railings, grown from a cutting taken from the Glastonbury thorn, itself said to have grown from the staff of Joseph of Arimathea. 'Bawming' means anointing or adorning it with ribbons and garlands. Children dance round the thorn after decorating it in early June, and villagers stage a fete, with stalls, sideshows and games. The custom may have been a last vestige of ancient midsummer rites, although the current festivities are based on 19th-century practices.

▶ *3 miles SE of Warrington.*

❹ Knutsford

According to legend, King Canute forded the River Lily here on his way north to fight the Scots, an incident that is recalled in the town's name. As he stepped from the water, he shook the sand from his shoes – and this, too, is remembered in a ceremony called sanding, when the townspeople make patterns of coloured sand outside St John's Church on May Day.

▶ *2 miles E of Junction 19 of M6.*

❺ Rostherne

Rostherne Mere is said to be the home of a Mermaid. On Easter Sunday she may be heard singing and ringing a sunken bell that lies at the head of the lake. The mermaid, traditionally a sea-dweller, purportedly reached the mere via a subterranean tunnel linked either to the Irish Sea or the river Mersey.

Overlooking the mere, on the corner of the church of St Mary, is a little carved head with

ANTROBUS SOUL CAKERS

horns or hair. The carving is the subject of much local speculation. Some say that it was once part of a shrine and was pulled out of the mere. It may be associated with Cernives, a horned God, or Coventina, a water goddess.

The wooden lych gate outside the church used to be carefully avoided by newly married couples, who believed that if they passed through it, one of them would die within a year – or that the marriage would be an unhappy one. The belief was once widespread and probably originated in the lych gate's association with death. 'Lych gate' means 'corpse gate', from the old English *lic*, meaning corpse, and is the roofed gateway at the entrance to a churchyard where the pallbearers with the coffin could shelter from the weather while awaiting the arrival of the priest. A few date back as early as the 13th century, though most were constructed from the mid 15th century onward

▶ *Just S of Junction 7 and 8 of M56.*

❻ Antrobus

In the Celtic calendar, winter and the New Year began on November 1, and this was a time when the spirits of the dead were believed to make a brief return to the world.

Later, this became the Christian All Saints' Day, while the following day became All Souls' Day when masses were said for souls in purgatory.

The pagan practice of leaving out food for the dead lingers on in the Cheshire custom of 'souling' or 'soul-caking' in late October to early November. 'Soul cakers' perform songs from door-to-door in return for small cakes and gifts.

Souling used to be made more lively by the Hodening Horse – a man in a sheet, carrying a horse's head, who pranced about at the doors, snapping its jaws. These days, in Antrobus, Comberbach, Acton Bridge and other local villages, a group of mummers enhance the proceedings with a soul-caking play. The mummers include a Letter-in, who starts the action by announcing: 'There is going to be a dreadful fight!' The Black Prince of Paradise in his spiked helmet is killed by King George and resurrected by the Quack Doctor. Other characters include Old Mary, Little Dairy Doubt and Beelzebub with his frying pan 'club'. But the most revered characters are the Wild Horse with his Driver. The Wild Horse appears in no other mummers' play in the country and is possible derived from the mount of the Norse god, Odin.

▶ *5 miles N of Northwich just off A559.*

❼ Alderley Edge

A natural spring flows forth from the sandstone ridge of Alderley Edge into a well, above which is carved: 'Drink of this and take thy fill, For the water falls by the wizards will.' The inscription evokes the legend of a wizard, who once waylaid a farmer on the way to market. The wizard offered to buy the farmer's white mare, but the farmer, thinking he could sell the mare for more in Macclesfield, turned his offer down. To the farmer's surprise, his mare did not tempt a single buyer, and the farmer was forced to take her home. As he trudged back along Alderley Edge, the wizard appeared once more, and requested that the farmer follow him. The wizard led the way to a huge rock, which he split with his staff to reveal a pair of iron gates. He bid the farmer bring the mare, and they made their way along a passage to a cave, filled with sleeping knights. He told the farmer that he needed the mare for one of the knights, whose

A CAVE BELOW THE RIDGE IS FILLED WITH SLEEPING KNIGHTS
ALDERLEY EDGE

role was to wake in a time of grave trouble and fight a battle that would save the country. The wizard gave the farmer gold and jewels in payment for the mare, and led him back to Alderley Edge. The farmer of the legend – and many more people since – have searched in vain for the iron gates.

The story of the wizard inspired author Alan Garner to write his famous work *The Weirdstone of Brisingamen*, published in 1960.

▶ *Just N of B5087, 2 miles S of Wilmslow.*

⑧ Macclesfield

The town was popularly known as 'Treacletown' or 'Sticky-town' allegedly because, at the turn of the 20th century, a barrel of treacle rolled off a cart in Beech Lane and burst as it hit the ground. The contents flowed down Hibel Road, whereupon all the townsfolk downed tools and rushed to scoop up the free syrup in cups, kettles, buckets and tin baths. Everyone lived on a diet of treacle for weeks afterwards.

It may be that the name comes from a more philanthropic act. The town was a great silk centre, and it is said that the mill owners provided unemployed weavers with barrels of treacle. Now a Treacle Market is held on the last Sunday of each month in the old cobbled market place, featuring arts, antiques, crafts and local produce.

A tradition that has recently been revived is the old Barnaby Festival, celebrating the feast day of St Barnabas. For one weekend in June, Macclesfield is given over to music and the arts, with concerts, street theatre and exhibitions in a modern-day take on the 13th-century fair.

▶ *30 miles E of Chester.*

⑨ Siddington

In the middle of Redes Mere, a vast lake that lies in the grounds of Capesthorne Hall near Siddington, is a large peat island, which visibly moves back and forth in strong winds. Local legend tells that a medieval knight, wrongly convinced that his lady was untrue to him, swore that he would never again look upon her face until the island had moved on the waters of the mere. Soon afterwards he grew very ill and was saved from death only through the devotion of the lady, who nursed him back to health. It is said that, as soon as he recovered, a violent storm uprooted the island as a sign of his lady's constancy, and the island has remained floating ever since.

Capesthorne Hall narrowly avoided being burnt down in 1861, but it was rebuilt to incorporate the two surviving wings. The Hall and grounds are open to the public.

▶ *5 miles SW of Macclesfield at junction of A34 and B5392.*

CUMBRIA

Among the magnificent lakes and mountains of Cumbria, giants and fiends of old have been joined by worrisome new entities – a monster in Windermere and unknown forces unleashed by a millennium stone.

❶ Seascale

A rare breed of sheep known as Herdwicks is found only in the Lake District. Their origins are unknown, but legend claims that they first appeared in Britain in 1588 when several swam ashore from a Spanish Armada ship wrecked near Seascale. Another legend says that they were brought from Scandinavia by Vikings who landed on the Cumberland coast many centuries earlier. Herdwicks always wander back to the same 'heaf', or plot of land, on which they have been reared. Once there, they will not stray.
▶ *12 miles S of Whitehaven on B5344.*

❷ St Bees

St Bega, from whom the town of St Bees takes its name, was an Irish princess who, according to legend, was shipwrecked on the Cumbrian coast during the 7th century. She took refuge with the lord of Egremont and begged him for land to build a nunnery. Mockingly, he offered her as much of his estate as should be covered with snow next morning, Midsummer's Day – and woke to find the land for 3 miles around deep in snow. True to his word, he granted Bega the land and helped to build the nunnery.

Long after her death, the people of Cumbria celebrated St Bega's feast. A bracelet or an arm ring, given to her allegedly by an angel, drew pilgrims all year.
▶ *On B5345 4 miles S of Whitehaven.*

❸ Workington

A traditional game called 'Uppies and Downies' is played in the streets of Workington every year on Good Friday, Easter Tuesday and the Saturday that follows. The game has no rules and consists of an heroic struggle to score goals with a football. One of the two goals is situated at the harbour and the other a mile away by the park wall surrounding ruined Workington Hall. Hundreds of men and women join in on each side. Formerly, the game was played between rival teams of coal miners and dockworkers, but it has now become an annual wild battle between the citizens of the Upper Town and the Lower Town.
▶ *7 miles N of Whitehaven.*

❹ Caldbeck

Although now gone far, far away, Cumberland's best-loved son will never be forgotten as long as school choirs can manage the descant. 'Once on a day', according to the song – or to be more precise, from 1776 to 1854 – John Peel lived at Caldbeck, where he was a farmer and horsedealer. But he was principally a hunting man, who, until his death following a minor fall, rode to hounds at least twice a week. When his son Peter died, he went hunting on the day of the funeral and brought back a fox's brush to place in the coffin as 'a fitting tribute'. The song was written by his friend J. W. Graves, after a hunt in 1832. 'By Jove, Peel!' said Graves. 'You'll be sung when we're both run to earth.' John Peel was buried in Caldbeck churchyard.
▶ *14 miles SW of Carlisle on B5299.*

❺ Penrith

St Andrew's churchyard contains two tall slender stones standing 4.5m (15ft) apart. They are believed to mark each end of the grave of the gigantic Ewan Caesarius, a notable slayer of boars and 5th-century ruler of Cumbria. Four 'hogback' stones on the grave itself are said to represent the creatures he slew. In the late 16th century, the grave was said to have been opened, to reveal the bones of a huge man. St Andrew's was designed by Nicholas Hawksmoor, a pupil of Sir Christopher Wren's, and modelled on St Andrew's in Holborn, London.
▶ *20 miles S of Carlisle close to Junction 40 of M6.*

❻ Little Salkeld

Long Meg and her Daughters is the name given to an impressive stone circle dating from around 1500 BC, just outside Little Salkeld. The 69 rhyolite boulders, the 'daughters', are accompanied by a tall outlier – Long Meg – made of sandstone with faint traces of spiral carvings. Meg was a witch, according to legend, turned to stone with her coven when found dancing on their sabbath. Meg is also said to bleed if damaged. Legend has it that if anyone can count the stones and get the same number twice, it will break the spell.
▶ *5 miles NE of Penrith on minor roads N of A686.*

'I CURSE
THAIR HEID
AND ALL THE
HARIS OF
THAIR HEID...'
MILLENNIUM SUBWAY, CARLISLE

❼ Carlisle

'I curse thair heid and all the haris of thair heid; I curse thair face, thair ene, thair mouth, thair neise, thair toung, thair teith, thair crag, thair schulderis, thair breist, thair hert, thair stomok, thair bak, thair wame, thair armes, thair leggis, thair handis, thair feit, and everilk part of thair body, frae the top of thair heid to the soill of thair feit, befoir and behind, within and without…'

So begins the text that inspired the Cursing Stone of Carlisle's Millennium Subway. This unusual monument by artist Gordon Young was unveiled in 2001 and is situated on a path inscribed with the names of the Reiver families – a group of robbers, sheep rustlers and highwaymen who plagued the Borders in the 16th century. So difficult did these families make life for the locals that in 1525, Gavin Dunbar, Archbishop of Glasgow, wrote a 1,069 word curse and laid it on the Reivers, instructing that it should be read aloud by priests from every parish to frighten the miscreant families into submission. Just 300 of the impassioned words appear on the stone.

Since its installation the stone has been blamed for devil worship, 'spiritual violence' and a number of local disasters, such as the foot-and-mouth outbreak in 2001, a fire at a local bakery and the 2005 Carlisle floods. The council met to discuss proposals to have the stone exorcised, or to have it removed completely, but it remains in place according to the original vision. A blessing also features in the walkway, taken from St Paul's epistle to the Philippians: 'Whatever is true, honorable, just, pure, lovely, gracious, If there is any excellence, if there is anything worthy of praise, Think about these things. What you have learned and received and heard and seen in me, do. And the God of peace be with you.'

▶ *W of M6. Access from Junctions 42, 43 and 44.*

❽ Edenhall

Long ago, a servant from the great house of Eden Hall, in the village of Edenhall near Penrith, was said to have surprised some fairies dancing around a goblet made of glass. He seized the goblet and ran, and the fairy queen cried out that if ever it was broken, Eden Hall would be destroyed. Although the hall was demolished in 1934, its 'luck' remained unbroken. The gold and enamelled beaker, thought to have been made in Syria in the 13th century, is now in its own display case in the glass gallery of the Victoria & Albert Museum, London.

▶ *3 miles NE of Penrith, just S of A86.*

⑨ Eamont Bridge

Giant's Cave, by the Eamont River between Eamont Bridge and Langwarthby, was said to be the lair of a man-eating giant called Isir, and was sometimes known as Isir's Parlour. It is also linked in legend with Tarquin, a giant knight who imprisoned 64 brave men in his cave and was eventually slain by Sir Lancelot. Some people also claim that Uther Pendragon, King Arthur's father, lived here, and that, like Isir, he ate human flesh. A circular ditch-and-bank earthwork in the village is known as King Arthur's Round Table, part of which lies under the road. It pre-dates the legendary king by more than 2,500 years. Just 400m (437yd) to the west is Mayburgh Henge, a circular earthwork with a solitary stone monolith in the centre. It is believed to have been a meeting place in prehistoric times.
▶ *1 mile S of Penrith.*

⑩ Cross Fell

A cairn marks the place where the moorland on Cross Fell was once surmounted by an early Christian cross, put up as protection for wandering travellers from the demons that haunted the moors. Cross Fell was once known as 'Fiends' Fell'. At 893m (2,929ft) it is the highest point in the Pennines, and the wailing demons are thought to be a supernatural

explanation for the Helm Wind, a powerful gale that manifests without warning in spring, taking unwary travellers by surprise.
▶ *10 miles E of Penrith.*

⑪ Tebay

Mary Baynes, the 'Witch of Tebay' who died in 1811 at the age of 90, is reputed to have prophesied that 'fiery horseless carriages' would speed over nearby Loups Fell, which is now the route of the London-Glasgow railway. She was greatly feared by her neighbours, who blamed her for everything that went wrong in the village. Local people claimed that she withered and died at the same moment that a number of eggs she had bewitched were fried in boiling fat.
▶ *Just E of Junction 38 of M6.*

⑫ Kirkby Lonsdale

The 14th-century bridge that spans the River Lune at Kirkby Lonsdale is known as the Devil's Bridge, and was supposedly built by Satan himself. Its legend is common to many bridges and tells of an old woman who lost a cow across the river. The Devil offered to build her a bridge in exchange for the first soul to cross it, but his plan was foiled. When the bridge was ready, the canny woman threw a bun for a dog to chase across it. The Devil is also associated with other local landmarks: the Devil's Neck Collar,

THEY SAW A SNAKE-LIKE SHAPE IN THE WATER

Castleton Fell and the Apron-full-of-stones are said to have been created when the Devil, in his bridge-building haste, dropped some of the stones.
▶ *12 miles SE of Kendal on A65.*

⑬ Grasmere

Traditional Cumberland and Westmorland wrestling, for which the annual Grasmere Lakeland Sports are famous, is said to date back to the days of face-to-face combat among Border inhabitants. Some of the greatest 18th-century champions were Lake District clergymen, and large bets were placed by workers and nobility alike. The Sports themselves date back to the mid 19th century, when farm hands, shepherds and other local young men had a chance to show their sporting prowess, while spectators socialised.

Today the event takes place on August Bank Holiday and includes hound trials, a dog show, children's races and fell running. In the spirit of the original 19th-century Sports, entries for all events are made on the day.

Grasmere is also famous for its gingerbread, and debate continues about whether the thick or thin variety is the original. The thick one may have been baked from the 18th century and given to church workers. The thinner one was first made by Sarah Nelson, who settled in the village in the 1850s. Her shop is still open, selling gingerbread made to her recipe.
▶ *3 miles NW of Ambleside on A591.*

⑭ Windermere

Windermere, 11 miles long and 67m (220ft) deep, has generated many legends, but the greatest modern myth is its monster.
Named Bownessie, the creature has been spotted eight times in recent years, more than the Loch Ness Monster. It is described as serpentine, or eel-like, about 5-6m (15-20ft) long. One sighting was made near the lake's deepest part, Gummer's Howe; photographer Linden Adams managed to take a picture of 'something' there in 2007. In February 2011, Tom Pickles and Sarah Harrington were kayaking when they spotted a snake-like shape in the water. Pickles managed to capture a picture of it on his mobile phone.
▶ *8 miles W of Kendal. A592 and A591 runs along E side of Windermere.*

⑮ Dunmail Raise

Dunmail was the last King of Cumbria, and his army was annihilated in AD 945 by the combined forces of Malcolm, King of Scotland, and Edmund, King of the Saxons. Edmund killed Dunmail, and ordered the captured Cumbrians to pile a heap of rocks and boulders – Dunmail Raise – over their slaughtered king. Dunmail's two sons had their eyes put out by the Saxons, and his golden crown was thrown into nearby Grisedale Tarn. It has never been recovered.
▶ *3 miles N of Grasmere on A591.*

Christian pageants

Strange goings-on in some local villages are re-enactments of ancient rituals with origins both practical and moral.

Christianity has been flourishing in these islands for the best part of 1,500 years, so it is not surprising to see it at the roots of many long-established celebrations. This is especially true of the industrial towns of the Lancashire cotton belt, so strongly adherent to Methodism and other non-conformist branches of Christianity, where traditions have grown and flourished that may have had their origins in religious ceremony, but have tilted well towards the secular, the eccentric and the jolly side of misrule.

Morris dancers with their thwacking sticks and jingling bells, their male bonding and loud singing and beery bonhomie, make for vigorous guardians of tradition. The morris sides (troupes) of industrial Lancashire have been responsible for reviving and

carrying forward two of the old semi-Christian traditions that fell victim to more sophisticated pastimes and tastes in the 20th century – Rush Bearing and Pace Egging.

A kindly edict issued by Pope Gregory VII 1,000 years ago caused churches throughout the Christian world to strew rushes on their chilly earthen floors for the comfort of worshippers. With the advent of better flooring and, later, heating the practice was discontinued, but a tradition had been established of bearing the rushes ceremonially to church on a decorated cart. Villages would compete to build ever more elaborate stacks on their carts, and timed the ceremonies to coincide with the annual mill and factory holidays known as Wakes Week. Undoubtedly, much drinking and rowdiness went on

during the rush bearings, which were a wonderful excuse for a party. Eventually, some events were banned, and others just died out because local youngsters saw them as parochial and old fashioned and so declined to take part.

However, in Cumbria, some rush bearings continue to this day. St Oswald's Church in Grasmere has the floor strewn on the Saturday nearest the saint's day, August 5, and at St Mary's in Ambleside the chosen day is the first Saturday in July. Six maidens carry offerings of rushes and flowers followed by anyone who wants to join in, carrying bearings, some made up into decorative crosses. A brass band and a choir add to the festivities.

Rush-bearing revival

In August 1975, the Saddleworth Morris Men revived the old ceremony in their valley, and in 1991, on a Saturday in late July, the Rochdale Morris followed suit with a Littleborough rushcart. Variations occur in the rituals followed by the two troupes, but the basic format is the same. A two-wheeled cart is cleaned and painted, and a stack of freshly cut green reeds built on it, up to a height of about 5m (16ft). The stack is in roughly the shape of a bishop's mitre, and is hung with banners and other decorations.

One of the morris men is elected to ride atop the stack, a precarious perch. In the case of the Saddleworth ceremony, the stack jockey is fortified with copious draughts of beer from a copper kettle. The Saddleworth cart eventually arrives at St Chad's Church in Uppermill, where the brightly coloured banners are removed from the cart and hung up in the church.

In both cases, the day invariably concludes with singing, dancing, gurning, clog-stepping, morris wrestling, worst singer contests and other such 'traditional' sports.

Easter ritual

The ceremonial play of Pace Egging is a different kettle of fish. Pace Egging is an Easter-tide ritual ('Pascha' is an old term for Easter), but it's essentially a pagan one with a lick of Christian respectability. A group of 'jolly lads' – morris dancers, almost without exception – look jovially threatening with their black-face makeup, masks, fancy dress and tall hats as they present their extremely boisterous play in the public bars of selected inns. As for the play they perform, that has many variations, but one central theme – the victory of good St George (wearing Crusader armour, in case there's any doubt) over a foreigner – either a Turkish knight (as played by the Pace Eggers of Middleton, North Manchester) or the King of Egypt and his son the Prince of Paradine (as presented in Abram, a mining suburb of Wigan). Subsidiary characters include a rascally Doctor, with a very rude medical bag, the Devil in various guises, and gallant but cowardly Captain Slasher.

At the end, after St George has been revived from a death wound by the Doctor and has dispatched all his enemies, the 'Tax-collectors' come round, some brandishing sticks with pantomime intent. Beer, money or eggs are equally acceptable, according to tradition. In the old days, the eggs were specially painted and decorated, and in some localities these were kept as treasured mementoes; in others they were rolled downhill to see whose egg would be last to break. Any broken shells had to be carefully powdered and dispersed, because if local witches should find a sizeable fragment, they could use it as a boat. Such lore, if known to today's Pace Eggers, is not too seriously regarded. Today, the fun and continuing the tradition are more important – and, of course, the beer.

RUSH BEARING IN GRASMERE

LANCASHIRE, LIVERPOOL & MANCHESTER

Easter has a special place in the annual activities of Lancashire, from egg-rolling to the weird and wonderful nut dance; but throughout the year, odd traditions and bizarre customs continue to thrive.

❶ Saddleworth

The Saddleworth Rushcart is a spectacular event believed to have pre-Christian origins. Each year on the second Saturday and Sunday after August 12, the flower-decked Saddleworth Morris Men haul a cart piled high with cut rushes through the local villages in a magnificent parade. The custom was all but abandoned in the early years of the 20th century. But it underwent a renaissance after Peter Ashworth, a local man, researched the old traditions and formed the Saddleworth Morris Men in 1975.

The rushes are cut from the nearby moors, and piled on to a cart, after which they are trimmed into mounds about 4m (13ft) high. On Sunday, the rushcart is taken to St Chad's Church in Uppermill, where the rushes, together with fragrant herbs, are scattered on the floor. After a service, celebrations include dancing, clog stepping and wrestling.
▶ *4 miles NE of Oldham.*

❷ Liverpool

In parts of the city, particularly around the predominantly Catholic dock area, children used to light bonfires on Good Friday and burn effigies of Judas Iscariot. Liverpool was the only city in Britain where this happened, although the custom is common in Spain, Portugal, Greece and Latin America; so it may have been introduced by sailors from overseas.

Dominating the River Mersey are the two towers of the Liver Building, topped by the 'Liver birds'. These mythical creatures are said to have frequented the pool near which the city was founded. In fact, the 'Liver bird' first appeared on the city's coat of arms about 700 years ago. It was intended to represent the eagle of St John the Evangelist, the city's patron, but owing to the artist's lack of skill, the bird's identity became part of the city's folklore. Local tradition has it that when a female virgin or an honest man pass the birds, they flap their wings. They were carved by the German sculptor Carl Bernard Bartels (1866-1955) and appear to be part eagle, part cormorant. Bartels was a long-time London resident, but spent the First World War in an internment camp on the Isle of Man. Such was the anti-German feeling at the time that Bartels is not widely known as the artist.

William McKenzie, a notorious 19th-century Liverpool gambler, pledged his soul to the Devil in a game of poker. When he died, in order that his soul be saved from harm, he was entombed in a pyramid in St Andrew's churchyard, sitting upright at a table, cards in hand, or so the legend goes. McKenzie does indeed have a pyramid for a tomb, but in life he was a successful railway engineer, who left a fortune – honestly earned – on his death in 1851. How the myth developed is as much a mystery as the story itself. His unusual tomb probably inspired the legend, although it is simply an example of Egyptian Revival architecture, which became popular at the time of Napoleon's early 19th-century explorations. St Andrew's is a Presbyterian church, known as the Scotch Church since it was built to serve the growing Scottish community. It was closed in 1975 and is on English Heritage's at risk register.
▶ *St Andrew's Church is at N end of Rodney St, close to the Metropolitan Cathedral in Liverpool city centre. Liverpool is 35 miles W of Manchester. Access via M62 and M58.*

❸ Croxteth

The Molyneux family, the Earls of Sefton, lived in Croxteth Hall from the 16th century until 1972, when the last earl died without leaving an heir. Local legend is attached to the second earl, William Philip Molyneux, who was a heavy gambler and friend of the Prince Regent. In 1829, he laid the foundation stone for Aintree Racecourse, burying a stash of sovereign coins underneath it. His ghost is said to wander around the grounds of Croxteth Hall at the time of the Grand National, and in 2009 CCTV footage appeared to show a luminous figure approaching the main entrance. The Hall and adjacent country park are looked after by Liverpool City Council and are open to the public.
▶ *Croxteth is a suburb of Liverpool, 5 miles NE of city centre. Croxteth Hall is within a country park, 1 mile S of the centre of Croxteth.*

④ Heysham

The ruins of St Patrick's Chapel stand raw and magnificent on top of the headland above St Peter's Church in the small village of Heysham, overlooking Morecambe Bay. Legend has it that St Patrick was shipwrecked here in the 6th century, and built the chapel in thanksgiving for having managed to stumble ashore. Nearby is a series of rock-cut graves – coffin-shaped lozenges hollowed out of a bedrock platform, believed to date from the 8th century. The ruins are now in the care of the National Trust.

▶ *4 miles W of Lancaster.*

⑤ Clitheroe

Stepping stones across the River Ribble at nearby Brungerley are said to be the haunt of an evil spirit who claims one life every seven years by dragging some unwary traveller to a watery grave. The tale is probably a warning to children, who are often told not to go near the water because, if they do, Jenny Greenteeth will pull them in. They associate the sprite with green plants growing in the river. Some of the stepping stones are missing in the middle of the river, so it is inadvisable to try crossing that way.

▶ *10 miles N of Blackburn, 2 miles W of A59.*

EMPTY COFFIN-SHAPED HOLLOWS IN THE BEDROCK
ROCK-HEWN GRAVES, HEYSHAM HEAD

⑥ Blackburn

Hollinshead Hall Holy Well lies on boggy ground around a mile from Abbey Village near Blackburn. It flows into a restored medieval well house, believed to have been used by a local Catholic family, the Radcliffes, when their beliefs were outlawed in favour of Anglican worship in the 16th century. The water wells up into a small pool behind the house and is said to be pure and good for the eyes.

▶ *10 miles E of Preston. Access from Junctions 4, 5 and 6 of M65.*

⑦ Bacup

On Easter Saturday, the Britannia Coconut Dancers perform their unusual Nut Dance over the 7 miles from one side of the town to the other. The Morris team of eight dancers have blackened faces (it is believed that in pagan times the dancers had to be disguised, otherwise the magic of the dance would be ineffective) and wear black breeches and clogs, with white shirts, stockings and plumed caps. Wooden discs called 'nuts' are attached to their waists, knees and the palms of the hands, and the dancers clap these together in a complicated rhythm as they move along, led by a 'whipper-in' who drives off evil spirits.

The dance is thought to have originated in Cornwall, brought there by Moorish pirates who settled in the West Country and were employed in the mines. Cornish miners took it up and when the tin ran low and the men moved to the stone quarries of Lancashire, they brought their traditions with them.

The Coconut Dancers also perform at the summer carnival.

▶ *7 miles N of Rochdale.*

⑧ Bolton

The footprint impressed on the stairs at the magnificent timber-framed Smithills Hall, near Bolton, Greater Manchester is alleged to have been made by the Protestant martyr George Marsh. This farmer-turned-preacher refused to renounce his faith and convert to Catholicism and was arrested. Marsh was brought before Robert Barton, owner of Smithills estate, and interrogated in the Green Room. Afterwards, he was sent to the Church Court and eventually condemned and burnt at Boughton, Cheshire, in 1555. The footprint reputedly is a divine reminder of the unjust persecution of Marsh, who was accused of preaching false doctrine, and is said to run with blood on the anniversary of his death; and the Green Room is allegedly haunted. Smithills Hall is open to the public, and the footprint can still be seen, protected by a metal grill.

▶ *Bolton is 10 miles NW of Manchester city centre. Smithills Hall is 2 miles N of Bolton town centre, just N of A58.*

COCONUT DANCERS OF BACUP

⑨ Winwick

The site of Winwick church was chosen by a mysterious pig, an effigy of which is carved on the church tower. The construction of the church was originally begun nearby, but when darkness fell, the pig would appear from nowhere and carry off the masonry in its mouth. The pig took the stones to the church's present site, said to be the place where St Oswald died in 642. As it ran to and fro, it squealed 'We-ee-wick, we-ee-wick', and this apparently inspired the name of the parish.

▶ *Just N of Junction 9 of M62.*

⑩ Ashton-under-Lyne

The old Easter Monday ceremony of Riding the Black Lad dates back over two centuries. It was abandoned in the 1960s and revived in 1995, becoming a key attraction of the Ashton carnival. In the traditional festivities the 'Lad' was the effigy of a knight in black armour, which was paraded around the town to the jeers of onlookers, then pelted with stones and refuse and, at one time, shot. The custom commemorated the people's antagonism towards Sir Ralph de Assheton, lord of the manor of nearby Middleton in the 15th century. Sir Ralph had the right to claim fines from people who let weeds grow on their land. Accompanied by bullying henchmen, and dressed in his black armour, Sir Ralph rode into town to carry out his lucrative annual inspection – and extortion – on Easter Monday, which became known among the local people as 'Black Monday'.

On the Friday following Whit Sunday, brass bands from all over the country descend on Ashton-under-Lyne and surrounding villages for the annual band contest. At each venue, each band plays a marching piece and a standing piece, and judges are often prevented from watching performances, so they make their decisions based on the music alone.

▶ *6 miles E of Manchester city centre, close to Junction 23 of M60.*

NORTHWEST MORRIS

THE NORTHWEST IS home to some of the most active and colourful morris sides in England. From Manchester in the south to Wigton near the Solway Firth, morris has developed its own distinct style – with processional dances that often accompany the traditional rushcarts of the old late summer Wakes holiday.

The sheer outlandishness and eccentricity of morris dancing (coupled with its strong drinking customs) led 19th century folklorists to suggest pagan origins for the performances, but while there is little doubt that pre-Christian societies had their own form of exuberant celebration, morris dancing as performed today can be traced directly to Spanish court entertainment of the 15th century. The name 'morris' is a derivation of 'moorish'. After the ten-year Granada war ended Islamic rule of Spain in 1492, the Moors were forced to convert to Christianity or be exiled. The resulting court celebrations included a 'Moresca', a specially devised sword dance still performed today in parts of Aragon.

The innovative dance spread quickly throughout Europe, was popularised at the English Court and was subsequently embraced by the populace – in 1567-8, port of London import records show a tally of 10,000 morris bells, such was the demand for the dances' accoutrements.

Over time, each region developed its own local dance flavour. Cotswold Morris uses sticks or handkerchiefs to emphasise hand gestures; Border Morris is more freeform in style; the Midlands and East Anglia favour Molly Dancing, the sides blackening their faces and wearing black costumes with coloured decorations, and Northumberland and County Durham remained true to the original spirit with short swords forming a key part of the performance. Northwest Morris is distinct not only in its association with the rushcarts, but in the adoption of a leader, or conductor, who dances at the head of the procession, signalling moves to his men.

NORTHWEST ENGLAND

THE 'NUTS' ARE CLAPPED IN INTRICATE RHYTHM

THE ISLE OF MAN

Belief in the supernatural is part of everyday Manx life. Respect is shown to the Little People, and heed always taken when guardian deity Manannan cloaks the island in a protective shroud of mist.

❶ Peel

The Moddey Dhoo or Black Dog, is a spectral hound said to frequent Peel Castle. From the late 17th century it was reported to lie before the guardroom fire. The soldiers came to take it for granted, although none would stay alone with it, or make the nightly round without a companion. According to legend, a drunken soldier boasted that he would patrol the castle by himself and find out whether the animal was a dog or devil. He returned gibbering and remained speechless until his death just three days later.

In an event that may – or may not – be connected to the phantom beast, builders working on the reconstruction of Peel cathedral in 1871 unearthed the body of Simon Arkadiensis, 13th-century Bishop of Sodor and Man. His embalmed body had been interred alongside that of a dog.

▶ *On W coast, 10 miles NW of Douglas.*

❷ St John's

The Isle of Man has one of the oldest parliamentary traditions in continuous existence in the world. The Norse Manx Court of Tynwald (from 'thingvalla', meaning assembly place) was held in the open air, where laws were read aloud. There are two houses: the elected House of Keys and the Legislative Council, members of which are elected by the House of Keys. The Tynwald meets annually, generally on July 5, at Tynwald Hill, St John's. The event is presided over by the island's Lieutenant Governor, and all laws are promulgated in English and in Manx Gaelic.

The hill itself is a four-tiered earth mound, covered in grass, directly linked to the chapel of St John by a processional way. According to legend, the mound was built by the Viking rulers, using soil from each corner of the island to construct the different tiers. It has been suggested that Tynwald Hill was originally a Bronze Age burial mound – certainly ancient graves have been found nearby and the site was always sacred. The chapel stands on the place of a cross, originally dedicated to the Norse sun god Lugh.

▶ *7 miles NW of Douglas on A1.*

❸ Castletown

Castle Rushen at Castletown, the island's ancient capital, was reputed to harbour a giant in its underground maze. According to legend, curious townsmen rallied with torches and staves and searched the labyrinth, where they found a blind giant with a long beard sitting on a rock. He enquired how things were in the island,

and asked that one of the party should shake hands with him. A visitor held out an iron bar, which the giant squeezed, saying, 'Ah, so there are still men in the Isle of Man,' after which the party left. Rushen is a fine example of a medieval castle, beautifully preserved and open to the public. Its labyrinth is, like its giant, no more than a myth.

The harbour is the venue for the World Tin Bath Championships, a race instigated in 1971 in which competitors attempt to paddle tin baths across the cold waters.

▶ *On S coast, 9 miles SW of Douglas.*

4 Santon

Few islanders will drive or walk over the bridge on the Douglas to Castletown road – known as the Fairy Bridge – without politely offering their greetings to the Little People. There are many tales of holidaymakers and visitors scorning the tradition, and being showered with bad luck for the duration of their stay. A simple 'Hello fairies' is sufficient.

The tree beside the bridge is tied with wishes – letters to the fairies asking for help and blessings, and giving thanks for luck and success. With no place to park save the roadside near the bridge, attaching the wishes requires both daring and a dose of fairy protection.

▶ *4 miles SW of Douglas.*

5 Maughold

The island abounds with holy wells and springs, many associated with ancient spirits and saints. Once, every church had its own baptising well, and for centuries before Christianity these wells were known for their associated guardian – and in many cases their curative properties. It was considered wrong to drink the waters without leaving a gift, and people cast small votive offerings, such as coins or pins, into the wells. At Chibber Mun Laa at Cardle Veg, Maughold, traditionally visited at the rising of the full moon, or the rising sun, petitioners would sprinkle themselves with the water as well as drinking some.

St Maughold's Well is situated on the cliffs at Maughold Head, its rocky basin thick with ferns and roofed with unhewn slabs. In the early 19th century, Manx people made pilgrimages there to drink the waters. Today, on St Maughold's Day, July 31, people still walk there from the church.

Maughold is the patron Saint of the Isle of Man, an Irish prince and bandit chief converted to Christianity by St Patrick. After his baptism the prince renounced his worldly ways and put to sea in a wicker boat, drifting to shore at the headland that bears his name. He retired to a cave, and such was his piety that he was chosen as bishop.

▶ *On E coast, 15 miles N of Douglas.*

SOLDIERS WOULD NOT PATROL ALONE
PEEL CASTLE

Northeast England

The folklore of the northeast has
a distinctive flavour, born of old
Viking tales and early Christian
deeds. Pageants and traditions
have an otherworldly air and are
played out with enthusiasm in
all four seasons.

Berwick-upon-Tweed
A1
A697
Bamburgh
Alnwick

Northumberland
National
Park

A68
Otterburn
A696
Morpeth
A189
A1068
NORTHUMBERLAND
and Tyneside
162-167

A69
Hexham
Newcastle-upon-Tyne
Gateshead
Sunderland
A692
Consett
A167
Durham
A1(M)

DURHAM
and Teesside
160-161

Barnard
Castle
A688
Bishop
Auckland
A689
Hartlepool

A66
Darlington
Middlesbrough
A66
A172
Whitby
A171

Richmond

Hawes
A1
A79
North York Moors
National Park
Scarborough
A165
Bridlington
A170
Thirsk
Pickering

Yorkshire Dales
National Park
A65
Settle
A61
Ripon
A168
YORKSHIRE
168-173
A64
A166
A59
Harrogate
A1237
York
A1035
A629
A658
A1(M)
A64
Leeds
Selby
A63
Kingston-upon-Hull
Bradford
A646
Halifax
M621
A63
A1079
A614
A58
M62
Wakefield
A638
A79
M62
Huddersfield
A635
M18
A628
M1
A1(M)
Doncaster
Rotherham
A631
A57
Sheffield

KEY
1 Main entry
   County boundary
   Motorway
   Principal A road

DURHAM & TEESSIDE

Apocryphal stories and old legends reflect the region's distinctive industrial heritage, while in one small town, most of the populace mark Lent with their version of the northeast's favourite game.

❶ Durham

The statue of Charles William Vane Stewart, 3rd Marquess of Londonderry (1778–1854) stands on a tall stone plinth in Durham's Market Square. The handsome electroplated copper statue is a famous city landmark, once a favourite meeting place of courting couples, yet it has been the focus of drama and discord since its erection in 1861. The statue depicts Lord Londonderry, aged 42, as a hussar, and was commissioned by his wife after his death. According to popular legend, the statue's Milanese sculptor, Raffaelle Monti, was so proud of his creation that he threatened suicide if anyone were to find fault with it. At its unveiling – an event attended by Benjamin Disraeli, among others – the statue was much admired. Then a blind man, examining the statue by touch, declared that it was imperfect, for the horse had no tongue, and in a dramatic gesture, Monti threw himself off a bridge. The tale is a fabrication – a blind man would have needed a scaffold to reach the statue on its plinth, the horse does indeed have a tongue and Monti (1818-81) went on to produce many more works of art in marble and porcelain.

The real drama lay in the statue's original proposition. Lord Londonderry was not a popular figure, despite his distinguished military career. He developed the coalfields on land that had come to him via his second wife's considerable inheritance, and as a colliery owner he was a harsh master. When the miners went on strike in 1831, he threatened to evict any merchants who supplied the men and their families, so there were many objections to his being honoured in such a manner. Not only were there complaints over the statue itself, but the siting was disputed and the council, surprised by its size – the statue and pedestal together stand over 6m (20ft) high –

A FOCUS OF
LORD LONDONDERRY, DURHAM

requested that it be placed on Palace Green instead. They were overruled, and the statue took its place in Market Square as planned.

In 2010, the square underwent a £5.5m refurbishment, part of which involved restoring and moving the statue by 19m (62ft). More than 6,000 people objected to the move, but the plans went ahead and the statue assumed its new place in September 2010.

▶ *2 miles SW of Junction 62 of A1(M).*

❷ Penshaw

The legend of the Lambton Worm has achieved something of the status of a fairytale. Set at some time in the Middle Ages it tells of a wild youth who was heir to Lambton Castle, which is near the village of Penshaw in County Durham. He went fishing in the River Wear one Sunday and caught a strange-looking worm. On his way home, he threw it into a well by the castle and forgot about it.

As he grew up he changed his wild ways and eventually joined a crusade to the Holy Land. During his absence, the worm grew to an enormous size and wriggled out of the well. It soon began to ravage the district, killing man and beast, and each night it slept coiled three times around Lambton Hill, which is now called Worm Hill. Attempts were made to slay the monster, but whenever it was cut in two the halves merely joined up again.

Seven years later, the lord's son returned. He was stricken with remorse at the result of his youthful folly, so he asked a witch what would be the best way of tackling the monster. She told him to cover his armour with razors, and then fight the worm in the middle of the river. The price of her counsel was that he should kill the first creature to greet him after his victory.

The plan was successful, for when the worm wrapped itself around the knight, the razors cut it into pieces, which were swept away by the river before they could join together. But when he signalled to his father on his bugle, the old man forgot to release a greyhound as arranged and ran to the river himself. The son refused to kill his father, so the witch put a curse on the family. In fact, from that day on, many Lambtons died violently – some in accidents and others in battle.

▶ *5 miles SW of Sunderland on A183.*

❸ Sedgefield

On Shrove Tuesday a traditional football match is staged between two teams of local people. The pitch is 500m (547yd) long, and the goals are a pond and a stream. It kicks off at 1pm, and ends when the first goal has been scored – this can take some time because the ball is often 'kidnapped' along the way. The northeast's oldest sporting tradition is taken very seriously by participants, and local businesses board up their windows in anticipation of a boisterous match.

▶ *2 miles E of Junction 60 of A1(M).*

❹ Hartlepool

A merman is on display in the Hartlepool Museum. This fabulous creature is made from wood with the head and body of a monkey and the tail of a fish, and is designed to give the impression of a mummified aquatic man. These creatures were traditionally made in China and purchased as souvenirs in the 19th century. The American businessman and entertainer P.T. Barnham exhibited such a merman in London in 1859, claiming it came from Fiji, and the craze for these sideshow exhibits grew. Many similar chimeras exist in museums and collections throughout the world and are known today as 'Feejee Mermaids'.

▶ *15 miles SE of Durham.*

❺ Darlington

Close to the River Tees, in the suburbs, are four deep pools called Hell's Kettles. Legend says 'spirits have oft been heard to cry out of them', and that a farmer who took hay wagons out on St Barnabas's Day (June 11), when pious folk should not work, was swallowed up in them – carts, horses and all.

▶ *3 miles E of Junctions 58 and 59 of A1(M).*

DRAMA AND DISCORD

NORTHEAST ENGLAND

NORTHUMBERLAND & TYNESIDE

Blazing fires and massed games hail the seasons in local versions of nationwide festivals. In folklore, Viking sagas of demons and dragons mingle with early Christian tales of miracles.

❶ Lindisfarne

Also known as Holy Island, Lindisfarne is famed as an important centre of early English Christianity. It was sacked by Danish raiders in AD 875, an event that was said to be preceded by storms and 'fiery serpents' flying through the sky. Legend claims that when the now ruined priory was built in the 11th century, the labourers fed on bread made from air and drank wine from a bottomless cup.

The old North Country marriage custom of jumping over the Petting Stone still occurs in Lindisfarne. The stone stands in the churchyard, and is believed to be the socket of St Cuthbert's Cross, which dates from the 7th century. Brides jump over it as they leave the church, symbolising a leap into a new way of life.

▶ *7 miles S of Berwick-upon-Tweed off A1. Causeway impassable at high tide.*

❷ Farne Islands

Demons or devils were said to haunt the isle of Wideopens – one of the Farne Islands off the Northumbrian coast. According to legend, when Cuthbert, Bishop of Lindisfarne, came to live there in the 7th century, he exorcised the spirits, only to have them retreat to the outlying islands, where their screams could still be heard. The hideously deformed, dark-featured wraiths were said to have been seen '…clad in cowls, and riding upon goats, black in complexion, short in stature, their countenances most hideous, their heads long - the appearance of the whole group horrible.' They were once believed to be the ghosts of drowned sailors, although today a more earthly – and poignant – origin has been suggested: that the devils were no more than the aboriginal islanders who might have once been part of a larger mainland group.

The magnificent and fearsome medieval knocker on Durham Cathedral's north door is reputed to have been modelled on the demons. The original 12th-century knocker represents the privilege of sanctuary once granted to Durham's criminals. Anyone seeking refuge had simply to knock, and would be given refuge by the watchers who were stationed in chambers overlooking the door. The original knocker is now in the Treasury Museum – the one to be seen at the cathedral is a copy.

▶ *Off coast at Bamburgh. Visit by boat from Seahouses on B1340.*

❸ Bamburgh

A tiny gold 7th-century plaque punched with the enigmatic figure of a strange beast was discovered during archaeological excavations in 1971 at Bamburgh Castle, and the 'beast' has since become the castle's motif.

Founded in AD 547, the fortified structure was the ancient royal residence of Northumbrian kings. In the 7th century, Oswald was the first Christian ruler to live there. His charitable works prompted St Aidan, Bishop of Lindisfarne, to take hold of his hand and say, 'Never let this hand consume or wither.' According to legend, Oswald was killed in battle, and in light of the bishop's

pronouncement, his hand was cut off and retained as a relic. Unfortunately, it was stolen in the 11th century, still uncorrupted.

An old Northumbrian ballad, 'The Laidly Worm of Bamburgh', also known as 'The Laidly Worm of Spindleston Heugh', tells the story of a monster that terrified local folk. In fact, the monster was the daughter of the king of Northumbria, who had been turned into a dragon by the wicked queen, her stepmother. Not knowing the queen was a witch, the king had married her in his old age. The Laidly Worm laid waste to the country for miles around. At last, the king's son, the Childe of Wynde, volunteered to fight the monster, unaware that the creature was his sister, but the Worm refused to fight him, and when it revealed its true identity, this proved to be the antidote to the spell. The princess resumed her former shape, and the evil queen was changed into a toad, and locked in a dungeon, where she is said to reside still. Her door is opened every seventh Christmas Eve, and it is said she will remain a toad until some hero enters and unsheaths the Childe of Wynde's sword three times. He must then blow three times on the Childe's horn, and finally kiss the toad.

▶ *4 miles E from A1, 14 miles SE of Berwick-upon-Tweed.*

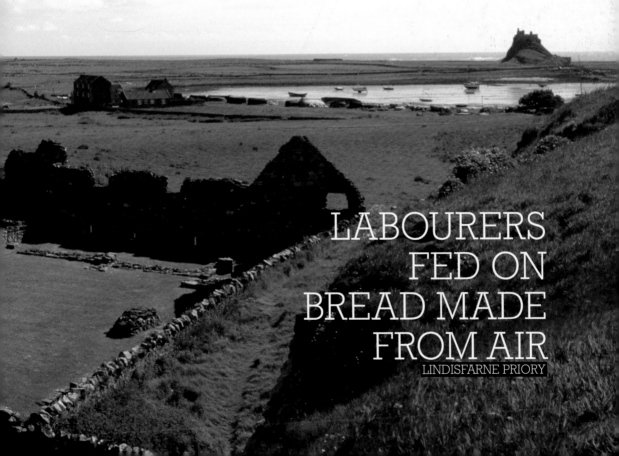

LABOURERS FED ON BREAD MADE FROM AIR
LINDISFARNE PRIORY

Proud industrial heritage

Hard manual work has garnered all manner of ceremonial displays, colourful traditions that are still keenly observed.

One area of serious human activity that underpins a number of long-established celebrations is the earning of daily bread by the sweat of one's brow. What could be more bound up with a community's identity, and its individual members' sense of themselves, than work and its dangers, its rituals and rewards? It may be hard to imagine pageantry evolving to celebrate the activities of IT experts or burger cooks, but the backbreaking work of heavy industry and farming has generated parades and public displays galore. And there's no region of Britain more steeped in industrial lore and traditions than Yorkshire and the northeast.

Filey's fishermen

The dangerous and demanding occupation of North Sea fishing seems to have produced extremes in its practitioners, especially among the fisherfolk of Filey on the East Yorkshire coast. In the early 19th century Filey's fishermen were notorious for fighting, swearing, drinking, fornicating and profaning the Sabbath – and their wives were just as bad. Then in 1823 'Praying Johnny' Oxtoby came to town on a mission from God. Praying Johnny had unshakeable faith and enormous courage. He braved abuse, threats and showers of rotten fish to make a stand and preach. The results were astonishing – the fisherfolk, almost to a man and woman, were converted to Primitive Methodism, and went about the countryside spreading the gospel. In the 1870s a huge Ebenezer Chapel, big enough to accommodate 900 souls, was built in Filey, and remained at the centre of the fishermen's religious and social life well into the 20th century.

In 1960 former fisherman Frank Hanson assembled a group of local men to sing for a Harvest of the Sea celebration at the Ebenezer Chapel, and that was the start of the far-famed Filey Fishermen's Choir. Nowadays, dressed in traditional blue ganseys, or woollen jerseys, they are in huge demand for their beautiful, soulful hymns and songs, many sea-themed. Although most choir members are Yorkshiremen, few are fishermen these days. But the Filey Fishermen's Choir takes pride in the fact that members of the Haxby family – fishermen, Methodists and singers since the 19th century – still perform with them.

Durham Miners' Gala

Up in County Durham it is the dirtiest, heaviest and most dangerous occupation of all that is celebrated every year in Durham city on the second Saturday in July. The Durham Miners' Gala – pronounced 'gay-la', and known to locals as 'The Big Meeting' – has been held annually, with breaks for wars and strikes, since 1871. The Gala is a celebration of trade unionism, a vital force in an industry full of dangers and one in which employees had to fight 'the masters' for decent pay and conditions.

In recent years, coal mining has declined in County Durham to the point that there are no more deep pits in production; yet men from closed collieries still parade in Durham. The historic banners of painted silk that they carry, depicting socialist heroes of Durham mining history, represent the local lodges of the National Union of Mineworkers. Brass bands play and defiant speeches are made. The Gala has diminished in size and intensity since the heyday of the Durham coalfield, when 25,000 miners would walk in from pit villages all over the county. But it's still a thrilling and colourful spectacle, a great day out, and a reminder of a bedrock industry's past pride and glory.

Farming's show

Heavy industry in the shape of fishing, coal mining and shipbuilding may have shaped the recent history of the northeast, but farming – especially sheep farming – has been the backbone of the region's more northerly area since before Roman times. The Alwinton Border Shepherds' Show, the Cheviot Hills' last agricultural show of the year, has been going since the 1860s. Held in Upper Coquetdale's northernmost village of Alwinton on the second Saturday in October, this is a superb occasion, enjoyed to the hilt by local shepherds, farmers and families. There are sheepdog trials, sheep judging, local produce displays and bouts of vigorous and skilful Cumberland and Westmorland wrestling. There's a fell race, tug-o'-war, a dog show and a hysterically funny terrier race, which sometimes results in a massed dogfight.

What is striking about these work-related traditions is that the industries they celebrate are either dead (coal mining in County Durham), in recession not far short of crisis (North Sea fishing) or very radically changed since the rituals took shape (farming). Yet they continue to be keenly supported – often, as with traditional celebrations in other parts of the country, not just by past practitioners and their families but also by enthusiastic outsiders, who help to breathe new life into old ceremonies.

DURHAM MINERS' GALA

❹ Chillingham

The white cattle with red ears that have grazed in the 121-ha (300 acre) park around Chillingham Castle ever since the 13th century are Britain's last surviving wild herd. They are the direct descendants of the wild cattle that once roamed freely over Europe and Britain prior to the Roman invasion. The last herds were found in Wales in Saxon times. They are said to have the same colouring as fairy cattle and legend has it that they will kill anyone who touches them.

▶ *5 miles SE of Wooler off A697 or B6348.*

❺ Allendale Town

The town signals the end of the Old Year with a ceremony said to be of pagan origin. Costumed men carrying barrels of blazing tar on their heads parade through the streets to the marketplace, where the barrels are thrown on a bonfire. The townspeople then dance until midnight, when 'first footing' begins. A dark-haired man must be the first to enter a home after midnight, carrying gifts of bread and coal, to bring good luck.

▶ *10 miles SW of Hexham on B6295.*

❻ Alnwick

Shrovetide football has been played in Alnwick since 1762. The game takes place on Shrove Tuesday between two teams of up to 150 players each. The goals, decorated with evergreens, are a quarter of a mile apart, and before play starts on the Pasture below the castle, the ball is piped on to the pitch by the Duke of Northumberland's own piper. The game is won by the first team to score two 'hales' (goals), and the ball is kept by whoever manages to carry it off the pitch. Often this involves swimming the River Aln.

▶ *1 mile W of A1, 34 miles N of Newcastle upon Tyne.*

❼ Whalton

The traditional festival of Whalton Bale is held each year on Old Midsummer's Eve, July 4. A great bonfire is lit on the village green, and there is morris dancing and sword dancing to the music of fiddlers and Northumbrian pipers. 'Bale' comes from the Anglo-Saxon 'bael', meaning a great fire. Midsummer Eve bonfires were once a popular custom. The alteration of the calendar in 1752 resulted in dates being moved

ALLENDALE TOWN

forward by 11 days, but in Whalton, traditionally minded countryfolk went on celebrating the festival at the old time.

▶ *5 miles SW of Morpeth.*

❽ Bellingham

The local legend of the Long Pack is associated with a curious tombstone shaped like a pedlar's pack, about 1.2m tall by 91cm deep (4x3ft), in the churchyard. The story of the tombstone dates from 1723, when a pedlar called at Lee Hall, a former riverside mansion between Bellingham and Wark, owned by a Colonel Ridley, who had made his fortune in India. The pedlar asked for a night's lodging. The colonel was away, so the maid refused, but she did allow him to leave his bulky pack in the kitchen until morning, and after he had gone she saw the pack move. In fright, she called for help. A ploughboy fired a gun at the bundle and blood gushed out. Inside the pack was the body of a man armed with pistols. Like many border towns in those days, Bellingham was plagued by marauders, and the servants realised that a robbery had been planned. They called the other servants and then blew a horn they found beside the body. When the robbers came they were ambushed and severely beaten. The unknown body in the pack was buried beneath the stone in the churchyard.

▶ *On B6320, 25 miles W of Morpeth.*

❾ Sewing Shields

Deep in the crags beneath the remains of Sewing Shields Castle there is said to be a cave where King Arthur and his knights lie sleeping until their country once again calls on their services. Northwest of the ruins are two outcrops of sandstone known as King's Crag and Queen's Crag. Legend says that Arthur, who was sitting on one rock, had a quarrel with Queen Guinevere, who was sitting on the other. He threw an enormous boulder at her that bounced off her comb and fell between the two crags. There it lies to this day, the teeth marks of the comb still plainly visible on the face of the rock.

▶ *On B6318, 10 miles NW of Hexham.*

❿ Newbrough

Legend tells that the ashes of Old Meg, a 16th-century witch, are buried a mile north of Newbrough in a burn called Meggie's Dene, which flows down from Torney's Fell. She was burnt alive for witchcraft and at her burial a stake was driven through her charred heart to prevent

her soul wandering. It is said that her grave is marked by a pink thorn tree which grows at the water's edge.

▶ *On B6319, 5 miles NW of Hexham.*

⓫ Hexham

Until the Dissolution in 1539, Hexham Priory was one of the chief sanctuaries in the north of England. Anyone within a mile-wide area around the priory – marked by crosses at each point of the compass – could claim sanctuary, and any person seizing the fugitive was fined by the church. But excommunication awaited a person who dragged a fugitive out of the 7th-century sanctuary seat in the abbey, known as St Wilfrid's Chair or the Frid Stool.

▶ *1 mile S of A69, 22 miles W of Newcastle upon Tyne.*

⓬ Bolam

In 2002, Bolam Lake in Bolam Lake Country Park, became the focus for a host of 21st-century monster hunters following a series of strange sightings of a Yeti-like creature in the nearby woods. Eyewitness reports suggested that some kind of human-like creature, around 2-2.4m (7-8ft) tall was lurking in the wilds. These encounters so unsettled the witnesses that few were prepared to return, even accompanied by researchers, several of whom saw the alleged creature running in woodland illuminated by car headlights, but were unable, in the darkness, to photograph the form. The creature has now acquired legendary status and goes variously under the name of The Beast of Bolam, the Geordie Yeti and the Geordie Bigfoot.

▶ *On minor roads 8 miles W of Morpeth.*

⓭ Jarrow

Bede's Chair, in St Paul's Church, Jarrow, Tyne and Wear, may have belonged to the Venerable Bede (AD 693-735), the chronicler who spent most of his life in Jarrow. For centuries, this ancient oak chair was popularly believed to influence marriage and childbirth. Unmarried girls placed splinters from the chair beneath their pillows so that they would dream of their future husbands. Brides sat in it after the wedding ceremony to ensure fertility, while mothers-to-be soaked chips carved from the chair in water, then drank the liquid in the hope it would ease the pangs of childbirth.

▶ *On S side of Tyne close to A19. 3 miles W of South Shields.*

YORKSHIRE

Romantic tales of sanctuary and escape from harsh justice are set amid ruined abbeys and imposing minsters, while enduring customs and curious relics hint at a way of life much different from today's.

❶ Bainbridge

For 700 years a hunting horn has been blown on the village green every evening at 10pm during autumn and winter – from September 27 (the Feast of the Holy Rood) to Shrove Tuesday. This custom originated when Bainbridge was surrounded by the once-great Forest of Wensleydale, and the sound of the horn was intended to guide lost travellers to the village.
▶ *4 miles E of Hawes on A684.*

❷ West Witton

Burning the Bartle takes place in West Witton each year on the Saturday nearest St Bartholomew's Day (August 24). The Bartle, a life-sized straw effigy of a man, is carried through the village to be burnt on a bonfire, accompanied by the following chant:

> On Penhill Crags he tore his rags
> Hunters Thorn he blew his horn
> Cappelbank Stee happened a misfortune and
>   brak' his knee
> Grassgill Beck he brak' his neck
> Wadhams End he couldn't fend
> Grassgill End we'll mak' his end
> Shout, lads, shout!

Bartle is variously an 18th-century sheep thief who was hunted over the surrounding fells before being captured and put to death; a holy man; a wooden statue of St Bartholomew that the villagers attempted to hide during the Reformation in the 16th century; or the son of the Norse god Thor, a pig-farming giant who was set ablaze by the villagers for blaming them when he lost his prize pig.
▶ *13 miles E of Hawes on A684.*

❸ Hubberholme

On the first Monday night of the year, a special auction takes place in The George, the local inn of the hamlet of Hubberholme. The vicar and churchwardens gather in the dining room, known as The House of Lords, and the village farmers meet in another room, The House of Commons. The two sides negotiate for the following year's tenancy of a 6.5ha (16 acre) field, Poor's Pasture. All the while a candle burns in the window (a local tradition, signifying the

WEST WITTON

vicar is present). The highest bid at the moment the candle flickers out wins the tenancy. The money is donated to the poor of the parish.
▶ *Just off B6160, 10 miles S of Hawes.*

❹ Giggleswick

Near Giggleswick Scar is an oddity of nature, the Ebbing and Flowing Well. An underground siphon is believed to be the cause of the phenomenon, although the water 'ebbs and flows' much less than it once did. Locals put it down to a nymph who, being chased by a satyr, prayed to the gods for help. The gods responded by transforming her into a spring, which ebbs and flows with her panting breaths.

According to legend, the 17th-century

highwayman, John Nevison, evaded capture after pausing at the well. He allowed his horse to drink the water, and it gave his steed such strength that it leaped clear over the nearby gorge, and galloped away. The gorge, now much widened and cut through by Ferrybridge road, is still known as Nevison's Leap. A Blue Plaque marks the spot.

▶ *1 mile W of Settle, just N of A65.*

❺ Summerbridge

Brimham Rocks, eroded by the weather into weird shapes, were once regarded as the work of Druids; several of the rocks bear such names as Druid's Altar and Druid's Head. It was thought that a narrow, tube-shaped hole in one rock had been gouged out to serve as an oracle: a Druid would stand behind the rock and speak through the hole.

In one of the many legends told about the rocks, an eloping couple named Edwin and Julia were pursued by the girl's angry father. At the top of a crag, he caught up with them. Preferring death to separation, the couple leapt into space. Miraculously, they landed safely, whereupon the relieved father gladly gave his consent to the marriage. The rock is still known as Lovers' Rock. Today the rocks – from which visitors can enjoy wonderful views over Nidderdale – are managed by the National Trust.

▶ *3 miles SE of Pateley Bridge at junction of B6451 and B6165. Brimham Rocks on minor road 1.5 miles N of village.*

❻ Fountains Abbey

A friar from the abbey who was renowned for his strength and for his skill as an archer is said to have challenged Robin Hood to a sword fight. Their battle was long and fierce, but finally the friar was obliged to surrender. He joined Robin's band, and later became famous as Friar Tuck.

▶ *On minor roads 4 miles SW of Ripon.*

❼ Ripon

Every night at 9pm, the City Hornblower of Ripon sounds the Wakeman's Horn at each corner of the obelisk in the market square and in front of the mayor's house. The custom began in AD 886, when Alfred the Great granted the first charter to the town and presented it with a Charter Horn, which is now on show in the mayor's parlour. A Wakeman was appointed to patrol the city after the curfew had been sounded each night, giving rise to the city's

SWORD DANCING

IN THE IRON-MINING VILLAGES around Sheffield and in the Cleveland district of North Yorkshire, traditional dances, performed with swords made of steel or wood, are practised still by teams of six or eight men. The dances vary between areas but all involve the mock decapitation of a leader.

The origins of Long Sword dancing, like those of mumming plays, are obscure. One theory is that the dances once formed part of an annual folk play, but as audiences grew increasingly sophisticated, they became bored with the play, which was discarded, and only the dances and some songs were retained. Today, village teams maintain their individual traditions, many performing on Boxing Day or Plough Monday in January – the start of the agricultural year.

motto: 'Except ye Lord keep ye cittie, ye Wakeman waketh in vain.' The 14th-century, half-timbered Wakeman's House stands on the southwest corner of the square.

▶ *12 miles N of Harrogate at junction of A61 and A6108.*

❽ Knaresborough

Ursula Sontheil, the grotesque woman who was destined to be England's most famous prophetess, was born in 1488 in a small cave in Knaresborough. Her mother, Agatha, died giving birth to her, and the death was apparently attended by 'strange and terrible noises'. Ursula was placed in the care of a townswoman. One day the woman left the infant alone in her cottage, and when she returned with several neighbours, they were attacked by supernatural forces. All of the men found themselves yoked to a floating staff from which a woman hung by her toes, and the women were compelled to dance in circles; whenever they tried to stop, they were pricked with pins by an imp in the form of a monkey. Ursula and her cradle were found inside the chimney, suspended in mid air.

Mysterious events continued to plague the cottage as the child grew up, according to reports passed down the generations. Furniture moved up and down the stairs of its own accord, and at mealtimes food vanished from the plates of startled guests.

Ursula married Toby Shipton of Shipton, near York, in 1512, and soon afterwards gained renown as a fortune-teller. She was called ▶

NORTHEAST ENGLAND

Mother Shipton, and by virtue of her appearance was well suited to play the role of a witch. It was said that 'her stature was larger than common, her body crooked and her face frightful, but her understanding extraordinary'.

Most of the prophecies ascribed to her, such as her predictions of railways and the radio telegraph, are now known to have been written by a man named Hindley in 1871. Despite this, she continues to be Yorkshire's most famous witch. Her cave and the petrifying well – where objects turn to stone over time by exposure to flowing mineralised water – are popular attractions in the town.

▶ *3 miles NE of Harrogate on A59.*

9 Nunnington

In Nunnington church is a tomb surmounted by a stone effigy of Sir Walter de Teyes, who died in 1325. Local legend, however, claims that it is the burial place of Peter Loschy, who is said to have killed a magic dragon in nearby Loschy Wood. Loschy and his dog fought with the beast for hours, but each time the dragon received a wound it rolled on the ground and the wound instantly healed. The creature was finally defeated when Loschy began to hack its body to pieces, for his dog carried off each piece until nothing remained of the monster.

▶ *On minor roads 10 miles SW of Pickering.*

10 Horcum

A natural amphitheatre alongside the Pickering to Whitby road, known as the Hole of Horcum, or the Devil's Punchbowl, is the result of glacial ice flow, but is said to have been caused when the giant Wade dug up a spadeful of earth. When he threw away the earth, it created the nearby hill of Blakey Topping.

▶ *On A169, 8 miles N of Pickering and 12 miles S of Whitby.*

11 Glaisdale

Lovers' Bridge crosses the River Esk and bears the initials TF and the date 1619. The initials are said to belong to Thomas Ferris, who used to wade or swim the river to meet his sweetheart. When he went to America to seek his fortune, he vowed that if he became rich, he would come back and build a bridge across the river. He became very rich indeed and, when he returned to marry his old love, he paid for the bridge to be built.

▶ *On minor roads 8 miles SW of Whitby.*

12 Whitby

The ancient ceremony of Horngarth, or the Planting of the Penny Hedge, is still observed each year in Whitby, on the day before Ascension Day. Bundles of stakes and osiers, which are cut in Eskdale Side, are carried at sunrise through the town to the harbour. Here, they are planted at the water's edge, and the 'yethers' (osiers) are woven through the 'stowers' (stakes) to form a 'hedge'.

The custom is said to have originated as a penance imposed by the abbot of Whitby in 1159 on three hunters who had beaten a hermit to death. Their lives were spared on condition that they and their descendants built a hedge each year on the water's edge, strong enough to withstand the onslaught of three tides.

The fame of Whitby Abbey goes back to Anglo-Saxon times. A 'double monastery' – for men and women – was founded here in AD 657 and its first abbess was St Hilda. One legend relates how she rid Eskdale of snakes by driving them to the edge of the cliffs and cutting off their heads with her whip. The ammonites – fossilised shellfish – found on the rocks below are said to be their remains.

Caedmon, an abbey cowherd in the late 7th century, was teased because he could not sing. One night he had a vision of an angel who asked him to sing of the creation of the world. From then on he became famous as a poet – perhaps England's first. One of his manuscripts is kept in Cambridge University Library.

No part of the old abbey remains standing. The ruins – famously atmospheric – are those of the 13th-century Benedictine Abbey church. They are managed by English Heritage.

▶ *20 miles N of Scarborough on A171.*

13 Scarborough

At noon on Shrove Tuesday, the pancake bell at 86 Newborough is rung to announce that pancake making may now begin. All day there are skipping matches on the foreshore; skipping ropes are provided, and anyone may join in the Skipping Festival.

A Scarborough tradition of Robin Hood tells how he joined the crew of a fishing boat. Ignorant of the ways of the sea, he neglected to bait his hooks before throwing them overboard. He made amends when a French man-o'-war attacked the boat. Robin led the crew in boarding the raider, killed her captain and captured a vast sum of gold, which he presented to the poor fishermen.

▶ *40 miles NE of York.*

THE RUINS ARE
FAMOUSLY
ATMOSPHERIC
WHITBY ABBEY CHURCH

⑭ Rudston

A 7.9m (26ft) tall late Stone Age monolith, thought to be the tallest in Britain, stands in the churchyard at Rudston. It is reputed to weigh 80 tonnes and to extend several metres below ground (although this has never been verified). One legend holds that it simply fell from the sky one day 'killing certain desecrators of the churchyard'; another states that it was thrown by the Devil, attempting to destroy the church, and it landed in its present position because of his bad marksmanship.

▶ *5 miles W of Bridlington on B1253.*

⑮ Beverley

During the Middle Ages, Beverley Minster was famous as an ecclesiastical sanctuary. Hunted men fled to it from all over England. Once within the bounds, fugitives were given sanctuary for 30 days, while the clergy tried to intercede for them. If this failed, the offenders were handed over to the coroner, who gave them the choice of trial or exile. Beverley was unique among ecclesiastical sanctuaries in offering a third alternative: the criminal might take an oath to become a servant of the Church, give all his property to the Crown and live within the town of Beverley for the rest of his life. Those who accepted were known as Frithmen.

A story is told of Toustain, a henchman of William the Conqueror, who at that time was laying waste to the North. Toustain violated Beverley's sanctuary by leading a band of soldiers into the Minster in pursuit of townsfolk, who had fled there. As he crossed the threshold, there was a flash of light and he fell, his head completely turned round and his limbs transformed to hideous lumps. After this, the Conqueror respectfully confirmed the Minster in its privileges.

The 1,000-year-old Frith-stol, or sanctuary chair, in Beverley Minster, was once the goal of hunted men from all over England. Anyone sitting in it could claim immunity from the law for 30 days.

▶ *10 miles N of Kingston upon Hull.*

⑯ Market Weighton

The annual Kiplingcotes Derby is held near Market Weighton on the third Thursday in March. Claimed to be the oldest flat race in England, the Derby dates from 1519 and is run over a 4-mile course that ends at Kipling Cotes Farm. Each rider must weigh over 10st (63kg) and pay an entrance fee. The money is won by whoever finishes second, while the winner receives the interest on a sum of money that was invested in 1618. Sometimes the entrance money amounts to more than the first prize.

▶ *10 miles W of Beverley on A1079.*

⑰ York

The York Mystery plays are performed every few years in the ruins of St Mary's Abbey, and are the most famous of their kind in Britain. They date from the middle of the 14th century, and tell the story of mankind from the Creation to Judgment Day. The fullness of the text and stage directions are the result of the chance survival of a complete manuscript, which is now kept in the British Museum.

One of the principal treasures of York Minster is the great ivory drinking-horn, over 60cm (2ft) in length, known as Ulph's Horn. Ulph was a Danish chieftain who held lands in western Yorkshire at the beginning of the 11th century. Legend relates how, after his eldest son, Adelbert, was killed in battle, Ulph attempted to bypass the claims of his other three sons and bequeath his domain to Adelbert's daughter, Adelwynne. She, however, persuaded him to bestow his lands on the Church. So Ulph rode to York, taking with him his largest drinking-horn. He filled it with wine and knelt at the high altar in the Minster. Then he drank the wine and laid the horn on the altar to be held by the Church for all time as title to his lands and to all his wealth.

▶ *12 miles E of Junction 47 of A1(M).*

⑱ Barwick in Elmet

At 26m (86ft), the maypole at Barwick in Elmet is considered to be the oldest and tallest maypole in England. On Easter Monday every three years, the pole is lowered by three 'pole men', who are elected for the task. Then, freshly painted and garlanded with flowers and ribbons, it is raised again for the traditional maypole dances on Whit Monday.

▶ *On minor roads 8 miles NE of Leeds.*

⑲ Guiseley

An ancient ceremony known as 'Clipping the Church' takes place on August 5, the feast of St Oswald, patron saint of the parish. The parishioners walk in procession around the church to symbolise their love for it. The word clipping is derived from the Old English word for encircling.

▶ *10 miles NW of Leeds on A65.*

⓴ The Cottingley Fairies

The village of Cottingley rose to international notoriety in 1920, when two girls, 13-year-old Elsie Wright and her 10-year-old cousin Frances Griffiths, produced photographs of what they claimed to be fairies in Cottingley Glen. The prevailing belief in spirits and the supernatural among many influential people of the time, coupled with the conviction that two young girls would not have the cunning, capability or even reason to fake such images, led the photographs to be championed by such public figures as Sir Arthur Conan Doyle. The girls maintained that the fairies were real, and for 50 years the story refused to fade.

In April 1983, Frances confessed to *The Times* newspaper that the fairies had been created by Elsie, tracing pictures from *Princess Mary's Gift Book*, published in 1914. She was surprised by the furore the images had caused. Elsie, while corroborating her cousin's story, always maintained that while four of the pictures might have been fake, the fifth was real and she and Frances really had seen fairies. She later retracted the 'genuine' claim for the picture, but held steadfast to the claim that the fairies were real. A film of the story, *Photographing Fairies*, was made in 1997.

▶ *Just S of Junction 1 of M621, 2 miles SW of Leeds city centre.*

㉑ Bradford

The hundreds of stone heads that came to light in the West Riding in the 20th century have never been comprehensively assigned to a particular period. Do they date from the pre-Roman Celtic times? Or were some of them carved just a century or two ago, indicating the survival of ancient Celtic beliefs into the modern world? The Celts who lived in the area 2,300 years ago, when it was part of the kingdom of Brigantia, revered the human head. The severed heads of enemies – or their replicas in stone – were set at the entrances of cattle-byres and houses. Large numbers of these Celtic masks have been dug from the ground in Scotland, Ireland and on the Continent. In the Bradford area, where many of them were placed in the drystone walls of fields and above cottage doors, they may still be serving their original purpose. It is thought that some of the heads are no more than 150 years old; if this is so, then an Iron Age cult – or the echo of it – may have survived in some form into the reign of Queen Victoria.

▶ *8 miles W of Leeds.*

㉒ Dewsbury

Every year on Christmas Eve, the 'Devil's Knell' is tolled at All Saints parish church in Dewsbury. The bell is rung once for each year since Christ's birth, and is said to have been given to the church by a local murderer, Sir Thomas de Soothill, hoping to atone for his enraged killing of a servant. The purpose is to keep the Devil away. The bell is nicknamed 'Black Tom of Soothill' and its final peal is planned to finish on the stroke of midnight. Since there are more than 2,000 years to mark, the ringing lasts for at least 2 hours.

▶ *8 miles S of Leeds.*

㉓ Denby Dale

Giant pies that can feed hundreds of people are the tradition at Denby Dale, which is also known as the Pie Village. The first was baked in 1788 to celebrate the recovery of George III from illness. Another was for victory at Waterloo. One containing everything from five sheep to '63 small birds' caused a near riot in 1846. It was drawn through the village by 13 horses before being tipped out of its cart by the crowd. The Hinchliffe family say that their ancestor, who cut the pie, made such a long speech that people chopped through platform supports and toppled him into the pie. The pies have featured in the *Guinness World Records* – in the year 2000, the Millennium Pie – filled with beef, onions, potatoes and best bitter – fed a total of 30,000 people.

▶ *At junction of A635 and A636, 8 miles W of Barnsley.*

㉔ Pontefract

Pontefract is famous for the round liquorice sweets known as Pontefract Cakes. Liquorice roots were probably first brought to Britain nearly 2,000 years ago by the Romans, but local legend insists that a Pontefract schoolmaster introduced the plant into England in 1588. He is said to have found a bundle of liquorice branches on a Yorkshire beach, washed ashore from a wrecked Armada galleon. They seemed admirably suited to birching the boys at his school; and while this painful process was going on, the boys bit on other liquorice branches to stifle their cries of pain. Thus they discovered the plant's flavour, and soon it was grown throughout the Pontefract area.

▶ *9 miles E of Wakefield. Access from Junction 32 of M62.*

KEY

1 Main entry
County boundary
Motorway
Principal A road

Holyhead
31
Anglesey
Llandudno
30 **29**
28
Rhyl
27
A55
26
Bangor
Caernarfon
23
3
2
Mold
22
Betws-y-Coed
25
A494
6
A5
Wrexham
A499
A487
Porthmadog
Snowdonia
National
Park
4
24
21
Llangollen
20
7
Bala
5
19
15
18
Dolgellau
A494
A458
Welshpool
Machynlleth
NORTH and MID WALES
176-183
A483
8
Newtown
16
9
A44
Aberystwyth
17
LLangurig
A470
Cambrian
Mountains
Llandrindod
Wells
A44
11
10
12
A487
A465
13
A483
Builth
Wells
8
Cardigan
14
9
11
A470
A438
Fishguard
4
5
6
Llandovery
Brecon
Black
Mountains
3
7
SOUTH WALES
186-191
A40
Brecon Beacons
National Park
A479
1
Pembrokeshire Coast
National Park
Carmarthen
Llandeilo
2
Haverfordwest
A40
13
Abergavenny
A4076
A477
14
A48
Monmouth
Milford
Haven
A465
Merthyr
Tydfil
21
Tenby
Llanelli
A449
10
A470
A4042
Chepstow
15
20
M48
Swansea
Neath
17
16
Newport
Port
12
Talbot
M4
18
Bridgend
Cardiff
19

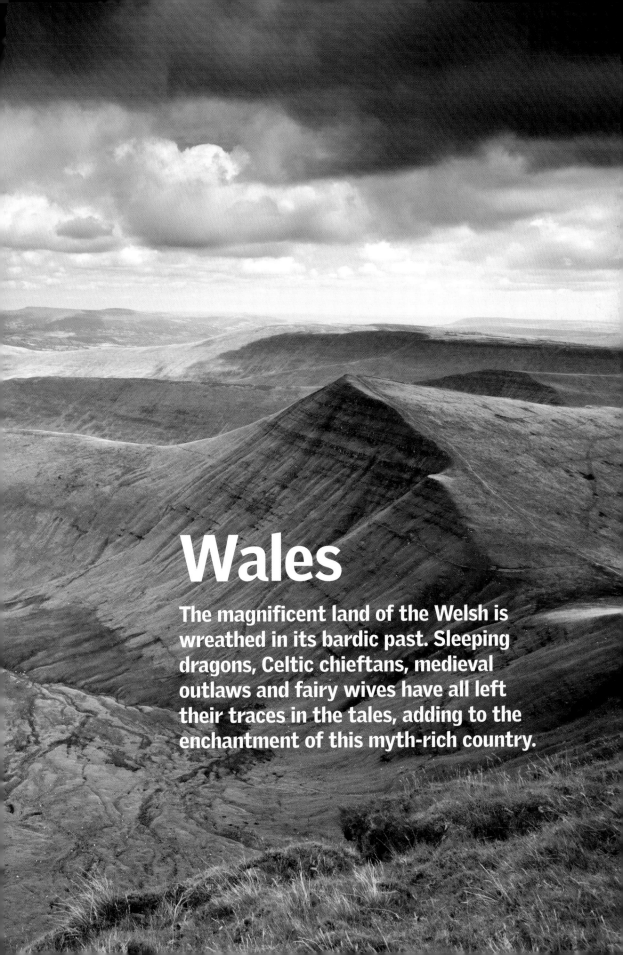

Wales

The magnificent land of the Welsh is wreathed in its bardic past. Sleeping dragons, Celtic chieftans, medieval outlaws and fairy wives have all left their traces in the tales, adding to the enchantment of this myth-rich country.

NORTH & MID WALES

In the observance of ancient customs and telling of old tales, Welsh imagination flourishes unchecked. Its roots lie buried deep in the Celtic past, and fabulous legends are only enhanced by time.

① Aberdaron, Gwynedd

A small farm cottage near Aberdaron on the Lleyn Peninsula was the birthplace in 1780 of Richard Robert Jones, better known as the folk hero Dic Aberdaron. With his pockets full of books, a cat at his side, a ram's horn slung round his neck, and often wearing a hare-skin hat, he spent his life travelling the length and breadth of Wales. Allegedly, he was able to summon and command demons, and once, when the reapers at Mathlem Farm near Aberdaron were working in a field full of thistles, he called for his satanic helpers and within minutes the whole field had been reaped. By his death in 1843, he is said to have mastered 15 languages.

By tradition, sheep rustlers were once hanged on Brynn y Crogbren, or gallows hill, near Aberdaron. Many of them were reputedly rounded up by the Cwn Annwn, the hounds of the underworld, led by the lord of the fairies.

On high ground stand the ruins of Capel Vair, the Chapel of Our Lady, and in the cliff below is a cave, Ogo Vair, with a well. At one time, the faithful believed that if they could carry a mouthful of water up a difficult path to the top of the hill, their wish would be granted.

▶ *14 miles SW of Pwllheli at end of B4413.*

② Betws Garmon, Gwynedd

The Pellings family, who lived near this small village in Snowdonia until the 19th century, were said to be descendants of a marriage between a man and a fairy, Penelope. The fairy consented to marry her mortal lover only on condition that he would never strike her with iron. They lived happily together for many years, and produced a son and a daughter. But one day Penelope was struck accidentally with a bridle as her husband tried to catch a pony, and she vanished for ever.

▶ *6 miles SE of Caernarfon on A4085.*

③ Llanberis, Gwynedd

Reputedly the strongest woman ever to have lived in Wales was born in Llanberis in 1696, and died there some 105 years later. At the age of 70, it is said, Marged vch Ifan could still out-wrestle every man in Wales. She kept a dozen hounds, and in a year she could catch as many foxes as the local huntsmen could in ten. Tradition maintains that she was a first-rate carpenter, blacksmith, cobbler, tailor, harp-maker, fiddle-maker and musician. After receiving many offers of marriage she chose the smallest and most effeminate of all her suitors. She is said to have beaten him twice; after the first beating he married her, after the second he became an ardent churchgoer.

▶ *7 miles E of Caernarfon on A4086.*

④ Llanfor, Gwynedd

According to local legend, the Devil was a frequent visitor to this little village, in which he generally used to appear in the shape of a pig. At last, the parson managed to quell the beast by reciting the service of exorcism while marching three times round the church, after which the Evil One was bound and taken to a pool in the nearby River Dee. There he was to remain as long as a certain lamp, hidden in the church, was kept burning. But the lamp burnt out for lack of oil, and the Devil returned in the form of a gentleman in a three-cornered hat, who constantly interrupted divine service in the church. Two magicians succeeded in capturing him again, and he was carried away, in the form of a cock, on the back of a horse. Once more he was thrown into the pool, but this time his stay was permanent, for he had to remain there until he had counted every grain of sand at the bottom of the pool, now called Llyn y Geulan Goch.

▶ *1 mile NE of Bala on A494.*

⑤ Llanuwchllyn, Gwynedd

A long time ago, the rich heiress of Llwyn Gwern manor fell in love with a peasant boy. Her father bitterly opposed the match, but told the young man that if he were to stand naked on a nearby hill throughout the coldest night of winter, he could marry his daughter in the morning. The boy accepted the challenge, and managed to keep himself warm by beating a pole into the ground with a sledgehammer. He married his sweetheart next day, and the hillside where he stood is still known as Bwlch y Pawl – the pass of the pole.

▶ *5 miles SW of Bala on A494.*

6 Nantgwynant, Gwynedd

The Iron Age hillfort of Dinas Emrys is associated with the story of how the red dragon became the Welsh national emblem.
The treacherous King Gwrtheyrn, when fleeing from his own people after betraying them to the Saxons in the 5th century, attempted to build a castle on the conical hillock of Dinas Emrys. But each night the building materials mysteriously disappeared, and the king's magicians told him that he must sprinkle the hill with the blood of a boy born of a virgin. After much searching, the boy was found, but before he could be sacrificed he revealed himself as Merlin. The wizard told the king that beneath the hill two dragons lay sleeping in a subterranean lake – a white dragon representing the Saxons, and a red one representing Wales. The lake was drained and the dragons began to fight, until the white one was defeated. This, it is said, is how the red dragon became the emblem of Wales.

Merlin, who was also known as Emrys, built a fort on the site and named it after himself, while the king withdrew and built his castle at Nant Gwrtheyrn instead.

▶ *8 miles N of Porthmadog. The valley runs NE from junction of A498 and A4085. Dinas Emrys is just N of A498, 2 miles NE of Beddgelert.*

THE DRAGONS FOUGHT BENEATH THE HILL
DINAS EMRYS, NANTGWYNANT

THE MABINOGION

THE PROFESSIONAL STORYTELLERS who entertained the nobility of Wales in the Middle Ages knew by heart an immense number of legends and traditional tales, some of which may have taken days to tell. Gradually, most of these stories were lost but a few were written down, and 11 of them survive today, a unique record of magic and mystery, which in Celtic imagination was as real as the everyday world. These stories, known collectively as the Mabinogion, have been preserved since the 14th century in the White Book of Rhydderch, now in the National Library of Wales at Aberystwyth, and the Red Book of Hergest in the Bodleian Library, Oxford.

The hero of the first four stories – the Four Branches – is Pryderi, son of Pwyll, Prince of Dyfed, and the beautiful Lady Rhiannon. The next five tales recount the adventures of King Arthur and his knights, as they ride through an enchanted land full of fabulous beasts and frightful monsters. Two shorter stories tell of the trials of Lludd, King of Britain, and the Roman emperor Magnus Maximus, who died about AD 388.

The earliest of the Arthurian tales dates from around the 10th century. It was prophesied that Arthur's cousin, Culhwch, would never marry unless he could win the heart of Olwen, daughter of Ysbaddaden, a fearful ogre who lived in the strongest fortress in the world. Culhwch, Arthur and six of his men rode to Ysbaddaden's castle to find the beautiful Olwen. She loved Culhwch at once, but Ysbaddaden refused to permit the wedding, because it had been foretold that when she married, he would die. Despite this, Olwen agreed to marry the brave young man, provided that he first obeyed all the giant's commands.

Ysbaddaden demanded 13 treasures, which could be won only through 40 dangerous adventures. Culhwch, Arthur and the knights performed superhuman feats in their quest until just one, the most perilous adventure of all, remained. They hunted a ferocious boar through forests and over hills from Wales to Cornwall, where the great boar was eventually driven into the sea. Before it died, Arthur tore the last treasure, a comb and scissors, from its head and the triumphant party returned to Ysbaddaden's castle. The giant had to agree to the marriage, and thus his own death, and his last words to Culhwch were, 'Thank Arthur for Olwen.' The giant's huge head was cut off and set up on a stake for all his enemies to mock, and Culhwch and his bride lived happily for ever.

❼ Llandderfel, Gwynedd

Medieval pilgrims used to visit the shrine of St Derfel, who was alleged to have been one of King Arthur's warriors. The shrine contained a wooden statue of the saint, the head, eyes and arms of which moved mechanically. The figure, which was shown holding a staff and placed on a horse, was widely believed to be capable of saving condemned souls from hell, and at the Reformation in the 16th century was taken to London to be burnt at Smithfield. A monk named Forest, who refused to deny that the statue had worked miracles, was burnt with it. The wooden horse and staff were left behind, though, and can still be seen in Llandderfel church.
▶ *4 miles E of Bala at junction of B4401 and B4402.*

❽ Aberdovey, Gwynedd

The tradition that Cardigan Bay was once a dry, fertile land is firmly based on fact; some 7,000 years ago, a forest covered what are now the shallows, and sunken fossil trees can still be seen there at low tide. Until about the 17th century, the lost land was called Maes Gwyddno, the land of Gwyddno, and was said to have been drowned when the guardian or priestess of a fairy well allowed the water to overflow. However, in the legend that holds sway today the lost land is Cantref Gwaelod, the lowland hundred, its king was Gwyddno Garanhir, and a drunkard called Seithennin looked after the sluices and embankments that protected it from the sea. One evening, after a great banquet, Seithennin left all the sluices open, and the land, the people and 16 noble cities were drowned. When the sea is calm and the wind quiet, some say that the bells of Cantref Gwaelod may still be heard tolling far beneath the waters of the bay, a legend kept alive by the folksong, 'Clychau Aberdyfi', 'The Bells of Aberdovey'.
▶ *10 miles SW of Machynlleth on A493.*

❾ Tre Taliesin, Ceredigion

Taliesin, the legendary 6th-century poet, is reputedly buried a mile east of Tre Taliesin, north of Aberystwyth, but the story of his birth is a classic mythic tale. For a year and a day the witch Ceridwen boiled a secret mixture of herbs in her cauldron, to make a magic potion for her son Morfran, because by swallowing three drops he would acquire all knowledge and power. But before he could take it, the potion was stolen and drunk by Gwion Bach. Ceridwen gave chase, and Gwion finally turned into a grain of wheat to escape her, but the witch turned into a hen and ate him. Nine months later, she bore a son. Ceridwen put the baby in a coracle and pushed it out to sea. The tiny boat was washed up near Borth and found by Elphin, son of King Gwyddno of the now drowned land of Cantref Gwaelod, who named the boy Taliesin, meaning 'beautiful brow'.

▶ *9 miles N of Aberystwyth on A487.*

⑩ Llanarth, Ceredigion

Local tradition claims that the Devil once tried to steal the bell from Llanarth church, but he made so much noise about it that he woke the vicar, who climbed up into the belfry armed with bell, book and candle. By solemnly repeating the name of Christ, the vicar succeeded in driving the Devil to the top of the tower, and forced him to jump off. In the graveyard, a stone bears the marks he made when he landed on it.

▶ *4 miles SW of Aberaeron on A487.*

⑪ Llanina, Ceredigion

The little church of St Ina in Llanina takes its name from an 8th-century king of Wessex. One day, so the story goes, a ship came to grief on the rocks during a raging storm. A local fisherman and his daughter, braving the rough sea, rowed out to the stricken vessel time and again, saving many lives. They could not understand the shipwrecked strangers, so a monk was called, who told the fisherfolk that they had saved none other than King Ina from England. In thanksgiving, the king built a church, which was known as Llan Ina, 'Ina's church', on the rocky promontory. Ina subsequently went on a pilgrimage to Rome and was later canonised. The promontory was eventually overwhelmed by the sea and a new church built farther inland, dedicated to St Ina. Cerrig Ina, 'Ina's stones', can be seen offshore, marking the spot where the original church once stood.

▶ *2 miles E of New Quay.*

⑫ Llanddewi-Brefi, Ceredigion

Christian missionaries were never more active in Wales than in the 6th and 7th centuries, and David, son of St Non, soon became one of the most important leaders of the new Celtic Church. Disciples flocked to him, in spite of his stern self-denial and the rigid discipline of his monastery, for he was noted for his gentle nature.

Like many Celtic saints whose biographies were written centuries after they had died, David was credited with the working of innumerable miracles. At a meeting of Celtic churchmen in Llanddewi-Brefi in 519, the assembled bishops could not make themselves heard above the noise of the crowd. But a hill is said to have risen up beneath David, and from this high vantage point he preached the gospel so that all could hear. A church dedicated to him still stands on top of the reputedly miraculous hill.

The famed Ychen Bannog oxen were brought to haul an enormous boulder up the hill to build the church. These were the strongest oxen in the world, but the work proved too much. One could not live without the other and, inseparable to the last, they both died from exhaustion.

▶ *8 miles NE of Lampeter on B4343.*

⑬ Lampeter, Ceredigion

In the 17th century the ancestral home of the Lloyds of Maesyfelin stood where Maesyfelin Street is today. Elen Lloyd, the only daughter of the family, became engaged to Samuel Pritchard, the son of Rhys Pritchard, a poet-priest from nearby Llandovery. One day, Elen's four brothers, fearing for their inheritance, tied Samuel head downwards on his horse, and galloped him from Lampeter to Llandovery. He died of his injuries, and they threw his body into the River Teifi. Elen was driven mad by grief, and died soon afterwards. Rhys Pritchard put a curse on the house of Maesyfelin, and within months it had caught fire and burnt to the ground. Either through remorse or because of Pritchard's curse, the eldest of the four Lloyd brothers murdered the other three and then hanged himself.

▶ *30 miles E of Cardigan at junction of A475, A482 and A485.*

⑭ Waen Rhydd, Powys

The annual Bog Snorkelling Championships take place every year on August Bank Holiday weekend on private land near Waen Rhydd, which also has the distinction of being Britain's smallest town.

Competitors, wearing flippers, mask and snorkel, proceed through a boggy channel cut in the peat; they can lift their heads only for orientation and cannot use any officially recognised swimming stroke. Many also compete in fancy dress. The prize is awarded to the entrant who completes two consecutive lengths of the 55m (60yd) ditch in the fastest time.

▶ *1 mile S of centre of Llanwrtyd Wells.*

wales

PENNANT MELANGELL, POWYS

15 Pennant Melangell, Powys

Brochwel Ysgythrog, a 6th-century prince of Powys, was hunting one day when his hounds set off in pursuit of a hare. Eventually, the exhausted creature found shelter between the feet of a strange young woman standing in the forest. The prince urged his hounds to make the kill, but they would not go near the woman. Brochwel, made uneasy by the dogs' behaviour, asked the woman her name. She told him she was Melangell, and that she had come from Ireland to worship God in peaceful Pennant. The prince realised that he was in the presence of a saint, and gave Melangell land on which to build a chapel.

St Melangell's encounter with the prince is recorded in 15th-century wood carvings on the screen of the Norman church. She became the patron saint of hares and, in the district, these creatures are sometimes known as 'wyn bach Melangell', or Melangell's little lambs.

▶ *10 miles SE of Bala, at end of minor road off B4391.*

16 Hyssington, Powys

The legend of the bull of Bagbury centres on the old church of St Etheldreda in Hyssington. A boot containing a tiny, savage bull is supposed to be buried below the church's doorstep, and if the step is ever moved, the bull will emerge, grow quickly to an enormous size and terrorise the parish as it once did years ago.

The creature is really the wicked squire of nearby Bagbury, turned into an evil bull. The parson confronted the monstrous animal, reciting prayers and reading aloud from the Bible, and gradually it began to shrink. He led it into the church and continued preaching at it until nightfall, by which time it was no larger than a small dog. But when the parson's candle burnt

out, forcing him to stop, the bull started growing again, until it became so large that cracks appeared in the walls of the church – they can be seen there to this day. Next morning, the parson had to start again from the beginning. After a long day's praying, he had made the bull small enough to be pushed into the boot, which he quickly buried beneath the church doorstep.

▶ *15 miles E of Newtown.*

17 Llangurig, Powys

The district is renowned for its 'white' witches who have helped country folk for years. During the 19th and early 20th centuries one family, whose descendants still live in the area, were particularly famed for their supernatural powers. People who thought they had been bewitched travelled to see Y Dyn Hysbys, 'the knowing one', for relief. The usual problem was sickness or death among livestock, and the white witch would curse the black witch responsible. The curse on one old woman, believed to have bewitched some calves, was to have a horn growing from her head until she removed her spell. Some farmers used to pay the white witch to give protection to their farms and their stock during the ensuing year.

▶ *25 miles E of Aberystwyth at junction of A44 and A470.*

18 Llanrhaeadr-ym-Mochnant, Powys

This, and other villages in the Tanad Valley, still maintain the plygain, a form of carol service once fairly common throughout Wales. Groups of singers wander from church to church during the Christmas season, and give unaccompanied performances of Welsh carols.

▶ *15 miles SE of Bala off B4396.*

⑲ Llansilin, Powys

Until the middle of the 20th century, the local carpenter was still making fish-shaped coffins. It has been suggested by some that the shape was intended to help the dead person to swim the last river on his way to paradise.

Llansilin's church is pockmarked by bullets, which were supposedly fired at Cromwell when he took shelter there. It is said that his army fled the church in terror when Royalist soldiers flung a beehive at them from a bedroom window of Ty Mawr house.

▶ *6 miles W of Oswestry on B4580.*

⑳ Chirk, Wrexham

Fourteenth-century Chirk Castle has been occupied since 1595 by the Myddelton family, whose coat of arms includes a red hand. According to one of the many legends associated with the 'bloody hand', it represents the family's past misdeeds, and cannot be removed until a prisoner survives ten years in the castle dungeons. Other stories tell of rivalry between two brothers, both desperate to inherit the estate, and one chopping off the other's hand in an attempt to win, or make the other lose, a deciding close-run race. The property is under the guardianship of the National Trust, and the magnificent 18th-century wrought-iron gates feature a red hand.

▶ *8 miles S of Wrexham on A5.*

㉑ Glyndyfrdwy, Denbighshire

On September 16, 1400, a band of Welsh rebels met at Glyndyfrdwy and declared Owain Glyndwr to be the rightful Prince of Wales, an event that sparked off a ten-year rebellion against Henry IV. Although Wales failed to establish itself as a kingdom in its own right, or achieve separation from England, Owain Glyndwr has ever since remained the country's most famous folk hero who, legend claims, will one day return to liberate the Welsh nation.

Glyndyfrdwy stands on the River Dee, which in pagan times was held to be the dwelling place of Aerfen, a martial goddess who presided over the fate of wars between the English and the Welsh. It was believed that three human sacrifices had to be drowned in the sacred river every year to ensure success in battle.

▶ *5 miles W of Llangollen on A5.*

㉒ Ruthin, Denbighshire

The Maen Huail, Huail's stone, is a large block of limestone, which stands in the marketplace at Ruthin. Legend has it that in the 6th century all the sons of Caw, except the historian Gildas, constantly rebelled against King Arthur. Huail, the eldest, was the ruler of Edeirnion in North Wales and proved to be the most troublesome of the brothers. When King Arthur held court at Caerwys in Flintshire, he used to visit a woman who lived in Ruthin. Huail learnt of this and began to pursue the woman himself, which soon led to a fight between the two warriors. Arthur was wounded in the knee, but agreed to forgive Huail on condition that the Welshman would never mention the wound. Shortly afterwards, the king disguised himself as a woman and secretly went to Ruthin where his mistress was attending a dance in the village. Huail recognised Arthur by his limp and remarked, 'Your dancing would be fine were it not for your clumsy knee.' Immediately, Arthur had him taken outside where he was beheaded on the stone.

▶ *16 miles NW of Wrexham at junction of A494 and A525.*

Wales

23 Llanddwyn, Anglesey

On the little island of Llanddwyn, there is a well and the remains of a 13th-century church dedicated to St Dwynwen, the patron saint of Welsh lovers. The story goes that in the 5th century, Dwynwen fell deeply in love with Prince Maelon, but her father refused to accept the match. Frantic with desire, the prince raped the girl then abandoned her. Dwynwen prayed to be relieved of her great love, so while they slept God gave Dwynwen and Maelon a drink that cured the girl but turned the prince to ice. God then gave Dwynwen three wishes. First, she wished that Maelon should be unfrozen; second, that God would answer all requests made by her on behalf of true lovers; and third, that she would never want to marry again. Her wishes were granted, and Dwynwen remained unmarried – she became a nun – until the day she died.

▷ *Access via minor road and footpaths off A4080, 12 miles SW of Menai Bridge.*

24 Cynwyd, Denbighshire

Between Cynwyd and Corwen stands the small parish church of Llangar. Now looked after by CADW, the church contains some impressive medieval wall paintings. Originally, it was to have been built where Cynwyd Bridge crosses the River Dee but each night the stones laid during the day mysteriously vanished, supposedly removed by the Devil. A wizard told the stonemasons that the site was not acceptable to God, and advised them to organise a hunt for a white stag and build the church where the stag first appeared. They did so, and Llangar church now occupies the place where the animal was first seen. Nearby Moel y Lladdfa, the hill of slaughter, is the place where the stag was finally caught and killed by the hunters.

▷ *2 miles S of Corwen on B4401.*

25 Betws-y-Coed, Conwy

The dreaded Afanc, a water monster, lived near Betws-y-Coed, in the River Conwy. The creature was enticed from its cave by a young girl it had fallen in love with, but although the townspeople managed to put chains round it, it clawed off one of the girl's breasts and escaped. Finally, it was left to the Ychen Bannog, two long-horned oxen, the strongest in the world, to haul the Afanc from its hiding place. Such was the struggle that the eye of one of the oxen fell to the ground. This was so large that it formed a pool, which is still known as Pwll Llygad Ych, the pool of the ox's eye.

▷ *15 miles S of Conwy at junction of A5 and A470.*

LLANDDWYN

㉖ St Asaph, Denbighshire

St Asaph's cathedral, named after its 6th-century bishop, is the smallest in Britain. St Asaph was said to have shone with 'virtue and miracles from the flower of his earliest youth'. One legend tells how Nest, the beautiful wife of Maelgwn Gwynedd, king of North Wales, one day lost a precious ring as she bathed in a pool. Nest was overcome with grief, for the ring had been given to her by Maelgwn and was the traditional ring always worn by the queen of the North. She went to St Asaph, hoping that he might be able to help her. The bishop invited the royal couple to eat with him the following evening. When they arrived, he told Maelgwn what had happened, but the king refused to believe his wife's story, and grew furious with her. Asaph immediately prayed to God that the ring might be found and the three of them sat down to eat. The meal began with fish, caught in the River Elwy on the same day; when Maelgwn cut in to his fish, the ring fell out on to his plate.

▶ *5 miles N of Denbigh on A525.*

㉗ St George, Conwy

Until the late 19th century, people used to sprinkle their horses with holy water from the village well. This was done both to bless the animals and to cure them of sickness. So powerful was the magic that if you had several horses, it was necessary to sprinkle only one, which would then pass the blessing on to the others. St George is the patron saint of horses, but this custom probably long pre-dated Christianity. Many of the place names in the district, such as Tremeirchion and Kinmeirch, are based on the Welsh word for horse, indicating that the area has always been sacred to these animals.

▶ *4 miles W of St Asaph on A55.*

㉘ Llanddulas, Conwy

A cave on Pen y Cefn mountain is said to have been the home of the Devil. While he lived there, he was a great worry to the people of Llanddulas, especially for his habit of scaring pregnant women. At last they could stand it no longer, so they held a service of exorcism outside the cave, after which he never troubled them again. It is alleged that at some time during the course of the service, the Devil fell into a deep, muddy pool, and that is why he has been black ever since.

▶ *4 miles E of Colwyn Bay on A55.*

㉙ Rhôs-on-Sea, Conwy

The tiny 6th-century chapel of St Trillo stands just below the promenade, next to the sea, and is little more than a simple altar built over a natural spring. This well has been in use since pre-Christian times and was once famous for its healing powers. Even today, the spring water is used for baptisms in other churches in the parish. St Trillo was a missionary from Brittany and he built his cell, probably of wood and wattle, over the holy well.

▶ *1 mile N of centre of Colwyn Bay.*

㉚ Conwy

Among Conwy's legendary links with the sea is the story of a mermaid who was washed ashore by a storm. She begged the fishermen who found her to help her back into the water, but they refused to do so. Just before she died, she cursed the people of the town, swearing that they would always be poor. When Conwy was suffering from a fish famine during the 5th century, many said that the curse had been fulfilled.

Another fish-famine story concerns St Brigid. While she was walking by the River Conwy, she threw rushes into the water, and a few days later they turned into fish. Soon the river was teeming with the miraculous fish, and ever since then they have been known as sparlings, or in Welsh brwyniaid, meaning 'rush-like'.

▶ *5 miles W of Colwyn Bay on A55.*

㉛ Penmynydd, Anglesey

Many centuries ago, according to legend, a huge dragon with poisonous fangs lived near the manor farm of Penhesgyn. A wizard prophesied that one day it would kill the estate's heir, so the young man was sent for safety to England. Then, one day, a clever local youth thought of a way of killing the monster. He dug a hole near the creature's lair and placed a large, highly polished brass pan in the pit. The dragon peered in, and mistaking its own reflection for another dragon, tried to fight it. The lad waited until it was exhausted, then killed and buried it. The heir came home and a great celebration followed at the manor, after which the heir wanted to see the monster's body. So the grave was reopened and, with justifiable pride, he kicked the dead dragon's head. Tragically, a poisonous fang pierced his foot, and the young man died, so fulfilling the prophecy.

▶ *3 miles W of Menai Bridge on B5420.*

wales

The great sitting together

A travelling folk festival devoted to excellence in the arts, the Eisteddfod has become an integral part of Welsh cultural life.

Eisteddfod: the word conjures up images of bards in long robes and head-dresses, enthronings, mysterious prizes known as chairs, and a rather forbidding solemnity, not to say impenetrability – a celebration accessible only to native Welsh speakers with high brows and higher minds. That might have been true of eisteddfodau of the past, and it is certainly true that the National Eisteddfod Council and the Gorsedd, or assembly, of Bards continue to set pretty rigorous standards in poetry, singing, musicianship and artistry. But eisteddfod today, as a celebration of Welsh culture, tries to live up to its meaning – 'a sitting together' – by reaching out to all comers.

What became known as the first Eisteddfod, a gathering of poets, musicians and singers to compete for prizes and glory, was held in Cardigan Castle at Christmas-tide 1176 at the behest of Rhys ap Gruffydd, ruler of the kingdom of Deheubarth in southwest Wales. Lord Rhys, a man of 'excellent wit and quick in repartee', was keen to underline his hard-won position as an ally and equal of the English king, Henry II, and here was the chance to project exactly the required image – a rich and beneficent lord in a mighty stronghold, powerful and independent, dispensing largesse while upholding the dignity and prestige of his native culture.

The competition had been announced a year previously to allow the cream of artists from all corners of the British Isles, Ireland and France to attend. In the event, a poet from North Wales and a musician from Rhys's own household claimed the chief prizes, a chair or place apiece at Lord Rhys's own table.

Relations with the Anglo-Normans across the border might be rocky from time to time – and they would get a lot rockier very soon as the English

began to impose their rule on the Welsh – but the message coming out of Cardigan Castle that Christmas time was clear: 'We're very strong and confident about ourselves.'

Decline and revival

A long-standing Celtic tradition already existed whereby contests were held between professional bards employed by noble families. So it's probably safe to assume that many more such gatherings were summoned in the following centuries. We hear of great eisteddfodau at Caerwys in 1523 and 1568, when participants competed for beautiful miniature prizes of silver – a tongue for singers, a crwth or bowed lyre for fiddlers, a harp for harpists, and a chair for poets.

But Welsh language and culture were in serious decline by then, swamped under the inexorable tide of Norman and Saxon influence. A decree by Elizabeth I, obliging bards to hold a licence for which they had to pass an examination, may or may not have been intended to maintain standards, but by

the 18th century the long years of devaluation and political absorption into the main British union had rendered Welsh culture a shadow of itself.

Then in 1789 an eisteddfod held in Corwen – the first one open to the general public – reawakened interest, and in 1792 a gorsedd, or assembly of Welsh bards, at Primrose Hill in London added weight to the idea of a nascent Welsh cultural revival, partly as a reaction against Methodism's dead hand of disapproval. The advent of the Romantic movement and of political radicalism in the early 19th century helped things along, and after the success of what was billed as a 'Great Llangollen Eisteddfod' of poems, essays and music in 1858, the revival got on to a more formal footing with the establishment of a National Eisteddfod Council as an organising body. A pioneering National Eisteddfod followed in 1860; held in Denbigh, it was a great success, the first in a succession of annual eisteddfodau that continues to this day.

Traditions upheld

Nowadays the National Eisteddfod of Wales is Welsh culture's flagship festival, held in the first week of August in venues that alternate between north and south Wales. This is the largest festival of competitive music and poetry in Europe, held entirely in the Welsh language, with several thousand entrants and up to 150,000 spectators. New members of the Gorsedd of Welsh Bards are inducted by the Archdruid in a purpose-built stone circle at the Eisteddfod ground, and the sight of a procession of bards in robes of green or white forms a remarkable link with the past. Eisteddfod is not just for grey-beards; the Eisteddfod yr Urdd, or youth eisteddfod, has proved a great draw for young poets, dancers, musicians and actors.

The tradition of eisteddfod has branched out far beyond the confines of the National Eisteddfod and the Gorsedd. Nowadays there are smaller, less formally structured eisteddfodau all across Wales. And then there is the International Eisteddfod, held every July in the superb setting of the Dee Valley at Llangollen in North Wales. This gathering has grown apace since its inauguration just after the Second World War as a means of bringing the nations together for peaceful celebration. Participants from all over the world come to the little Welsh town to show off their national costumes, their dances and songs. There are children's parties, processions, street theatre and rock concerts, all in a party atmosphere. Only purists of a very stern stamp would fail to succumb to this demonstration of the modern spirit of eisteddfod, inclusive, international and joyous.

The Gorsedd of bards at the National Eisteddfod of Wales.
NEWPORT, GWENT

SOUTH WALES

Ceremonies commemorating saints and their miraculous deeds, stories of legendary characters exhibiting wildly eccentric behaviour, whispers of fairy curses – these are the beating heart of Welsh folklore.

❶ St David's, Pembrokeshire

This small cathedral city is situated in Glyn Rhosyn, the vale of roses. A legend about Glyn Rhosyn tells that 30 years before David was born, St Patrick came to settle. But an angel sent him on to Ireland, since the place was already reserved for David.

When David and his followers first arrived, the area was terrorised by an Irish brigand, Boia, whose shrewish wife urged him to drive out the monks. But David tamed the wild Irishman, and even, according to some accounts, converted him to Christianity. Enraged by her husband's lack of fire, Boia's wife sent her maidservants naked to the monastery, in order to tempt the monks to break their vows of chastity. But David's self-control never wavered, and by his example he made it easy for the monks to disregard the girls.

▶ *16 miles NW of Haverfordwest on A487.*

❷ Roch (Y Garn), Pembrokeshire

Roch Castle occupies a solitary position on the summit of a rocky outcrop. It was built in the 13th century by the Lord of Roch. A witch had foretold that his death would be caused in a certain year by a viper, so the lord retreated to the top of the castle, never venturing out. On the last day of the year, a basket of firewood was brought up to him and a snake concealed among the logs bit him. He was found the next morning, lying dead in front of his hearth.

▶ *6 miles NW of Haverfordwest on A487.*

❸ Newton Cross, Pembrokeshire

Half a mile outside the village, standing in a circular churchyard, 19th-century St Edren's church occupies an ancient religious site. Inside is an old stone slab carved with a cross and the Greek letters alpha and omega, the beginning and end. In the churchyard, a dried-up holy well testifies to the site's mystic origins. When the water was flowing, it was said to restore those afflicted by madness to good health, but once it became polluted, those powers magically infused the surrounding grass. Legend has it that eating a grass sandwich from St Edren's is a cure for rabies.

▶ *9 miles NW of Haverfordwest on B4330.*

❹ Goodwick, Pembrokeshire

One of Pembrokeshire's best-known storytellers, Shemi Wad (or James Wade) is buried in Pencaer. Even though he died towards the end of the 19th century, many of his 'white lie' tales are remembered to this day. On one occasion, he said, a great carrion crow swooped down out of the sky while he was fishing and grabbed him in its beak. It carried him to Ireland and dropped him in a cannon, where he spent the night. Just as he was waking up next morning, the cannon was fired, and he was rocketed across St George's Channel to land unharmed right next to his fishing rod on the shore at Goodwick.

▶ *1 mile NW of Fishguard.*

❺ Fishguard, Pembrokeshire

The last foreign invasion of British soil took place on February 22, 1797, when a French expeditionary force landed at Strumble Head near Fishguard. The commanding officer, an American named Tate, had hopes of starting a peasants' rebellion against local landowners, but his troops, who were mostly ex-convicts, stole drink from the inns and began to loot nearby farms. The tiny contingent of local militia and volunteers were powerless to stop them, and the invaders set up headquarters near Goodwick.

Two days later, Lord Cawdor advanced on them with the Castlemartin Yeomanry. According to local tradition, several women of the district, led by Jemima Nicholas, dressed in red cloaks boldly marched towards the drunken French soldiers, who fled in terror, mistaking them for the British army. The French retreated to the beach below Goodwick and surrendered on February 24. On the invasion's centenary, an inscribed stone was erected at Carregwastad Point to mark the spot where the French first landed.

The sequence of events is commemorated in the Last Invasion Tapestry, 30m (100ft) long and 50cm (20in) deep, which was sewn in 1997 and is displayed in the town hall. Jemima Nicholas, who became famous as 'the General of the Red Army', died in 1832 and is buried at the Church of St Mary in Fishguard.

▶ *15 miles N of Haverfordwest at junction of A40 and A487.*

6 Preseli Hills

Bedd Arthur, or Arthur's grave, crowns the Preseli Ridge, the high point of the open uplands in the Pembrokeshire Coast National Park. The grave is a prehistoric ditch and bank, dotted with 13 standing stones, and is one of many supposed burial places of the mythical king. Close by, and visible from the monument, is Carn Menyn, or Butter Rock, an outcrop identified by geologists as the source of the bluestones of the inner horseshoe of Stonehenge. The area bears the traces of ancient quarrying, although the question of why stone from the Welsh hilltop was transported more than 250 miles to the southern English plain remains unanswered. Many springs in the Preseli area were believed to have healing properties in historical times, and it has been suggested that the area was seen as a healing sanctuary by the prehistoric population. If so, the stones themselves may have been thought to hold special powers.

In 2005, Robyn Lewis, Archdruid of the Welsh Gorsedd of Bards, wrote to the *Daily Telegraph* requesting the bluestones be returned to Wales.

▶ *Approx 10 miles E of Fishguard. A487 runs along N edge and A478 along E edge. B4329 runs through the hills.*

BLUESTONES WERE MINED HERE AND CARRIED TO STONEHENGE
PRESELI HILLS

❼ Cwm Gwaun, Pembrokeshire

Before the Gregorian calendar was adopted in Britain, in 1752, the New Year began on what is now January 12. The people of Cwm Gwaun still celebrate the old New Year's Day, Hen Galan, on that date. In the morning, children go out to collect the traditional 'calennig', meaning a New Year's gift, and later, a 'noson lawen', or merry evening, is held in several of the farmhouses and in the local hostelry, The Dyffryn Arms, where homemade food and beer are served in a convivial atmosphere of singing and storytelling.

▶ *4 miles SE of Fishguard, just off B4313.*

❽ St Dogmaels, Pembrokeshire

At Netpool on the River Teifi, the Abbot of St Dogmaels used to bless the fishing fleet before it set out, praying for an abundant catch. The stone of blessing, Carreg y Fendith, was rediscovered in the 1960s and the custom revived, but it lapsed again after a poor season. The lack of success was blamed on the presence of too many clergymen at the service, which was said later to have been ill-omened. Since then, however, the tradition has been re-established and the annual river blessing takes place at Netpool in the summer. The stone is still to be seen, just below the Teifi Inn.

▶ *2 miles W of Cardigan on B4546.*

❾ Nevern, Pembrokeshire

In St Brynach's churchyard stands a tall, intricately carved 10th-century stone cross. Every year on April 7, St Brynach's day, a cuckoo is said to land on the cross, singing to announce the arrival of spring. Villagers used to gather nearby to await the annual event.

Also in the churchyard stands the bleeding yew, one of an avenue of ancient yew trees. Blood-like resin drips from its twisted, damaged trunk. A wrongly convicted monk is said to have been hung from the tree, and with his dying breath, he prophesied it would bleed ever after to prove his innocence.

▶ *10 miles E of Fishguard, just N of A487.*

❿ Tenby, Pembrokeshire

On New Year's Day, the children of Tenby sprinkle passers-by with fresh raindrops from twigs of box or holly. This custom probably dates back to a pre-Christian purification rite, but by the Middle Ages the practice was associated with the Virgin. It is still considered lucky to be sprinkled, and the children are rewarded with money.

Another ancient custom still followed in Tenby occurs on July 31 when St Margaret's Fair is opened by the mayor and council walking in procession round the town walls.

▶ *30 miles SW of Carmarthen.*

PENNARD CASTLE, OVERRUN BY SAND
PENMAEN, SWANSEA

⑪ Ystradffin, Carmarthenshire

A cave about a mile west of Ystradffin was reputedly the hideout of Twm Sion Cati, or Thomas Jones, whom legend transformed from a 16th-century landowner and antiquary into a notorious outlaw and trickster. In some of the stories that are told about him, he is a man to be feared, but in others he is the Welsh equivalent of Robin Hood – a popular hero who robbed from the rich and gave to the poor.

One story tells how Twm, angered by the wickedness and cruelty of a fellow highwayman, decided to teach him a lesson. He disguised himself as a poor farmer and rode a tired old nag, its saddlebags full of shells, to a place where he knew his rival lay in ambush. Sure enough, the wicked highwayman sprang from the bushes and held him at gunpoint. Twm pretended to be terrified but instead of meekly handing over his saddlebags, he threw them over a hedge. As the highwayman scrambled after them, Twm leapt from his own horse on to the highwayman's beautiful mare, whose saddlebags were already packed with stolen money, and galloped away.

Twm is thought to have gone to Geneva in 1557 and returned two years later when he received a royal pardon for all his past crimes. In his seventies, he allegedly became Sheriff of Carmarthenshire, having married the widow of the previous incumbent.

▶ *On minor road 9 miles N of Llandovery.*

⑫ Penmaen, Swansea

Among the sand dunes of the Gower Peninsula lie the ruins of Pennard Castle, which was once the fortress of chieftain Rhys ap Iestyn. According to legend, a prince of North Wales gave Rhys his daughter in marriage as a reward for his valour in battle. On the wedding night, as the sentries outside Pennard's walls listened to the revels, they became aware that, close by, they could hear the strains of unearthly music. In the moonlight, the soldiers saw a host of fairies dancing on the grass near the gatehouse. A sentry ran to tell Lord Rhys, who, now drunk, ordered his men to drive the little folk away.

His new wife was aghast, and warned him that terrible misfortune would befall everyone if such a thing were done. Her lord told her arrogantly that he feared no one of this world or any other and, followed by the bravest of his men, went out to battle with the fairies. But the little people faded before them, and not one of them was touched. Suddenly, a warning voice rang out: 'Thou hast wantonly spoilt our innocent sport, proud chief. Thy lofty castle and town shall be no more.' And at once, a terrible sandstorm blew up, burying the castle, the town and all its inhabitants.

The basis of the legend is that during its 300 year occupation, Pennard Castle's only battle was with the encroaching sand dunes. They finally destroyed it in the 16th century.

▶ *9 miles W of Swansea on A4118.*

⑬ Llandeilo, Carmarthenshire

At one time, people who suffered from whooping cough or consumption used to visit this spot near Maenclochog to drink the waters of St Teilo's Well. For a cure to be effective, the water had to be drunk from St Teilo's skull, which had to be handed to the patient by the heir to Llandeilo farm. The skull disappeared in 1927. When Teilo died in the 6th century, his body was claimed by three churches: Penalun, where he was born; Llandeilo, where he died; and Llandaf, where he was bishop. Unable to decide which one should have it, the monks prayed all night, and in the morning, miraculously, there were three saintly bodies, one for each church.
▶ *15 miles E of Carmarthen on A40.*

⑭ Gorslas, Carmarthenshire

The 63 ha (158 acre) Llyn Llech Owain Country Park is to be found on the slopes of Mynydd Mawr, a mountain that lies a mile north of Gorslas. Nature trails snake around a beautiful lake, the origins of which are the subject of legend. Long ago, a well on Mynydd Mawr was tended by a man called Owain. One day, after watering his horse, he forgot to replace the huge stone slab with which the well was always kept covered, and a torrent of water poured down the mountain. It would have drowned the whole area had Owain not galloped around it, using magic to check the flood. The lake that was created became known as Llyn Llech Owain, the lake of Owain's stone slab.
▶ *1 mile N of junction of A48 and A476 at Cross Hands.*

⑮ Llanwonno, Rhondda Cynon Taf

In St Gwynno's churchyard, in the tiny settlement of Llanwonno, a headstone marks the last resting place of Griffith Morgan (1700-37), better known as Guto Nyth Bran, who was, in his day, the greatest runner in Wales. Legend has it that he paced himself against hares and slept in a dunghill to strengthen his legs. He would run for prize money but when the number of his challengers dwindled, he gave up racing. Some years later, he was persuaded to race again over a distance of 12 miles for a prize of 1,000 guineas. Guto won in 53 minutes, but when an admirer slapped him on the back in congratulation, he suffered a fatal heart attack. Now, every New Year's Eve, the Nos Galen races are held in his memory – people come from far and wide to race through the local streets, finishing at a bronze statue of the legendary runner in the nearby village of Mountain Ash.
▶ *On minor roads 5 miles NW of Pontypridd.*

ST FAGAN'S NATIONAL HISTORY MUSEUM

ALSO KNOWN AS THE WELSH FOLK MUSEUM and the Museum of Welsh Life, this treasury of Welsh folklore, custom and tradition is located in the grounds of St Fagan's Castle, just outside Cardiff. The land and castle – in reality a late 16th-century manor house – were given to the Welsh nation by the Earl of Plymouth in 1946, and the open-air museum has become one of the largest in Europe. The aim is to preserve as many aspects of Welsh rural and industrial life as possible. More than 40 buildings, which range from a tollgate house to a tannery and include the medieval church of St Teilo as well as a Workmen's Institute, have been moved stone by stone from their original sites. Craftsmen, such as weavers, basket makers and coopers, demonstrate their skills, using centuries-old techniques, and there is a small working farm that specialises in preserving native breeds of livestock.

The exhibits in the folklore section of the museum are a vivid reminder of an age not long past when few people thought to question the reality of magic and the supernatural. For instance, the widespread pagan custom of 'Hunting the Wren' – the bird was supposed to embody the evils of winter – persisted in Wales until at least the end of the 19th century. The hunting took place around Twelfth Night and when a bird was captured, it was placed in a carved, be-ribboned cage, known as a wrenhouse. The one in the museum is from Marloes in Pembrokeshire. Four men carried it around the town, singing of the hunt and their willingness to sell the wren in order to buy beer. The singers were greeted at every house, and given money or a drink.

Another relic of past culture to be seen at St Fagan's is a piece of wood with the letters W.N. – or Welsh Not – carved into it. In the late 19th century, the native traditions of Wales were held to be so valueless that children speaking Welsh in school were punished and humiliated by having a Welsh Not hung around their necks. Today, the situation is very different, and Welsh is taught as a first language in schools.

⓰ Llantrisant, Rhondda Cynon Taf

Llantrisant is the home town of Dr William Price (1800–93) whose eccentricities and wild behaviour became famous far beyond his native country. Generally, he wore a fox skin on his head, and he often conducted ancient Druidic ceremonies at the Rocking Stone on Pontypridd Common. But his greatest claim to fame is as a pioneer of cremation. His teenaged housekeeper gave birth to their child in 1883, but when the infant, a son, named Jesus Christ, died the following year, Price burnt the body on a bonfire in the fields near his home with due Druidic ritual, but no Christian ceremony. This aroused considerable local opposition, and Price was arrested and tried in Cardiff. He won his case and, after this incident, cremation became legal – the cremation act finally being passed in 1902.

The people of Llantrisant are still sometimes called 'The Black Army'. This is because some of the men fought for the Black Prince at Crécy during his French campaign of 1346 and were ridiculed by other Welshmen for fighting for the English.

▶ *10 miles E of Bridgend close to junction of A473 and A4119.*

⓱ Pencoed, Bridgend

A Christmas season horse ceremony, known as Mari Lwyd, the grey mare or grey Mary, combined with the ancient custom of wassailing, was once widespread throughout Wales. Today, the tradition still survives in Pencoed and other parts of South Wales. It is believed that this ceremony, which bears a strong resemblance to English mumming rituals, stems from pagan rites to welcome the return of the sun after the winter solstice. In medieval times, it became associated with the wassail tradition and may have been adopted by the Church to commemorate the purification of the Virgin Mary. Many of the characters taking part are similar to those found in medieval miracle plays.

The Mari Lwyd is a decorated horse's skull, carried on a pole by a man draped in a white sheet. He is led by a party of people, which, in some districts, used to include a Leader, Sergeant, Corporal and Merryman. They select a house and stand outside, singing a verse. The people inside the house reply with a verse of their own and this carries on until the ritual is completed. The Mari Lwyd is then allowed into the house, and the whole party is given food and drink, before moving on.

▶ *5 miles E of Bridgend just N of Junction 35 of M4.*

⓲ Penmark, Vale of Glamorgan

The name of the village is an Anglicised version of Pen March, which means 'horse's head'. In King Arthur's time a prince of North Wales owned a strong and very swift horse, which was used to carry messages to the king's court in Somerset. One day, the horse was galloping so fast that it slipped at a place now called Cefn March, the horse's ridge, near Gilfachrheda in Ceredigion. In falling, the horse was decapitated and its head carried on, coming to rest at a place that became known as Pen March.

▶ *10 miles SW of Cardiff at end of A4226.*

⓳ Penarth, Vale of Glamorgan

It was once the tradition at Hancock's brewery for cooper apprentices, when they had completed their five years of training, to undergo a centuries-old initiation ceremony. Each new cooper had to make a 54 gallon hogshead cask. He was then put inside it, covered with soot, wood shavings, beer and water, and the cask was rolled over three times on the ground, after which the apprentice was hauled out and tossed in the air three times. Now wooden barrels have been replaced by metal casks, and no initiation has been performed since 1962.

▶ *4 miles S of Cardiff.*

⓴ Risca (Rhisga), Caerphilly

Twmbarlwm Hill, near the village of Risca, is the site of a Celtic fortress. It is said that the Druids held their courts of justice on the hill, and that the bodies of those found guilty of serious crimes were thrown into the valley below. The name of the place, Dyffryn y Gladdfa, means 'valley of the graves'.

▶ *On B4591, 4 miles NW of Junction 27 of M4.*

㉑ Kilgwrrwg, Monmouthshire

The isolated church of Holy Cross stands in a circular churchyard on a rise in the middle of a field, half a mile or more from the nearest road. According to a local tale, the location was chosen by tying two cows together and building the church where they first lay down to rest. In Celtic times, burial sites were usually circular, so the place may have been a site of pre-Christian religious activity. Richard Morgan is buried here, thought to be the last British serviceman to be killed in the First World War.

▶ *5 miles NW of Chepstow on minor road off B4293.*

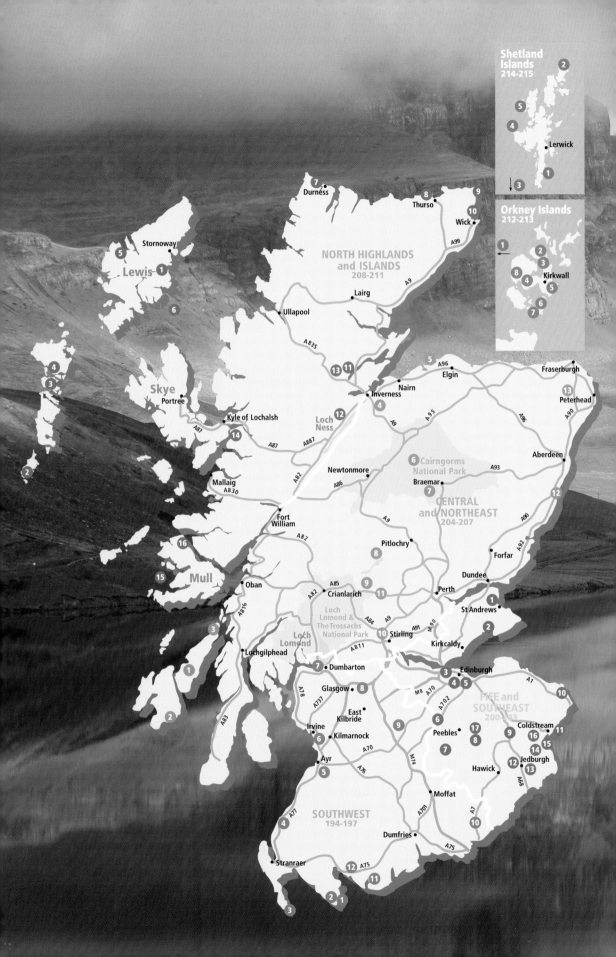

Shetland
Islands
214-215

Orkney Islands
212-213

Lerwick

Kirkwall

Stornoway

Lewis

Skye

Portree

Kyle of Lochalsh

Mallaig

Fort
William

Oban

Lochgilphead

Mull

Durness

Thurso

Wick

NORTH HIGHLANDS
and ISLANDS
208-211

Lairg

Ullapool

Elgin

Fraserburgh

Peterhead

Nairn

Inverness

Loch
Ness

Newtonmore

Aberdeen

Cairngorms
National Park

Braemar

CENTRAL
and NORTHEAST
204-207

Pitlochry

Forfar

Dundee

Perth

St Andrews

Crianlarich

Loch
Lomond &
The Trossachs
National Park

Loch
Lomond

Stirling

Kirkcaldy

Dumbarton

Edinburgh

Glasgow

FIFE and
SOUTHEAST
200-203

East
Kilbride

Coldstream

Irvine

Peebles

Kilmarnock

Hawick

Jedburgh

Ayr

Moffat

SOUTHWEST
194-197

Dumfries

Stranraer

Scotland

Vanishing islands, walking stones, votive cairns
and medieval monsters vie with legends of
kings and conquerors in Scotland's folklore.
As the northern nights grow long,
the Scots take to the streets
with passion and fire.

KEY

1 Main entry

━━ County boundary

Motorway

Principal A road

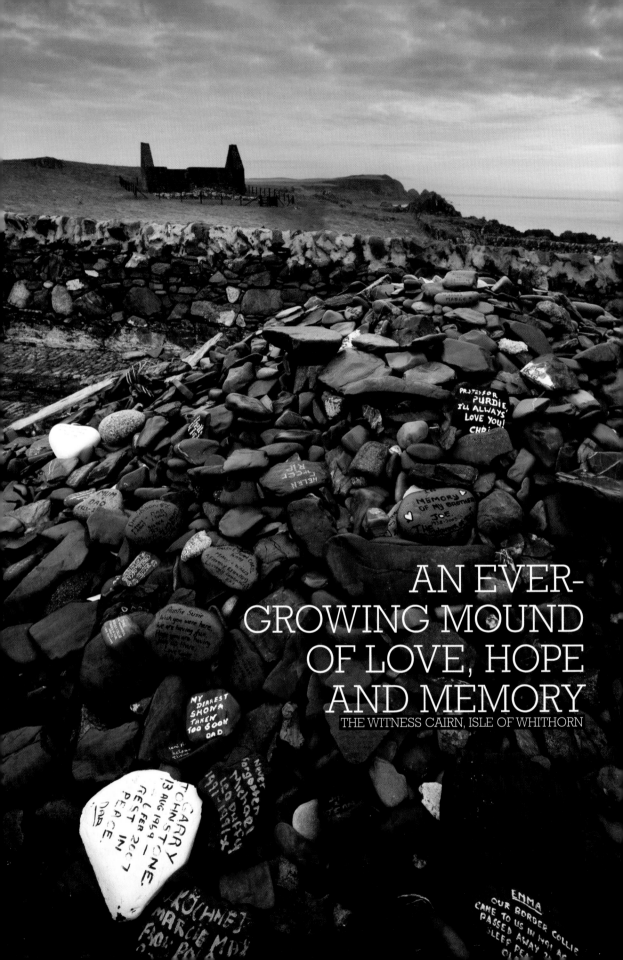

AN EVER-GROWING MOUND OF LOVE, HOPE AND MEMORY

THE WITNESS CAIRN, ISLE OF WHITHORN

SOUTHWEST SCOTLAND

Love and faith are prominent in tales of southern Scotland, and although happy endings tend not to feature, old customs are still enthusiastically observed in modern-day fairs and annual rituals.

❶ Isle of Whithorn, Dumfries & Galloway

On the shore of the Isle of Whithorn, near the site of the old lifeboat house and within view of the 2nd-century roofless chapel of St Ninian, lies a heap of sea pebbles created by visitors. Each one is marked with a message for the saint. These modern prayers, wishes and mementoes for the departed make up the Witness Cairn, an ever-growing mound of love, hope and memory begun in 1997 to celebrate 'The Year of Celtic Saints'.

▶ *20 miles S of Newton Stewart at junction of B7004 and B7052.*

❷ Glasserton, Dumfries & Galloway

Small carved crosses pepper the rocks at the entrance to St Ninian's Cave, a coastal cavern and retreat of the 1st-century Irish saint, who built the first Christian church in Scotland in AD 397. The church was known as the Candida Casa, or white house, and gave the nearby town of Whithorn its name. Stone cross sculptures on loose stones and boulders discovered at the site are now in Whithorn's Priory Museum. In the Middle Ages, Christian pilgrims journeyed to the cave with offerings; today it is still the destination of an annual pilgrimage on the last Sunday in August. Visitors leave wooden crosses, beach pebbles marked with a cross and coins in rock crevices.

▶ *2 miles SW of Whithorn on A747. St Ninian's Cave is 2 miles S of the village: car park at Kidsdale then footpath down Physgill Glen to beach.*

❸ Mull of Galloway, Dumfries & Galloway

According to legend the last Picts lived in the Mull of Galloway, where they jealously guarded the secret of heather ale, passing the recipe down from father to son. War with the Scots reduced the Picts to just two, and the Scots' king tried to prise the recipe from them, under threat of torture. The father agreed, but insisted the king first kill the son, in case the boy gave in. Then he hurled himself from cliffs to his death, and the secret of heather ale died with him.

▶ *20 miles S of Stranraer via A716.*

❹ Ballantrae, South Ayrshire

In the early 16th century, during the reign of James I, people living in the country around Ballantrae were deeply perturbed by the disappearance of merchants and wayfarers. Several innkeepers had been accused, and even hanged, but the disappearances continued. Then one evening, as a farmer and his wife came home from market, they were attacked by a host of tattered, blood-smeared ghouls, who cut the woman's throat and drank her blood. The farmer managed to escape. Word was sent to the king (then James VI of Scotland), who sent soldiers and bloodhounds, and the terrible band was tracked down to a cave by the seashore. In its depths were found smoked and pickled human limbs, and a vast quantity of treasure. The cave's inhabitants, members of a single family led by a man called Alexander 'Sawney' Bean, were bound and brought before the king. For years they had lived by highway robbery and cannibalism; a trial seemed superfluous for such heinous crimes, so the women were burnt while the men had their hands and feet cut off, and bled to death. So, according to legend, lived and died the tribe of Sawney Bean. Whether there is the smallest grain of truth in this gruesome tale, or whether it is a fiction devised by 18th-century sensation seekers to generate sales of their chapbooks, no one knows.

▶ *18 miles N of Stranraer on A77.*

❺ Dalrymple, East Ayrshire

Near Dalrymple stands the privately owned Cassillis House. Local tradition claims that the heroine of the ballad 'The Gipsy Laddie' was the wife of a 17th-century Earl of Cassillis. When Johnnie Faa and six other gypsies arrived at the castle gate, they sang so sweetly that Lady Cassillis came out to listen to them and, entranced by their music, followed them into the forest. Her distraught husband searched desperately for her, until at last he found his wife and her new companions by a stream. He begged her to return home, but she told him she had finished with the fine life and desired only to live as a gipsy girl with Johnnie Faa. Her husband's answer was to arrest the gypsies, and hang them all.

▶ *5 miles S of Ayr at junction of B7034 and B742.*

SCOTLAND

❻ Irvine, North Ayrshire

The town's colourful Marymass Fair, held each August, dates from the 12th century. The name of the fair links it to the parish church, which was dedicated to the Virgin Mary, but ever since Mary, Queen of Scots visited Irvine in 1563 the Marymass Queen has always been dressed to represent Mary Stuart. A feature of the fair is the amateur horse-racing, put on by the Irvine Carters' Society, which includes an unusual race for carthorses. The races may have been started before the fair and, if so, this must be one of the oldest race meetings in Europe.

In the River Irvine, a boulder known as the Grannie Stane, can be seen at low water. This may be the last survivor of a stone circle, saved by popular protest when others were removed during construction of the weir in 1895. Legend suggests that some stones were removed much earlier and used as stepping stones at Puddleford, so that monks from a Carmelite priory that once stood here could cross the river to reach the church. Another tale attached to Puddleford is that it was the site of a skirmish between William Wallace and the English.
▶ *12 miles N of Ayr.*

❼ Dumbarton, West Dunbartonshire

Some legends claim that St Patrick was born near Glasgow, and his ministry flourished there. But St Patrick's great piety so offended the Devil that he ordered every witch in Scotland to rise up against the saint. This macabre army pursued the unfortunate holy man until he came to the banks of the Clyde where he found a boat and hastily set off for Ireland. Witches cannot cross running water, so his frustrated pursuers tore a huge rock from a nearby hill and hurled it at the retreating saint. Their aim was poor and the huge boulder fell short to become the rock on which Dumbarton Castle was built.
▶ *14 miles NW of Glasgow just off A82.*

❽ Glasgow

Once considered the jewel of western Scotland, Glasgow's name is derived from the Celtic 'glas ghu', meaning 'dear green place'. Many ancient legends of this bustling modern city are centred on its 6th-century patron saint, the gentle and kindly Kentigern. In his youth, Kentigern was cared for by St Serf, who renamed him Mungo, meaning 'dear friend'.

Unfortunately, St Serf's other disciples were jealous of the favour shown to Mungo, and did their utmost to make trouble for him. Once, a robin belonging to St Serf was accidentally killed, and the other boys blamed Mungo. But Mungo took the bird in his hands and prayed over it, whereupon it was restored to life.

In about AD 550 Mungo finished his training and travelled to the house of a holy man named Fergus, at Kernach. Fergus had been told that he would not die until he met someone who would convert the whole district to Christianity. Soon after Mungo greeted him, Fergus fell dead. Mungo placed the body on a cart drawn by two wild bulls, and ordered them to go to the place ordained by God. They stopped at Cathures, and here Mungo buried Fergus and founded the church that later would become Glasgow Cathedral.
▶ *M74 from SE, M8 from E and W, M77 from SW.*

❾ Lanark, South Lanarkshire

Every March 1 at 6 pm, the children of Lanark gather in St Nicholas's churchyard and when a bell rings, race around the church three times, in an anti-clockwise direction, waving a ball of paper tied with string above their heads. Afterwards, they scramble for coins thrown for them by local dignitaries. This is Whuppity Scoorie day, the origins of which are unknown. It may have originated in a pagan rite of spring, or have been some sort of a penance.
▶ *25 miles SE of Glasgow.*

❿ Langholm, Dumfries & Galloway

Since the 1700s, when Langholm was awarded rights to common land, the town has staged a Common Riding to mark out its boundaries. Now Langholm's fair and Common Riding take place on the last Friday in July. The Cryer proclaims the town's rights to the common land and the Cornet, or master of riding, spurs his horse up a steep hill, followed by attendant riders. Once at the top, they follow a centuries-old route to inspect the boundaries while processions march through the town behind recognised symbols – a spade, a wooden fish nailed to a wooden bannock (large scone), a crown made of plaited roses, and a huge thistle made up of scores of real thistles. Eventually, the Cornet and his party return to the square for a second proclamation by the Cryer:

'So now I will conclude and say nae mair,
And if ye're pleased, I'll cry the Langholm Fair.'
▶ *On A7, 20 miles N of Carlisle.*

BILLY MARSHALL'S HEADSTONE, KIRKCUDBRIGHT

⓫ Kirkcudbright, Dumfries & Galloway

Billy Marshall, king of the tinker-gypsies of Galloway, is buried in Kirkcudbright church, where his monument still stands. He died in 1792, claiming to be 120 years old. Seven times lawfully married, he fathered four illegitimate children after his hundredth year. Sir Walter Scott's character Meg Merrilees, from *Guy Mannering or The Astrologer*, published in 1815 is probably modelled on Flora Marshall, one of Billy's wives. Billy commanded a tinker army of cavalry and infantry, which was defeated by tinkers from Argyll in a battle at Newtown of Ayr in 1712.

According to author Dorothy L. Sayers, 'In Kirkcudbright one either fishes or paints,' for by the early 20th century, the town had become a magnet for distinguished artists of the day, either as residents or summer visitors. Kirkcudbright is still known as 'Artists' Town'.

▶ *At junction of A762, A711 and A755, 10 miles SW of Castle Douglas.*

⓬ Anwoth, Dumfries & Galloway

Near the village of Anwoth stand the ruins of Cardoness Castle, a 15th-century tower house built by the McCullochs. The property came into the family by marriage and the story goes that the previous castle was so expensive to maintain that it impoverished three successive lairds. A fourth had to roof the building with heather, which he collected on Glenquicken Moor, some 4 miles away, and carried home on his back. Once that was done, the laird's luck began to improve. Other lairds swore fealty to him, and many reivers (cattle rustlers) and broken men (outlaws) took service with him. Just one thing spoilt the laird's happiness – he had nine daughters, but no son. His luck held, however, and his tenth child was a boy. The celebrations that followed were the grandest that had ever been held in Cardoness Castle.

The laird decided that the time had now come for his eldest daughter to marry his closest friend, Graeme the Outlaw, and after the marriage, the celebrations continued unabated. After a week, the laird suggested that the party should end with a feast on the nearby Black Loch, which was frozen over at the time. All his followers and friends were invited, but since the day appointed for the feast was a Sabbath, none of them came. Undaunted, the laird, his family and servants went out on the loch, and after some hours of sport, sat down to eat and drink. At that moment, there came a crack like a gunshot. The ice gave way, and laird, family, servants and all, disappeared into the depths of the loch. One tale says that none of the family was ever seen again. In another, the youngest daughter survived, and later married a McCulloch. The castle is now in the care of Historic Scotland.

▶ *1 mile W of Gatehouse of Fleet, just off A75.*

SCOTLAND

197

The fires of midwinter

In northern parts, parading with flaming torches and lighting bonfires remains a spectacular way to welcome the new year.

The bushy-bearded Vikings who roar through the streets of Lerwick once a year look as if they have come to plunder and pillage the capital town of the Shetland Isles. Swords gleam, metal link armour shines and jingles, and the dragons inlaid on the round shields seem fierce enough to spring to life. It's all show and sham, though. These guizers, or mummers, are members of the Jarl Squad, right-hand men to the Guizer Jarl himself – a Shetland-born man chosen to play the part of a Viking warlord and the Lord of Misrule on the last Tuesday in January, the most important of all days in the Shetland calendar. This is when the annual midwinter fire ceremony of Up Helly Aa is held.

The Guizer Squad, and many other groups around Lerwick, will parade and drink the short winter day away. At nightfall, in a huge torchlight procession, they will drag a full-sized replica Norse longship, built with loving care over the previous year, to the burning site. There they will hurl the burning torches into her hull, and watch her burn to ashes. Then it's back to dancing, mumming and partying.

The closer to the Arctic Circle, the longer the winter nights and the shorter the days. In Lerwick in the middle of winter, the sun doesn't rise till after 9am, and has set by three in the afternoon. Scandinavian countries, way up towards the frozen roof of the world, have always reveled in winter fire ceremonies. Shetland's capital is just 200 miles from Bergen in Norway – far nearer than Edinburgh. So it's hardly surprising that these northeastern isles are more Norse by tradition and history than Scottish. The Up Helly Aa ceremony itself may not be much more than a century old (it replaced a dangerous and sometimes violent ritual involving rival gangs with blazing tar barrels), but the fine, defiant chorus of the Up Helly Aa song confirms the Shetlanders' strong affinity with their neighbours just across the North Sea:

> A full-sized replica Norse longship is dragged to the burning site and flaming torches are hurled into her hull.
> UP HELLY AA FESTIVAL, LERWICK, SHETLAND ISLES

'Grand old Vikings ruled upon the ocean vast; Their brave battle-songs still thunder on the blast; Their wild war cry comes a-ringing from the past; We answer it "A-oi!" '

Blazing defiance

It is not only in Shetland that inhabitants of Britain's northern regions keep old fire rituals alive. At Burghead on the Moray Firth, not far from Inverness, the local Presbyterian church as far back as the 18th century was condemning the Hogmanay ceremony of Burning the Clavie as 'superstitious, idolatrous and sinful, an abominable heathenish practice.' Yet it survived and still continues. Every January 11, on 'Old Hogmanay', a flaming barrel, the Clavie, is carried through the town to Doorie Hill where onlookers scramble for pieces of it as it disintegrates, to take back home and ignite a new fire for good luck.

All sorts of pagan superstitions are bound up with this – the fire itself, the election of a Clavie King, the re-use year after year of the same iron nail to fix the barrel to its carrying stave (iron being a sacred mineral), the clockwise direction in which it is paraded round the town ('widdershins' or anti-clockwise being an unlucky direction), and the spreading of the gift of fire, light and heat from the central 'fire god' of the Clavie itself.

Torchlight processions

At Biggar in the Scottish Borders a giant bonfire as large as a house is assembled in the days leading up to Hogmanay. On the night, kilted pipers lead a procession of flaring torches through the streets to the bonfire, where the burning brands are thrown to set the stack alight (see page 202). In the normally neat and respectable Perthshire town of Comrie on the same night, much the same sort of ritual is played out with a parade of fiery flambeaux or burning torches, which are brought to Dalginross Bridge and hurled to fizzing extinction in the waters of the River Earn.

One of the most spectacular events takes place in the Aberdeenshire fishing port of Stonehaven. Here 'swingers' parade up and down with fireballs, large lumps of flaming combustibles on the end of a wire, circling them round their heads in a splutter of smoke and sparks for up to half an hour before sending the burning remains hissing into the sea.

These Scottish midwinter fire ceremonies may have dubious origins and contradictory conclusions, some participants dousing their fiery burdens as if quelling or purifying evil spirits, others using them to ignite more fires. But there's no doubt about what each of them represents – a bold shout in the face of General Winter.

199

FIFE AND SOUTHEAST SCOTLAND

This once-troubled region inspired Sir Walter Scott to write stirring tales of derring-do. Its turbulent history is encapsulated in flourishing traditions, and remembered with vibrant festivals and fairs.

❶ St Andrews, Fife

In the early 16th century, St Andrews castle was the home of Cardinal David Beaton, the Catholic martyr or bloody oppressor of Protestantism, according to differing points of view. In the early days of the Reformation, he ruthlessly stamped on the slightest manifestation of the Lutheran heresy and, in the process, created the earliest Protestant martyrs in Scotland. One of the first was Patrick Hamilton, a young priest who objected to the Church selling indulgences – remission of punishment for sins – and got married in defiance of Church law. He was burnt to death at St Andrews, but there was not enough wood and the rain kept putting the fire out although the logs were smeared with gunpowder. He took six hours to die, but his courage made him a popular hero. It is said that Beaton calmly watched the burning of another married priest, George Wishart, before going on to attend the wedding of his own illegitimate daughter. Two months later, in July 1546, a group of Fife Protestants broke into the castle and murdered the cardinal; afterwards, his body was suspended over the walls by an arm and a leg, so forming a St Andrew's Cross. A rhyme of the period concluded: 'For stickit is your cardinal, and salted like a sow' – apparently the conspirators pickled his body in brine during the weeks they held the castle against the forces of the government.

The town fair in St Andrew's, held every August, has a charter dating from the early Middle Ages. Originally, it was a 'feeing-fair', where farm workers met prospective employers.
▶ *12 miles S of Dundee, at junction of A91, A915 and A917.*

❷ Kirkton of Largo, Fife

The village is built on the southern slopes of a hill known as Largo Law. Volcanic in origin, it is said to have been created from a rock dropped by the Devil as he flew past. At the top is a formation known as the Devil's Chair, with seven steps leading up to it.
▶ *11 miles SW of St Andrews on A915.*

❸ Queensferry, City of Edinburgh

The festivities of the August Ferry Fair are led by the Burry Man, a curious character clad from head to toe in sticky burrs. He wanders round the streets with two attendants, collecting money for charity. In the past, after a poor fishing season, the Burry Man may have been a scapegoat, led through the town and then expelled in the hope of removing the bad luck.
▶ *At S end of Forth Road Bridge on A90, 10 miles W of Edinburgh.*

❹ Edinburgh

Each April 30, the Beltane fire festival takes place on Calton Hill, a modern interpretation of an ancient rite marking the end of spring, and the moving of cattle to summer pastures. The livestock were driven through a purifying fire to protect them from harm, and women collected embers from which they would light their own fires for the coming year.

Today's fabulously theatrical spectacle, revived in the mid 1980s, features the May Queen and the Green Man, who lights the 'Neid Fire' from a spark kept burning from the previous year. There are Blue Men, White Women and acrobatic Red Men, whose efforts to woo the White Women initially meet with failure. After the Green Man's death and rebirth, the Red Men finally succeed in persuading the women to dance.
▶ *A1 from E, M8 from W, A68 and A702 from S.*

❺ Liberton, City of Edinburgh

According to legend, the parish of Liberton is named after 'Leper Town'. This idea is probably associated with the Balm Well, the waters of which were said to cure skin diseases. The water contains drops of a black oily substance, which is produced by a coal seam at the well's source. But tradition claims that the well sprang from a drop of miraculous oil brought to St Margaret, the 11th-century Queen of Scotland, from the tomb of St Catherine of Siena on Mount Sinai.
▶ *3 miles S of city centre.*

BURRY MAN, QUEENSFERRY

⑥ Biggar, South Lanarkshire

The annual torchlight procession that winds its way through Biggar every New Year's Eve, culminating in an enormous bonfire, is believed to have originated in a Druid fire festival. So the ancient tradition of burning away the evils of the old year and ushering in a fresh start continues. The ritual was even observed during the Second World War, when rather than the usual huge conflagration, a candle was lit in a tin.
▶ *28 miles SW of Edinburgh on A702.*

⑦ Tweedsmuir, Borders

A single-track road from Tweedsmuir to Fruid Reservoir passes three ancient standing stones. The one on the right is known as the Giant's Stone. From behind it, according to legend, Jack the Giant Killer shot his last victim, but in his death throes, the giant killed the hero. Jack is said to have been buried by the Giant's Stone, and late in the 18th century, a grave was discovered there, containing a burial urn.
▶ *15 miles N of Moffat on A701.*

⑧ Traquair, Borders

The great gates of 10th-century Traquair House, one of the oldest inhabited houses in Scotland, have been closed in mourning, some say, ever since Bonnie Prince Charlie's defeat in 1746. In fact, they were closed in 1796, when the wife of the 7th Earl of Traquair died. He swore they would never be re-opened until the next countess came to take her place. But his son died without heirs, and the title is now extinct.
▶ *7 miles E of Peebles on B7062.*

⑨ Earlston, Borders

Scotland's legendary prophet and seer, Thomas the Rhymer of Ercildoun (the old form of Earlston), is reputed to have lived here some time in the 13th century. In later centuries his name became associated with witchcraft, and in 17th-century trials several witches swore they had dealings with him. The old ballad of 'Thomas the Rhymer' relates how the seer acquired his prophetic powers. He met the Queen of Elfland and, ensnared by her magic kiss, followed her to her fairy domain. There he remained, bewitched, for seven years, before returning to earth gifted with his knowledge of future events.
▶ *8 miles E of Galashiels at junction of A68 and A6105.*

⑩ Eyemouth, Borders

Eyemouth's Herring Queen festival began as a Peace Picnic, or Fisherman's Picnic, organised to mark the end of the First World War. So successful was it that the picnic became an annual summer event, a local holiday for everyone connected with the fishing industry. Since 1939, the festival has had a Queen, who is crowned in a ceremony that symbolises the life of a fishing community.
▶ *8 miles N of Berwick-upon-Tweed.*

⑪ Coldstream, Borders

The mid point of the bridge spanning the Tweed here marks the border between Scotland and England. An old toll house stands at the Scottish end of the bridge and here, as at the better-known border crossings of Gretna

GREYFRIARS BOBBY, EDINBURGH

ON THE PAVEMENT near Greyfriars churchyard stands a granite fountain, topped with a statue of a Skye terrier. This is Greyfriars Bobby, and the fountain was erected by Baroness Angelia Georgina Burdett-Coutts, President of the Ladies Committee of the RSPCA, in 1873, a year after Bobby's death. She had visited Bobby several times and commissioned the statue from William Brody, who sculpted it from life.

For some eight years, Bobby had been the constant companion of John Gray, a nightwatchman in Edinburgh, and after his master died in 1858, the little dog guarded his grave until his own death, 14 years later. Bobby became famous and crowds would

gather at the gate of the churchyard to watch him run to the local coffee house for his midday meal. When a byelaw was passed requiring all dogs to be licensed, or destroyed, the Provost bought a licence and also a collar for Bobby. The collar is now in the museum in Edinburgh, along with Brody's original sculpture. The story of the faithful dog has captured popular imagination and he has been the subject of books and films. A red granite headstone marks his grave, just inside the gate of Greyfriars church, close to John Gray's grave. The stone was erected by the Dog Aid Society of Scotland and unveiled by the Duke of Gloucester in 1981, and the inscription reads: 'Let his loyalty and devotion be a lesson to us all'.

Green and Lamberton, runaway marriages used to be celebrated. An ancient Scottish law stated that a couple who made marriage vows before independent witnesses were legally wed. Such marriages continued to be legal until 1940, but the last marriage in the Coldstream toll house took place in 1856. In that year an Act was passed making it obligatory to spend three weeks north of the border before the wedding.

▶ *15 miles SW of Berwick-upon-Tweed.*

⑫ Ancrum, Borders

In 1545 a Scottish army led by the Earl of Angus defeated 5,000 English troops at the Battle of Ancrum Moor. Local tradition asserts that one of the bravest warriors on either side was a young girl, Lilliard, who fought and died in the Scottish ranks. One story says that she took up arms in fury after seeing her lover cut down. Lilliard's Edge, part of the battlefield, is supposed to have been named after her, although in fact, it was already known as Lillyat long before the battle was fought. Lilliard's Stone, a 19th-century monument, marks her grave, replacing an earlier one that was damaged.

▶ *4 miles NW of Jedburgh just off A68.*

⑬ Jedburgh, Borders

The border town of Jedburgh has two annual festivals. Every February for more than 250 years, young men of the town have taken to the streets to play Jethart Handba'. They are divided into two teams, the Uppies and the Doonies, depending on where they live, and have to carry, or 'hail', the ball by any means possible to either the castle (the Uppies) or the Jedwater at the bottom end of town (the Doonies). The ball, about the size of a baseball, is decorated with ribbons, and legend has it that, originally, the severed head of an English soldier was used after a particularly bloody border battle.

The second annual event, the Callant's Festival, began in 1947 and also commemorates border fighting, especially the battle of Redeswire in 1575 when the arrival of the Jedburgh men ensured victory over the English. The festival starts at the end of June and lasts for two weeks. A young man is chosen each year to be the Callant, or host of the proceedings, and he leads several horse rides to various places of historical significance on the outskirts of town. The festival ends with a day of ceremonial and an all-night ball, and is followed by the annual Jedburgh Games, which were inaugurated in 1853.

▶ *On A68, 45 miles S of Edinburgh.*

⑭ Linton, Borders

Long ago, on Linton Hill, a ferocious worm terrorised the countryside. With ever-open mouth, it careered through fields, devouring cattle, sheep and people, until a local hero named Somerville stepped in. He hit on the idea of fixing a wheel daubed with a fiery mixture of pitch, resin and brimstone to the tip of his lance, and running it down the worm's throat to kill it. Somerville's deed is recorded in a carving above the door of Linton church.

▶ *7 miles SE of Kelso on B6436.*

⑮ Kirk Yetholm, Borders

Long celebrated as the headquarters of the Scottish gipsies, Kirk Yetholm is just over a mile from the English border. The last gipsy king, Charles Faa Blythe, was crowned on the village green in 1898 and reigned until his death in 1902, by which time his people had been assimilated into the population.

▶ *8 miles SE of Kelso on B6352.*

⑯ Ednam, Borders

Half a mile west of the village stands a knoll known as the Piper's Grave. In fact, it is a Pictish burial mound, which was once called Picts' Knowe. Local people believed it was a fairy hill into which a piper crept, eager to learn the tunes of the little folk. But the foolish man had entered without a protective talisman, and he was never seen again.

▶ *2 miles N of Kelso on B6461.*

⑰ Innerleithen, Borders

Long before the 18th century, when Robert Burns described the place as a famous spa, the sulphurous waters of the local well were renowned for their ability to cure eye and skin complaints. In Burns' day, the dark peaty spring was known as the Dow Well, taking its name from the Gaelic 'dubh', meaning black, but since the early 19th century it has been known as St Ronan's Well.

According to legend, St Ronan caught the Devil by the leg with his crook, ridding the town of evil, and a 'cleiking the De'il' ritual takes place each year in July, during St Ronan's Border Games, which were started in 1827. A local boy is chosen to play St Ronan, and there is a ceremony in the churchyard beside a runic cross. Following a torchlight procession to a nearby hill, an effigy of the Devil is burned on a big bonfire.

▶ *12 miles W of Galashiels on A72.*

SCOTLAND

CENTRAL AND NORTHEAST SCOTLAND

The distant past tugs persistently at the present. Ancient Celtic festivals are still celebrated with torch parades and huge bonfires, and emotive legends cling to the names of Wallace and Culloden.

❶ Jura, Argyll & Bute

The island of Jura is renowned for whisky, deer and three smooth hills known as the Paps. Two of these – Beinn an Oir, the Mountain of Gold, and Beinn Shiantaidh, the Sacred Mountain – can be clearly seen from a distance and in ancient times may have been regarded as the breasts of the Mother Goddess. One legend tells of Fair-haired Murdo of the Deer, who spent his life hunting on Beinn an Oir. His quarry, a stag, turned into a fairy, who mocked his white hair. Murdo, a good Christian, replied that God could easily make him young again, and he was instantly transformed into a young man. What happened to the fairy, the story does not say. Now the Paps form part of the challenging Jura Fell Race, held every spring. The tough, 16-mile course takes in all three Paps plus four other hills.

▶ *By car ferry from Port Askaig on Islay to Feolin Ferry on Jura.*

❷ Ardbeg, Islay, Argyll & Bute

The Gaelic name for this island is Ile, said to be derived from Ila, a Danish princess who walked there from Ireland, on stepping stones that miraculously formed in her path. She drowned while bathing, and her grave is marked by a standing stone above Knock Bay, a mile northeast of Ardbeg. According to legend, three people tried to open her enchanted grave and went mad as a result.

The local Hill of Ile is reputed to be a fairy dwelling, home of the Fairy Queen herself. The story goes that she once invited women from all over the land to her magnificent halls within the hill, and dispensed wisdom from a magic cup. Latecomers who missed the draught remained stupid. Dull-witted people are said to have been 'still on the hill when wisdom was handed out'.

3 miles E of Port Ellen which can be reached by ferry from Kennacraig.

❸ Corryvreckan whirlpool, Argyll & Bute

Between the islands of Jura and Scarba lies the treacherous Corryvreckan whirlpool – Breccan's Cauldron. According to legend, a man named Breccan died there, along with many others, some 1,500 years ago, when his entire fleet of 50 ships was sucked beneath the swirling water. Later, when his kinsman St Columba sailed past the spot, one of Breccan's ribs rose from the whirlpool to greet him.

Another tale tells how Breccan accepted a challenge to anchor his boat in the maelstrom for three days and nights in order to win the hand of a fair princess. He had three ropes with which to make the boat fast and while those made of hemp and wool stood the test, the one made of maiden's hair broke and he drowned. He was laid to rest in what is now known as King's Cave – one of a series of sea-facing caverns, which is also claimed to have sheltered Robert the Bruce in 1307.

The whirlpool is caused by the sea crashing against a huge needle of rock that rises from the seabed to within about 30m (100ft) of the surface. When wind and tides are strong, this creates a powerful natural vortex. In autumn, when at its fiercest, the churning water can allegedly be heard up to 20 miles away. This is the time when the Cailleach, literally the veiled one, the ancient hag goddess, is said to wash her plaid there, marking the transition from autumn to winter. Now daily boat trips leave from Loch Craignish to view the whirlpool and the King's Cave as well as the wildlife and many scenic glories of the area.

▶ *Boat trips from Ardfern on Loch Craignish, 25 miles S of Oban.*

❹ Culloden, Highland

Just east of Inverness is the site of the last battle fought in Scotland when, on April 16, 1746, Bonnie Prince Charlie and his clansmen were put to flight in under an hour, bringing the Jacobite rebellion to a bloody end, and sending the Young Pretender into exile. A stone cairn, erected in 1881, is a memorial to the ruthless massacre that broke up the clan structure and the highland way of life. After the Battle of Culloden, new laws reduced the power of the chiefs, and the Highland Clearances soon followed. In this eerie place no birds sing, no heather grows on the burial mounds and, unsurprisingly, it is said to be haunted. According to legend, a huge black bird, the Great Scree, occasionally appears, bringing bad luck.

▶ *The battlefield is just S of the B9006, 5 miles E of Inverness.*

JURA FROM THE BALLOCHROY STANDING STONES, KINTYRE

❺ Burghead, Moray

Before the Scottish calendar changed in 1660, January 11 was Hogmanay, and in Burghead, on the Moray Firth, an old fire festival is still observed to mark the occasion. The ceremony, known as Burning the Clavie, may go back to the Druids, and may also be related to Norse fire worship. Similar rites were once common to all northern peoples – lighting fires at midwinter was a plea for the sun to return, bringing with it the new growth of spring.

The clavie is made from a whisky barrel sawn in half and daubed in creosote. This is fixed to a salmon fisherman's pole, called a spoke, with a big nail – supposedly the same one each year. The half-barrel is filled with tar and wood shavings, set alight and carried round the streets by 11 men in turn. The last one, the King of the Clavie, carries it to an ancient stone altar at the top of Doorie hill. More fuel is heaped on, and finally the glowing embers are scattered, to be collected by onlookers. They are said to bring good luck for the year, and act as charms against evil spirits.

▶ *8 miles NW of Elgin.*

❻ Ben Macdui, Aberdeenshire

The satellite map of the Cairngorms shows the mountains and valleys in a spectacular graphic display. Peaks rise stark white against the variegated green of the surrounding landscape. In the centre is Ben Macdui, at 1,309m (4,296ft) second in height only to Ben Nevis. On the map, its mighty crags are reduced to an abstract pattern. On the ground, it is credited with a curious and persistent legend. The Grey Man of Macdui is said to lurk near a cairn and pursue unsuspecting wayfarers. Eerie presences have been sensed by climbers who make the ascent to the summit, including one account, given in 1925, of a professor from London University who ran down the mountain to escape the footsteps that he felt were pursuing him. The creature has been sighted several times since, notably in the 1990s.

▶ *12 miles SE of Aviemore.*

❼ Inverey, Aberdeenshire

One of the most swashbuckling characters on Upper Deeside was John Farquharson, known as the Black Colonel, whose flights from the law became part of the legend of the area. Once, when English troops burnt down his home, the colonel escaped, naked, with a huge leap over the River Ey. A hump-backed bridge at the spot is known still as the Bridge of the Leap.

Farther up the river, a ledge in a deep chasm, known as the Colonel's Bed, is where he is said to have hidden while on the run after the Battle of Killiecrankie, in 1689. One of the colonel's favourite tricks, when at home, was to summon his servants by firing his pistol at a shield on the wall, which rang like a bell.

▶ *5 miles W of Braemar on minor roads.*

❽ Fortingall, Perth & Kinross

Halloween is derived from the ancient festival of Samhain, held on October 31 to mark the eve of the Celtic new year. Samhain was associated with burial mounds, which were thought to be entrances to the other world. One of these was the Bronze Age barrow at Fortingall at the head of Glen Lyon, but the celebrations took place on an unusual date – November 11. A bonfire was built on the mound, which was believed to contain the bodies of plague victims, and the whole community held hands and danced round it. Youngsters held leaping competitions over the bonfire's dying embers. The festival was stopped in 1924 by a gamekeeper who said that stripping the cover from the hill to build the fire was interfering with the gamebirds that nested there.

The Celtic festival of Beltaine (May 1) was celebrated in Fortingall, too, and the bonfires may have damaged the famous ancient yew tree that still stands in the churchyard. The tree is thought to be around 5,000 years old. The main trunk has gone and the offshoots form what appears to be a grove of trees. They are enclosed by an old stone wall, and posts show the huge circumference of the tree in the 18th century, as described by naturalist Thomas Pennant. Another legend of Fortingall is that Pontius Pilate was born there in 20 BC, the son of a high-ranking officer in the Emperor Augustus's employ and a local girl.

▶ *8 miles W of Aberfeldy.*

❾ St Fillans, Perth & Kinross

At one end of this quiet village on the shore of Loch Earn, a large rock stands in the centre of a small park, just by an estate of new houses. Originally, the developer was going to bulldoze the rock out of the way but this caused such an outcry that he had to change his plans. According to ancient legend, the rock is home to a colony of fairies and the villagers said that moving it would harm the little people. In 2005, the council agreed, and the developer had to redesign the estate.

▶ *12 miles W of Crieff on A85.*

THE HORSEMAN'S WORD

A SECRET SOCIETY WITH PAGAN UNDERTONES has existed for centuries in northeast Scotland. In the days when the horse reigned supreme in agricultural life, until a young man had been initiated into the brotherhood, he was hardly regarded as a man at all. The cult was centred on Huntly in Aberdeenshire and was most active around the 1870s. It fell into decline as mechanisation took over from the horse, but interest was renewed after author Nicholas Evans revealed that the idea for his 1995 novel *The Horse Whisperer* came from the practices of the old secret society.

Then in 2008, the last man to have been initiated into the society went public in a bid to prevent knowledge of the ancient skills from dying with him.

Originally, farmhands and blacksmiths had an interest in keeping quiet about the knowledge of how to care for and get the best out of their horses, passing it on just to the next generation of horsemen, to make sure they stayed in work. The elaborate initiation, oaths and gestures of the Horseman's Word all evolved to ensure secrecy was maintained. The Word – 'two as one' – encapsulated the society's philosophy of treating the horse kindly, and controlling it through an intimate knowledge of its behaviour. For example, the horse's response to various scents was used to keep it standing still or encourage it to move forward. After his initiation, a young man would receive years of instruction in good horse management.

⑩ Stirling

The impressive Wallace monument, a tower 67m (220ft) tall, stands at Abbey Craig, overlooking the city. From this spot, in 1297, William Wallace, erstwhile outlaw, watched the advancing forces of Edward I. When they were halfway across the bridge, he led his army against them and won an overwhelming victory. After the Battle of Stirling Bridge, Wallace was nominated 'Guardian of the Kingdom of Scotland', and led the rebellion against English rule. He was captured in 1305, tried and executed. Not much is known factually about Wallace, not even where he was born – Elderslie in Renfrewshire and Ellerslie in Ayrshire both lay claim. Much of the romantic legend is based on an epic poem of uncertain accuracy, written in 1470 by Blind Harry, 'The Acts and Deeds of Sir William Wallace, Knight of Elderslie'.
▶ *Access from Junctions 9 and 10 of M9.*

⑪ Comrie, Perth & Kinross

An ancient fire ceremony to drive out evil spirits and welcome in the New Year is re-enacted every Hogmanay in this small village on the River Earn. Its roots probably lie in paganism but no one knows when the Comrie Flambeaux actually began. As the clock strikes midnight, the torches are lit – long birch poles tied with petrol-soaked rags – and paraded round the streets, these days accompanied by a pipe band and fancy-dress parades. Eventually, the flambeaux are thrown into the river.
▶ *20 miles W of Perth on A85.*

⑫ Stonehaven, Aberdeenshire

As midnight strikes on New Year's Eve, a dangerous-looking procession sets off through the streets of Stonehaven. The marchers, enthusiastically swinging balls of fire encased in wire mesh cages, are cheered on by hundreds of onlookers. When they reach the harbour, the fireballers throw their flaming offerings into the sea.
▶ *16 miles S of Aberdeen off A90.*

⑬ Old Deer, Aberdeenshire

An annual cattle and horse fair held at Aikey Brae, near Old Deer, was once the largest fair in the north of Scotland. Traders and showmen gathered to sell their wares and stock and folk came from miles around, treating it as holiday. Its origins are supposed to lie in an accident that occurred when a wandering packman, crossing the river on stepping stones, dropped his pack in the water. He spread out his goods to dry and sold it all to passersby. He promised to return the following year, others heard of his success and came along, too, and so it escalated. In the 18th century the fair went on for three days, but latterly was reduced to one.

Aikey Brae is also known for a stone circle of uncertain origin and purpose. It is thought to be about 4,000 years old. Most of the stones are of local granite but the recumbent stone and the standing stone at each of its ends are of a different, darker stone, so must have been carried there by some means.
▶ *11 miles W of Peterhead on A950.*

NORTH HIGHLANDS & ISLANDS

Heroic tales passed down in song mingle with stories of bloodshed and clan feuds, but water is the dominant force. Sprites lie in wait for the unwary while sea caves echo with the memory of past misdeeds.

❶ Loch Rèasort, Lewis, Western Isles

Long ago a herdsman on the loch shore killed a survivor from a shipwreck for the bundle he was carrying. It contained some menacing little carved images, which the killer buried, convinced they were malevolent gods. A crofter found them in 1831, and they were recognised as ancient walrus ivory chess pieces from Norway. Today, the Lewis chess set – actually thought to be the partial remains of about five sets, possibly made in Trondheim in the 12th century – is considered one of Britain's greatest treasures. The figures are kept in the Royal Museum of Scotland in Edinburgh, and the British Museum in London.

▶ *25 miles SW of Stornoway.*

❷ Barra, Western Isles

Waulking, or hand-shrinking woollen cloth, was a long and laborious process, relieved by communal songs that passed on local legends and stories. The women who sang these songs as they worked preserved the tales of heroes of long ago, and many of the songs are still remembered on the island.

St Bride, or Brigid, was much revered in the Western Isles. Local people would construct Bride's Bed out of rushes on February 1, the saint's day. The saint's spirit was then invoked to watch over the house for the rest of the year, by saying, 'Bride, come in, your bed is ready.'

▶ *Ferry from Oban and Lochboisdale, South Uist.*

❸ Benbecula, Western Isles

Somewhere on the shore, above high-water mark, a mermaid lies buried. In 1830, some women were gathering seaweed when they saw her in the sea. She easily evaded attempts to catch her, but was hurt when a boy threw stones at her. A few days later her body – 'top half like that of a child, the lower like a salmon but without scales' – was washed up. The local bailiff apparently thought her sufficiently human to order a special shroud and coffin for the burial, although a religious service was omitted.

▶ *Access by causeway from N and S Uist.*

ANCIENT CHESS PIECES WERE FOUND BURIED IN THE SAND

LOCH REASORT, LEWIS

❹ Carinish, North Uist, Western Isles

From a car park by the main road through the village, a track leads to the ruins of Teampull na Trionaid, Church of the Holy Trinity, which was originally built in the 13th century. This is also the site of the Battle of Carinish, fought in 1601 by the MacDonalds, who lived on the island, and a marauding band of MacLeods from Harris, to the north. A feud had started when a MacDonald slighted his wife, who happened to be the sister of a MacLeod. The MacDonalds were victorious in the battle and the deeply scarred skull of a slaughtered MacLeod was kept in the church for years afterwards. The ferocity of the battle is still remembered in the name of part of the battlefield – the ditch of blood.
▶ *10 miles SW of Lochmaddy.*

❺ Callanish, Lewis, Western Isles

The magnificent megalithic monument at Callanish is set on a ridge overlooking Loch Roag. It comprises a circle 11m (37ft) in diameter with radiating stones – including an avenue – forming the shape of a cross. A central tomb that was found to contain human bones is believed to be a later addition, and the monument itself was probably built in several phases, beginning in the Bronze Age around 2200 BC. Near the main monument are two other smaller circles.

The stones at Callanish have variously been linked to Druids, said to be responsible for creating the monoliths (Fir Cherig, or False Men) by turning men to stone, and to priests clad in feathers and bird skins, who were supposed to have brought the stones to the island and had them erected by 'black men'. British archaeologist Aubrey Burl suggests that these 'black men' were dark-haired Irishmen who had travelled from the south. A more recent belief is that any marriage consummated at Callanish would be a very happy one. Scottish Engineer and antiquarian Alexander Thom (1894-1985) believed the monument to be a lunar calendar, and long into the 20th century locals made regular visits to the stones, on the grounds that it would be wrong to 'neglect' them.
▶ *On A858, 15 miles W of Stornoway.*

❻ The Shiant Isles, Western Isles

The Shiant or 'Charmed' Isles lie in the Minch, the channel that divides the Western Isles from the Isle of Skye and the mainland. They are surrounded by turbulent seas churned by storm kelpies known as the Blue Men of the Minch. These glossy blue figures with grey bearded faces bob in the waves, especially in the tideway between the Shiant Isles and Lewis, which is called Stream of the Blue Men. They attack any vessel the skipper of which cannot answer their riddles. Afraid of being lured to their doom in the Blue Men's undersea caves, local fishermen avoided the Stream. Like so many legends, this one may be founded on fact. Norse pirates who plagued the Scottish isles used slaves taken from Moorish ships – Berbers who wore blue garments and veils, just as their descendants, the Tuaregs of North Africa, do today.
▶ *The islands lie between Skye and Lewis.*

SCOTLAND

❼ Durness, Highland

Along the dramatic shoreline near Durness is Smoo Cave, which has three chambers, one leading into the next, and a spectacular waterfall where the Smoo Burn enters the cave on its way to the sea. It was here that the first Lord Reay, also known as Donald, the Wizard of Reay, had a narrow escape from the Devil.

Like many 17th-century noblemen, Lord Reay was a well-travelled man, and in Italy he had studied the Black Arts under the Devil himself. Back in Scotland, Donald was exploring Smoo Cave one night when his dog, which had run ahead, came back yelping and hairless, and Donald guessed that his old professor was awaiting him in the cave's depths. Fortunately, just then a cock crowed and the Devil and three witches who were with him realised that their time was up. They blew holes in the cavern roof and all four of them flew away.

This is said to be the origin of the holes through which the Smoo Burn flows into the cave. In the 17th century, highwayman Donald McMurdo allegedly got rid of his victims by pushing them down into the cave through these holes. He now lies buried at nearby Balnakiel Church, overlooking Balnakiel Bay. Smoo Cave is accessible on foot and by boat.
▶ *On A838, 65 miles N of Ullapool.*

❽ Thurso, Highland

How a rare grass, called Holy Grass, comes to be growing on the banks of the Thurso River is explained by a local story. The plant was so named because this species was used on the Continent to strew in front of church doors. It is said that the floor of a chapel that once stood by the Thurso was covered with Holy Grass cut in Norway. The area was damp, and the seeds germinated and took root.
▶ *A9 from S, A836 from E and W.*

❾ John o' Groats, Highland

The name John o' Groats is said to be derived from John Groat, or de Groot, a Dutchman who ran the Orkney ferry in the late 15th century. Legend tells that John Groat had eight sons who cared so much about precedence that their father built an octagonal house with eight doors, and containing an eight-sided table. Each son could then enter by his own door and sit at his own 'head' of table. The site of the house is marked by a mound and a flagpole. The graves of the De Groots are in Canisbay churchyard.

Another legend concerns a local seal catcher, who was invited by a dark stranger to do business with his master. The stranger led the man to the cliff edge, where he was suddenly seized and plunged down beneath the waves. On the seabed the hunter was confronted by an old grey seal with a gaping wound in its side, while the hunter's own knife lay nearby. Ashamed of the pain he had inflicted, the man tried to staunch the wound with his hand, whereupon it healed. The hunter swore he would never kill again, and the dark stranger guided him safely home, leaving him with a bag of gold at his cottage door.
▶ *20 miles E of Thurso and 17 miles N of Wick.*

❿ Wick, Highland

At the end of the 17th century, when Campbell of Glenorchy tried to take land he thought himself entitled to from the unwilling Sinclairs, he deliberately allowed a ship loaded with whisky to be stranded near Wick. The Sinclairs found the vessel and spent the night in happy carousal. Next day, suffering from terrible hangovers, they were easily routed by Glenorchy and his men. The story is discredited locally, for it is said a mere single cargo could never have affected Caithnessmen so badly.
▶ *A99 from S and N, A882 from W.*

⓫ Conon Bridge, Highland

A fearsome water horse once made its lair in the River Conon, and the otters that sported on the riverbanks there had supernatural powers. Anyone who caught a King Otter, which was lighter in colour and bigger than other otters, was granted a wish if he gave it back its freedom. On the other hand, he would achieve immunity to bullets or sharp steel if he killed it and wore its pelt. By licking the liver of a freshly killed black otter, a man could acquire the power to heal burns with his tongue.
▶ *12 miles NW of Inverness.*

⓬ Drumnadrochit, Highland

Situated on the shores of Loch Ness, Drumnadrochit is not only the main centre for monster spotting but also the location of the Glenurquhart Highland Gathering and Games. Since 1945 the games, now strictly amateur, have been held on the last Saturday in August, featuring cycling, athletics, tossing the caber and tug o' war. Pipe bands and Highland dancing add to the entertainment.
▶ *16 miles SW of Inverness on A82.*

⑬ Strathpeffer, Highland

The Devil may well be an unholy figure, but not, it seems, unhygienic. There is ample evidence in this part of the world that he is fond of a bath, and washes his clothes all the time. At least, this is how local people have accounted for the hot sulphur springs smelling of brimstone, and the iron springs, too, that abound in this once-volcanic area. Wherever these waters mingle together they run black, and there, they say, the Devil is constantly washing his black clothes.

▶ *On A834, 18 miles NW of Inverness.*

⑭ Glenelg, Highland

In Glenelg, near Scallasaig farm, is a mound associated with serpent cults. Snakes were sacred to the Celtic goddess Bride, an earlier incarnation of St Brigid, and on the saint's day, February 1, the 'serpent queen' is supposed to emerge from the mound.

▶ *On minor road W from Shiel Bridge at head of Loch Duich.*

⑮ Staffa, Argyll & Bute

Vikings regularly raided the Hebridean islands and, once landed, built houses with wooden tree staves, which stood upright and somewhat resembled the striking columns of volcanic basalt lining Staffa's 41m (135ft) cliffs. The island's name is Norse for Stave Island, but marauding Norsemen would have been wary of the place, if the legends are to be believed. Fingal – Fionn of Celtic legend – allegedly used the island as his base in his successful defence of the Hebrides and in his campaigns against the sea raiders in the 3rd century. The sound of the waves in Fingal's Cave, one of the largest that riddle the cliffs, inspired Mendelssohn to write his famous overture 'The Hebrides' after he had visited Staffa in 1829.

▶ *Off W coast of Island of Mull.*

⑯ Tobermory, Mull, Argyll & Bute

One day, a farmer was walking with his small daughter and looking at the ships in the Sound, when she asked him what he would give her if she sank all the vessels they could see. He thought she was joking, so he asked her how she would set about the task. The child bent down and looked at them backwards between her legs. At once, all the ships except one whirled around, then sank. The little girl explained that she could not sink the remaining vessel because

it had a piece of rowan wood on board. Asked where she had learnt this terrible skill, she said her mother had taught her. The farmer had both of them burnt as witches.

It is probably true that the *Florencia*, one of the ships of the ill-fated Spanish Armada, was blown up or sunk in Tobermory Bay in 1588, but how the tragedy occurred is the subject of many differing legends. According to one account, Viola, the King of Spain's daughter, dreamt that she loved a man who lived on the far-off island of Mull, so she commissioned a vessel and set sail. When she reached the island, she recognised MacLean of Duart as the man of her dreams, but MacLean was already married, and his jealous wife ordered the galleon to be blown up. Only the cook survived, carried by the explosion to Strongarbh. Viola herself was buried at Lochaline. When the news reached Spain, a Captain Forrest was sent with another ship to avenge the atrocity, but as it dropped anchor at Tobermory, MacLean's wife summoned all the 18 witches of Mull to her aid. Disguised as seagulls, they raised a terrible storm, and the ship sank, it is said, opposite Coire-na-theanchoir Bay.

▶ *Ferry from Oban.*

A MONSTER'S MIRACLE HISTORY

LOCH NESS is a deep, dark body of water. At 228m (750ft), its peaty depths have yet to yield conclusive evidence of its much sought monster, first seen, records tell, by the Irish monk St Columba in the 6th century. According to his biographer, Adomnán of Iona, St Columba encountered local Picts burying a man near the River Ness. They told the monk their dead companion had been attacked by a water beast. To their surprise, St Columba then asked one of his monks to swim across the cursed lake. Halfway across, a monster appeared, and rushed at the swimmer with a roar. Columba cried: 'Go no further, nor touch the man! Go back!' The monster fled in fear, and the Picts proclaimed it a miracle.

The story was written a century after events, and may be a simple account of a popular medieval motif – monsters and dragons are common in early tales of the saints. Detractors claim the story's setting – by the river, not the lake – make it a different monster altogether, possibly even something as ordinary as a walrus.

To believers, Adomnán's account adds veracity to more recent sightings and suggests not one, but a family of monsters, appearing sporadically at the surface over the centuries.

ORKNEY ISLANDS

Not so very long ago, many Orcadians summoned magical help to safeguard cattle and crops from the spirits. Now prehistoric stone circles and a traditional ploughing match capture the imagination.

❶ Sule Skerry

One of Orkney's most haunting ballads tells of the grey selkie of Sule Skerry – a rocky islet 60km (37 miles) west of Mainland. A maiden fell in love with a seal man, but shortly after their son was born, he disappeared. Then a grey seal came to shore and said to her, 'I am a man upon the land, I am a selkie in the sea; and when I'm far frae every strand, my dwelling is in Sule Skerry.' She realised that this was her lover, but he vanished again and returned after seven years, bringing a gold chain for his son, who went away with him. The woman later married. One day her husband went out hunting and shot two seals – an old grey one and a young one. Round the young one's neck was a gold chain, which the hunter gave to his wife, who then knew that her son was dead.

▶ *37 miles W of Mainland.*

❷ Yetnasteen, Rousay

On Rousay, the giant's stone known as Yetnasteen is said to walk to the Loch of Scockness to drink on New Year's morn. Another Rousay legend tells of a giant who kidnapped three princesses, two of whom he flayed alive, keeping the third to weave his wool. This girl restored her sisters to their skins, and helped them to escape by persuading the dull-witted giant to carry them home concealed in baskets of grass. The princesses and their mother revenged themselves by scalding the giant to death.

▶ *NE Rousay. By ferry from Tingwall, Mainland.*

❸ Wyre, near Rousay

The 12th-century castle on Wyre, now in ruins, once belonged to an influential Norse chief named Kolbein Hruga. He is thought to be the ruler on whom the legendary giant Cubby Roo is based. Cubby Roo is supposed to have used islands as stepping stones, and when angered, threw huge boulders, which can be seen on Rousay and Stronsay.

▶ *By ferry from Tingwall.*

❹ Summerdale, Mainland

The last battle to be fought on Orkney island soil took place here in 1529, when the troops of the Earl of Caithness were defeated. The Earl discovered a witch unwinding balls of red and blue wool. The red was exhausted first, and she told him this meant that the side to shed the other's blood first would win. So the Earl killed a cowherd who was unfortunate enough to be in the vicinity. However, the man was a visitor from Caithness, and the Earl's cause was doomed.

▶ *10 miles W of Kirkwall.*

ONCE LOOSELY NAMED
THE TEMPLE OF THE SUN
THE RING OF BRODGAR, MAINLAND

⑤ Kirkwall, Mainland

Every year at Yuletide, the young men of Kirkwall gather for a ball game played through the streets of the town, similar to the annual scrum held in Jedburgh. Its origins are lost in time, but legend has it that it began when a young man heroically defeated a tyrant by the name of Tusker. The lad tied the evil one's severed head to his saddle to take back to Kirkwall, but a protruding tooth scratched his leg, fatally wounding him. The townsfolk vented their anger by kicking the head around the town. A plaque commemorating the game is to be found in St Magnus Cathedral.
▶ *N coast of Mainland.*

⑥ St Margaret's Hope, South Ronaldsay

Since time out of mind, the boys of the island have engaged in a mimic ploughing contest, once held at Easter, now on a Wednesday in August. The contest has two sections – Ploughmen and Horses. The Horses, usually girls, are judged on their elaborate costumes, after which everyone moves down to the beach where the ploughing contest takes place. The Horses take no part in this, and each boy has his own plough, often of ancient and beautiful workmanship. Genuine skill is shown in turning an unbroken furrow of even width in the smooth, firm sand. The day ends with tea, dancing and prizegiving. How this custom started and what exactly it means has been long forgotten but, as a spectacle, it remains captivating.
▶ *N coast of South Ronaldsay. Access from Mainland via causeways.*

⑦ Swona

This uninhabited island in the Pentland Firth is home to a herd of rare feral cattle. When the last inhabitants left in 1974, they left their cattle behind and the hardy creatures survived with little or no human help.

Near the island, a pair of lovers once drowned. A witch who loved a Ronaldsay man determined to kill his sweetheart, and pushed the girl out of a boat. In trying to save her, the man fell in, too. The witch locked her hand in his, but the lovers were lost, with the witch still holding on. Now, on an ebb tide, a small whirlpool forms, known as the Wells of Swona, which is said to be caused by the witch's efforts to free herself.
▶ *Off SW coast of South Ronaldsay.*

⑧ Brodgar, Mainland

The vast ditch-and-bank megalithic monument known as the Ring of Brodgar is the third largest stone circle in Britain, after the outer ring at Avebury in Wiltshire and the greater ring at Stanton Drew in Somerset. Set on a rise between the Lochs of Harray and Stenness, its huge slabs of Orcadian sandstone are set in a perfect circle 103m (340ft) across. It was probably erected between 2700 and 2000 BC, although its purpose is unknown. Brodgar was once loosely named the Temple of the Sun – the standing stones at Stenness formed the Temple of the Moon. The stones were also said to have been dancing giants, turned to stone by the rays of the rising sun. A short distance away on another rise lies the giants' fiddler, known today as the comet stone. Of the 60 original megaliths, just 27 remain.
▶ *8 miles N of Stromness.*

A STEEP
FLIGHT OF
NARROW
STEPS LEADS
TO THE TOP
MOUSA BROCH

SHETLAND ISLANDS

Norsemen once held sway here, and now their mythology dominates these timeless islands, ever linked to the caverns, rocks and towering brochs of this magical archipelago.

❶ Mousa

No one really knows who built the round towers the islanders call brochs, or why. Some 500 are scattered across the north and west of Scotland, as well as in the Shetlands, but the best preserved stands on the uninhabited island of Mousa, a mile or so from Mainland. Mousa broch, built around 2,000 years ago, remains over 13m (42ft) tall, and a steep flight of narrow steps leads to the top. Legend has it that one tempestuous spring about AD 900, a Norwegian named Bjorn eloped with the beautiful Thora Jewel-hand, but their ship was wrecked on the Isle of Mousa. While the sailors repaired the vessel, the couple married and set up home in the broch. The following spring they sailed north to Iceland, where their daughter Asgerd was born.

No archaeological excavations have been undertaken on the broch, so facts on the ancient islanders and their imposing architectural wonder remain a mystery.

A ferry operates from Mainland, weather permitting, and the RSPB has a reserve on Mousa, which is open in spring and summer.
▶ *Off SE coast of Mainland. Ferry from Leebotten, Mainland.*

❷ Burrafirth, Unst

Unst is the most northerly of the Shetland Isles, and the island giants are descended from the Norse jotner – lumbering, quarrelsome creatures, always half-building bridges and dropping stones, and occasionally making love with pathetic clumsiness to princesses or mermaids. The giants Herman and Saxie lived on opposite sides of Burrafirth. The pair quarrelled one day and became so enraged that each hurled a huge rock at the other. Saxie's rock, now known as Saxie's Baa, dropped into the water just short of Herman's home, Hermaness, while Herman's rock, now called Herman's Hellyac, embedded itself in the cliffs at Saxafiord. One day, both giants fell in love with a mermaid, who offered herself to the one who would follow her to the North Pole. The two of them plunged into the sea and neither were ever seen again. Hermaness is now a national nature reserve.
▶ *N coast of Unst.*

❸ Fair Isle

The unique, multicoloured knitting designs used in the island's famous woollen sweaters are claimed to have been copied from the clothing worn by shipwrecked Spanish sailors from the Armada. These men landed on the island when the storm-driven *El Gran Grifon* ran on to the rocks below the cliffs at Stromshellier in 1588. The crew and soldiers, in their armour and unusual clothes, made such an impression on the astonished islanders that they were regarded with awe as the advance guard of the Heavenly Host.
▶ *Fair Isle lies N of Orkney and S of Shetland. Access by air from Lerwick (Shetland) and Kirkwall (Orkney) and by ferry from Shetland.*

❹ Papa Stour

The Maiden Stack, a precipitous rock pinnacle, has a ruined house on its summit, said to have been built to secure the Laird of Papa Stour's daughter from a bold and persistent suitor, who managed nevertheless to scale the cliffs and complete his conquest.

It is said that a fisherman named Herman Perk, hunting seals on the nearby Ve Skerries, was cut off by a storm from his companions. However, a huge seal appeared and carried Herman home on his back, on condition that the fisherman gave him the sealskin he had found the previous day. The skin belonged to the seal's mate, who was unable to return to the sea without it. Shortly after the skin was handed over, Herman, hiding by the shore, saw a beautiful seal-woman hurrying to the beach, where she put on her lost garment and swam out to sea to join her waiting lover.
▶ *Off W coast of Mainland. By ferry from West Burrafirth, Mainland.*

❺ Esha Ness, Mainland

The Holes of Scraada at Esha Ness are the result of a collapsed sea cave, the work of the Devil, according to legend. The Devil was being punished for wrecking ships on the Ve Skerries by being made to carve out the long, narrow fissure, and his groans as he labours at his task can still be heard echoing through the Holes.
▶ *NW coast of Mainland.*

Index

Page numbers in **bold** refer to main entries. Page numbers in *italic* refer to pictures.

A

Abbots Bromley 128, **134**
Abbots Bromley Horn Dance 128, 134, *135*
Abbot's Chair 99
Abbotsbury 30, **34**
Abbotts Ann **56-7**
Aberdaron **176**
Aberdovey **178**
Abingdon **73**, *73*
Abram 151
Aconbury **118**
Acton Bridge 143
Adams, Fanny 57
Aerfen 181
Afanc 182
Aikey Brae 207
Aintree Racecourse 152
Alderley Edge **144-5**, *144-5*
Aldermaston **52**
Alderney 46
Aldington **67**
Aldworth **52**
Alfred, King 41, 169
Alfriston **78**
All Saints Church, Chalgrave 51
All Saints Church, Dewsbury 173
All Saints Church, Godshill 58
All Saints Church, Odell 50
All Stretton 133
Allendale Town **166**, *166*
Allington Castle 61
alms-collecting 63
Alnwick **166**
Altarnun **24**
Alton **57**
Alwinton Border Shepherds' Show 164
Ambleside 151
Ancrum **203**
Annakut 91
Antrobus **143**
Anwick **125**
Anwoth **197**
Apple Pie Fair 29
Appleton Thorn **142**
Apron-full-of-stones 149
Ardbeg 204
Arthur, King
  Cadbury Castle 42
  Eamont Bridge 148
  Glastonbury 45
  Mabinogion 178
  Merbach Hill 119
  Mons Badonicus 38, 70
  Preseli Hills 187
  Ruthin 181
  Sewing Shields Castle 167
  Tintagel 23
  Winchester 57
Arthur's Stone 119
ash trees 39
Ashbourne **113**, 128
Ashingdon **103**
Ashperton **119**
Ashton-under-Lyne **155**
Athelney 41
Atherstone **136**
Atlantis 14
Avebury Stone Circle **80**, *80-1*
Avening **114**
Axminster **33**
Aylesford **61**

B

Bacup **154**
Badbury Rings **38**
Bainbridge **168**
Baker Street, London **84**
Bakewell **112**
Bald Faced Stag 100
Baldock 60
Ballantrae **195**
Balm Well 200
Balnakiel Church 210
Bamburgh **163**
Bamburgh Castle 163
Bampton, Devon **28**
Bampton, Oxfordshire **70**
Bannaventa 126
Bardney **124**
Barnaby Festival 145
Barnstaple **28**
Barra **208**
barrows *see* burial chambers and mounds
Barton, Elizabeth 67
Barwick in Elmet **172**
bat-and-trap 76-7
Batcombe **37**
Bath **42**
Bawming the Thorn 142
Bayard 124
Bean, Alexander 'Sawney' 195
Beast of Bolam 167
Beating the Bounds
  Leighton Buzzard 51
  Poole 37
  St Albans 60
Beaton, David 200
Beauchamp, Sir John 138
Becket, Thomas 61
Becket's Well 61
Bedd Arthur 187
Bede's Chair 167
Bedford **50-1**
Bedfordshire 50-1
Beeley **112**
Beinn an Oir 204
Beinn Shiantaidh 204
Bellingham **167**
Beltane 30, 200, 206

Belton **120**
Ben Macdui **206**
Benbecula **208**
Bennet, Elizbaeth 102
Bentley, Nathaniel 88
Berkshire 52-3
Berkswell **136**
Bettiscombe **34**
Betws Garmon **176**
Betwys-y-Coed **182**
Beverley Minster **172**
Bible Orchard 98
Biddenden **67**
Bidford-on-Avon **137**
Biggar 199, **202**
Billingsgate, London **88**
Bilston **136**
Bincombe **35**
Birkland Wood 130
Bishopsgate, London **88**
Bisley **116**
Bisterne 57
Black Annis 120
Black Army 191
Black Loch 197
Black Mere Pool 134
Black Prince's Well 63
Black Shuck 96, 98
Black Tom of Soothill 173
Blackburn **154**
Blakey Topping 170
Blaxhall **109**
Bleadon 41
bleeding yew 188
Blessing of the Sea and Fisheries 66, 79, 188
Blessing of the Throats 87
Blidworth 130
Blind Harry 207
Blockhouse Point 58
Blue Ben 42
Blue John 112
Blue Men of the Minch 209
Blythburg **109**
Boar's Head 72
Bodmin **21**
body snatching 51
Bog Snorkelling Championships 179
Boggans 122
Bolam Lake **167**
Boleyn, Anne 61, 67
Bolton **154**
Bootie Night 30
Boscastle **23**
bottle-kicking 121, 128
bottom-pinching 128
Boudicca 86
Bourne **125**
Bourton-on-the-Water **117**
Bownessie 149
Boxley **61**
Boy's Grave 108
Bozwell, Edward 54
Bradford **173**
Bradle Stone 133
brass band competitions 155

Braughing **60**
Braunston-in-Rutland **121**
Braunstone **120**
Braunton **26**
Bread and Cheese Dole 114
Breamore **56**
Breccan's Cauldron 205
Bree Shute Well 21
Breeds, John 78
Bride's Bed 208
Bridge of the Leap 206
Bridgwater **40**, *40*
Brigg **122**
Brightling **78**
Brightlingsea **102**
Brighton 68, **76-7**
Brimham Rocks 169
Bristol **42**
Bristol Channel **42**
Britannia Coconut Dancers 154, *154*
Broadhalfpenny Down 58
brochs 215
Brodgar **213**
Bromsgrove **138**
Brooklands 74
Broughton **127**
Bruce, Robert the 205
Brutus Stone **29**
Brutus the Trojan 20, 29, 88
Brynn y Crogbren 176
Buckhurst Hill **100**
Buckinghamshire 54-5
Buckland St Mary **41**
Bull of Bagbury 180
bull-baiting 74
Bunbury **142**
Burghead 199, **206**
burial chambers and mounds
  Carne Beacon 19
  Fortingall 206
  Hob Hurst's House 112
  Kit's Coty House 61
  Long Stone 58
  Music Barrows 35
  Picts' Knowe 203
  Preseli Hills 187
  Rillaton 21
  Silbury Hill **80**
  Six Hills 60
  Tynwald Hill 156
  Wayland's Smithy 70
  Zennor Quoit 16
buried towns and cities
  Atlantis 14
  Cantref Gwaelod 178
  Dorstone 119
  Langarroc 17
  Lyonesse 14
Burley **57**
Burnham Green **60**
Burnham-on-Sea **41**
Burning the Ashen Faggot 39
Burning the Bartle 168
Burning the Clavie 199, 206

216

Burning the Clocks 68, *68-9*, 77
Burrafirth **215**
Burry Man 200, *201*
Bury St Edmunds **108**
Butter Rock 187
butterbur 50
Bwlch y Pawl 176

C

cadaver tombs 124
Cadbury Castle **42**
Caedmon 170
Caerwys 185
Cailleach 205
Caistor **122**
Caldbeck **146**
Callanish **209**
Callant's Festival 203
Cambridge **97**
Cambridgeshire 96-9
Camelot 42
candle auctions
Aldermaston 52
Hubberholme 168
Canisbay 210
Cannon Street, London **88**
Canterbury **63**
Cantref Gwaelod 178
Canute, King 142
Capel Vair 176
Capesthorne Hall 145
Caratacus 54, 119
Cardigan Bay 178
Cardoness Castle 197
Carhampton **39**
Carinish **209**
Carlisle **147**
Carn Menyn 187
Carne Beacon 19
Carreg y Fendith 188
Carregwastad Point 186
Cassillis House 195
Castle Dore **18**
Castle public house, London 87
Castle Rising **106**, *106*
Castleton **112**
Castleton Fell 149
Castletown **156-7**
caves
Blue John 112
Fingal's Cave 211
Giant's Cave 148
King's Cave 205
Kynaston's Cave *132*, 133
Merlin's Cave 23
Mortimer's Hole 130
Ogo Vair 176
Peak Cavern 112
Royston Cave **59**, *59*
St Ninian's Cave 195
Smoo Cave 210
Thirst House 113
Treak Cliff **112**
Wookey Hole **44**
Celtic masks 173

Centre Tree 130
Ceridwen 178-9
Cerne Abbas Giant **36**, *36*
Cerrig Ina 179
Chalgrave **51**
chalk figures
Cerne Abbas Giant **36**, *36*
Long Man of Wilmington 78
White Horse of Uffington 70
Chanctonbury Ring **75**
Channel Islands 46-7
Chapel Carn Brea **17**
Chapman, John 107
Charles II 37, 77, 85, 128
Charlie, Bonnie Prince 202, 205
Charlton 72
Chastleton House **72**
Chattering Charteris 112
Chawleigh **28**
cheese-rolling
Cooper's Hill 116, 128, *129*
Randwick 114
Stilton 99
The Cheesewring **24**, *24*
Cheshire & The Wirral 142-5
Chester **142**
Chester Cathedral 142
Chevauchee 46
Chibber Mun Laa 157
Childe of Wynde 163
Chillingham Castle **166**
Chillingham white cattle 166
chimney sweeps 62, *62*, 68-9
Chinese New Year 91
Chipping Campden **116**, 128
Chirk Castle **181**
Christian traditions 69, 150-1
Christmas Bull 38
Chulkhurst, Elisa and Mary 67
Church Gift 35
Church of the Holy Cross, Avening 114
Church Stretton **133**
Cinque Ports 102
City Livery Companies 92
Civil War 25, 35, 61, 72, 181
Clipping the Church
Guiseley 172
Painswick 115
Clitheroe **153**
cloth fair 98
Club Walks 28
Cobleigh, Uncle Tom 29
cock-in-the-pot 79
Colchester **101**
Coldstream **202-3**
Colnbrook **52**
Colonel's Bed 206
Combe Martin **27**, 30

Comberbach 143
Combwell **61**
Common Riding 196
Comprigney 18
Comrie **207**
Comrie Flambeaux 207
Conon Bridge **210**
Conwy **183**
Cooper's Hill **116**, 128, *129*
Coppinger, David 25
Coppinger's Tracks 25
Corfe Castle **35**, *35*
Cormoran 20
Cornwall 14-25
Corryvreckan whirlpool **205**
Corwen 185
Cotswold Olympiks 116, 128
Cottingley Fairies **173**
Countless Stones 61
Court Baron 32
Court Leet
Laxton 130
Sidbury 32
Wareham 37
Coventry 137
Cowcross Street, London **87**
Crabbe, Stephen 66
Cranwell **124**
cricket 58
Cross Fell **148**
Cross Keys public house, White Notley 100
Cross-and-Hand 37
Crown Jewels 89
Croxteth Hall **152**
Croydon Hill **42**
Crying the Neck 17
Crystal Palace **92**
Cubby Roo 212
Cuckoo Pen 72
cuckoos 78, 188
Culhwch 178
Culloden **205**
Cumberland and Westmorland wrestling 149, 164
Cumbria 146-9
Cunobelinus, King of the Britons 54
Cursing Stone **147**, 147
Cwm Gwaun **188**
Cwn Annwn 176
Cymbeline's Castle 54
Cynwyd **182**

D

Daddy Witch 96
Dalrymple **195**
Dando 20
Dane Hills 120
Danes/Vikings 30, 39, 41, 60, 108, 146, 156, 162, 198, 199, 211
Danes' Stream 57
Darlington **161**

Dashwood, Sir Francis 55
Davenport, George 121
Daventry 126
Daynes, Mercy 148
de Assheton, Sir Ralph 155
de Mohun, Reginald 33
de Shurland, Sir Roger 63
Deepdale **113**
Deerhurst **116**
Deliberately Concealed Garments Project 126
Denbigh 185
Denby Dale **173**
Derbyshire 112-13
Devil
Aldworth 52
Blythburg 109
Castleton 112
Chanctonbury Ring 75
Chester 142
Croydon Hill 42
Cymbeline's Castle 54
Helston 16
Holes of Scraada 215
Innerleithen 203
Kirkby Lonsdale 148-9
Lincoln 124
Little Baddow 101
Little Comberton 138
Llanarth 179
Llanddulas 183
Llanfor 176
Newington 62
North Marston 54
Odell 50
Rudston 172
Shebbear 28
Shrewsbury 133
Silbury Hill 80
Smoo Cave 210
Stevenage 60
Stonehenge 81
Strathpeffer 211
Sutton St Nicholas 119
Veryan 18
Wallasea Island 102
Devil Door 101
Devil's Bridge 148
Devil's Chair 200
Devil's Hole 46
Devil's House 102
Devil's Knell 173
Devil's Neck Collar 148
Devil's Punchbowl 170
Devil's Stone 119
Devil's Wedding 44
Devon 26-9, 32-3
Devons Road, London **93**
Dewsbury **173**
Diana, Princess of Wales 84
Dic Aberdaron (Richard Robert Jones) 176
Dinas Emrys 177, *177*
Dirty Dick's public house, London **88**
Diwali 91
Dodman 14
Dorset 34-8
Dorstone **119**

Dovers Hill 116
Dowsing, William 109
dragons
  Blue Ben 42
  Burley Beacon 57
  Deerhurst 116
  Henham 100
  Laidly Worm 163
  Lambton Worm 161
  Linton 203
  Nantgwynant 177
  Nunnington 170
  Penmynydd 183
Drake Stones 125
drinking competitions
  137
Druids
  Callanish 209
  Llantrisant 191
  Mottistone Hill 58
  Stonehenge 81
  Twmbarlwm Hill 191
Druid's Altar 169
Druid's Head 169
Drumnadrochit **210**
Dumbarton **196**
Dumbarton Castle 196
Dunmail Raise **149**
Dunmow Flitch Trial 100
Dunster **39**
Durham **160-1**
Durham Cathedral 163
Durham Miners' Gala
  164, *165*
Durness **210**

E

Eagle public house,
  London 92
Eamont Bridge **148**
Earl Sterndale **112**
Earlston **202**
East Dean 78
East Dereham **107**
East Grinstead **75**
Eastwell **67**
Eaton Socon 99
Ebbing and Flowing Well
  168-9
Ebenezer Chapel, Filey
  164
Edenhall **147**
Edinburgh **200**, 202
Edington Monastery 41
Edmondthorpe **121**
Ednam **203**
Edward III 119
Edward, Prince of Wales
  (Black Prince) 23, 63
Edwinstowe 130
Egloshayle **21**
Eisteddfod **184-5**
Eleanor, Queen 89
elf bolts 72
Elizabeth I 121
Ellesmere **133**
Ely Place, London **87**
Enderby **120**
Endon **134**

entombed train 92
Epping Forest **100**
Esha Ness **215**
Essex 100-1
Eton **53**, *53*
Eustace the Monk 66
Ewan Caesarius 146
Eyemouth **202**
Eynesbury **99**

F

Faa Blythe, Charles 203
Fair Isle **215**
Fairford **117**
fairs
  Apple Pie Fair 29
  Bampton Charter Fair
    28
  Barnstaple 28
  Easter cloth fair 98
  Goose Fair 130
  Henham Fair 100
  Honiton 28
  Langholm Fair 196
  Marymass Fair 196
  Pack Monday Fair 38
  Ram Roasting Fair 29
  Rose Fair 96
  St Andrew's Fair 200
  St Margaret's Fair 188
  Trinity Fair 109
  Widecombe 29
Fairy Bridge 157
fairy-folk 35, 41, 42, 46,
  70
  Ardbeg 204
  Betws Garmon 176
  Bincombe 35
  Bristol Channel 42
  Buckland St Mary 41
  Cottingley Fairies **173**
  Deepdale 113
  Edenhall 147
  Ednam 203
  Jura 204
  Pennard Castle 189
  Pezeriez Point 46
  Rollright Stones 70
  St Fillans 206
  Santon 157
Falmouth **17**
Farne Islands **162-3**
Farquharson, John (Black
  Colonel) 206
Faversham **63**
feeing-fairs 200
Feejee Mermaids 161
Ferris, Thomas 170
fertility rites 22, 38, 121,
  134
Fielder, Richard 98
Filey 164
Filey Fishermen's Choir
  164
Fingal's Cave 211
Finstock **70**
fire festivals
  Allendale Town 166,
    166

Beltane 30, 200, 206
Biggar 199, 202
Brighton 68, 77
Burghead 199, 206
Chapel Carn Brea 17
Comrie 207
Edinburgh 200
Fortingall 206
Golowan 14
Hatherleigh 29
Lewes 78
Ottery St Mary 32
Stonehaven 199, 207
Up Helly Aa 196,
  196-7
first footing 166
Fisherman's Picnic 202
Fishguard **186**
Fishtoft **125**
Fitzwilliam Museum 97
Fleam Dyke 96
Folkestone **66**
Fonaby Stone 122
football
  Alnwick 166
  Atherstone 136
  Bourton-on-the-Water
    117
  Corfe Castle 35
  Kirkwall 213
  Sedgefield 161
  Shrovetide football 113,
    113, 128, 161, 166
  Wall Game 53
  Workington 146
Fortingall **206**
Foulness Island 102
Fountains Abbey **169**
Friar Tuck 130, 169
Frid Stool 167
Friendly Societies 28
Friston **78**
Frith-stol 172
Frithmen 172
Fuller, 'Mad' Jack 78
Furry Dance 16

G

Galley Hill 51
Gallows Wood 122
Gatcombe **58**
Geoffrey of Monmouth
  81, 96, 101
George IV 87, 121
Gerbygge, Sir William
  and Lady 107
Gerrans Bay 19
ghosts
  Aintree 152
  Batcombe 37
  Brooklands 74
  Gracedieu Priory 120
  Merlin's Cave 23
  Nottingham 130
  St Albans 60
  Sherborne Castle 38
  Smithills Hall 154
  Whittlesford 96
ghouls 195

giant squid 16
giants
  Aldworth Giants 52
  Anthony Payne 25
  Burrafirth 215
  Castletown 156-7
  Cerne Abbas Giant **36**,
    36
  Cormoran 20
  Ewan Caesarius 146
  Eynesbury 99
  Gog and Magog 29, 96
  Horcum 170
  Jack o' Legs 60
  Rousay 212
  Ysbaddaden 178
Giant's Cave 148
Giant's Cave, Lamorna 20
Giant's Chair 20
Giant's Cradle 20
Giant's Stone 202
Giggleswick **168-9**
Gingerbread, Grasmere
  149
glacial erratics 109
Glaisdale **170**
Glasgow **196**
Glasserton **195**
Glastonbury **45**
Glastonbury thorn 45,
  142
Glastonbury Tor 45, *45*
Glenelg **211**
Glentham **122**
Glenurquhart Highland
  Gathering and Games
  210
Gloucester **116**
Gloucestershire 114-17
Glyn Rhosyn 186
Glyndwr, Owain 181
Glyndyfrdwy **181**
Godiva, Lady 125, 137
Godmanstone **37**
Godshill 58
Gog and Magog 29, 96
Gog Magog Hills **96**
Golowan 14
Goodwick **186**
Goodwin Sands **65**
Goose Fair 130
goosebell 66
Gorslas **190**
Gospel Oak 126
Gracedieu Priory 120
Gradbach New **134**
grampus 56
Grandison, Katherine 119
Grandmother of the
  Churchyard 46
Grannie Stane 196
Grantchester **98**
Grasmere **149**, *150-1*, 151
Grasmere Lakeland Sports
  149
Great Dunmow **100**
Great Kimble **54**
Great Mere 133
Great Ness **133**
Great Scree 205
Green Chapel 134

Green Meadows of Enchantment 42
Grey Man of Macdui 206
Greyfriars Bobby **202**
Griffiths, Frances 173
Guernsey **46**
Guildford **74**
guise dancers 14
Guiseley **172**
Gumb, Daniel 24
Gunpowder Plot 61
Guto Nyth Bran (Griffith Morgan) 190
Guy Fawkes 32, 40, 78
gypsies 54, 127, 195, 197, 203

H

Hadleigh **103**
Hal-an-Tow 17
Hallaton **121**, 128
Halloween 206
Hambledon **58**
Hamilton, Patrick 200
Hampshire 56-8
Hand of Glory 136
Hangman's Stone 32
Harbledown 63
Hardy, Thomas 86
Hare Pie Scramble 121, 128
Harp Hill 72
Hartland Point **26**, *26-7*
Hartlepool **161**
Hastings 68, **79**, *79*
Hatherleigh **29**
Hathersage **112**
Hawksmoor, Nicholas 146
Haxey **122**
Hay Sunday 120
Hayes Common **93**
heather ale 195
Heathfield **78**
Hellfire Club 55
Hell's Kettles 161
Helm Wind 148
Helston **16-17**
Hen Galan 188
Henfield **76**
Henham **100**
Henry II 130
Henry VIII 61, 67
Hentland **118**
Hercules 26
Herdwick sheep 146
Hereford Beacon **119**
Herefordshire 118-19
Hermaness 215
Herring Queen 202
Hertfordshire 59-60
Herward the Wake 125
Hexham Priory **167**
Hexton 128
Heysham **153**
Highclere **56**
Highdown Hill **76**
Highland Clearances 205

hillforts
  Badbury Rings 38
  Cadbury Castle 42
  Chanctonbury Ring **75**
  Dinas Emrys 177, *177*
  Gog Magog Hills 96
  Hereford Beacon 119
  Luton 51
Hilton **98**
Hinton St George **44-5**
Hob Hurst's House 112
Hobby Horses 30, *31*, 39, *39*
  see also Obby Oss
Hocktide Festival 52
Hocktide Revels 128
Hodening Horse 143
Hole of Horcum 170
holed stones 15, 76
Holes of Scraada 215
Hollinshead Hall Holy Well 154
Holmes, Sherlock 84
Holy Cross Church, Kilgwrrwg 191
Holy Grail 45
Holy Grass 210
Holy Island **162**, *162-3*
Holy Maid of Kent 67
Holy Thorn 45, 142
Holy Trinity Church, Blythburg 109, *109*
holy wells 20, 21, 26, 50, 54
  Altarnun 24
  Blackburn 154
  Bodmin 21
  Hartland Point 26
  Llandeilo 190
  Malvern 139, *139*
  Maughold 157
  Newark-on-Trent 130
  Newton Cross 186
  Otford 61
  St Neot 20
  Stevington 50
  Walsingham 107
  see also medicinal springs and wells
Honiton 28
Hood Game 122
Hooden Horse 63
Hoodening 63
Hooper, John 116
Horcum **170**
Horngarth 170
Horning **107**
horse cult and traditions 183, 207
horse racing
  Kiplingcotes Derby 172
  Marymass Fair 196
Horseheath **96**
Horseman's Sunday 90
Horseman's Word 207
horseshoes 121
hot cross buns 93, *93*
Huail 181
Hubberholme **168**
human sacrifices

Glyndyfrdwy 181
London 84
Hundreds 99
Hungerford **52**
hunky punks 45
Hunting of the Earl of Rone 27, 30
Hunting the Wren 190
Huntly 207
Hurling the Silver Ball
  St Columb Major 21
  St Ives 16
Hurstingstone 99
Hyssington **180**
Hythe **66**

I

Ightham **61**
Image House 142
Innerleithen **203**
Inverey **206**
Irvine **196**
Isabella, Queen 106
Isir's Parlour 148
Isle of Axholme 122
Isle of Man 156-7
Isle of Portland **35**
Isle of Whithorn **194**, **195**
Isle of Wideopens 162
Isle of Wight 58

J

Jack o' Legs 60
Jack of Batsaddle 127
Jack the Giant Killer 202
Jack the Painter 58
Jack-in-the-Green 68, 69, *79*, *79*
Jack's Hill 60
James II 133
Jarrow **167**
Jedburgh **203**
Jedburgh Games 203
Jeffries, Anne 23
Jersey **46**
Jesus Christ 39, 45
Jethart Handba' 203
John, King 52, 74, 125
John of Gaunt 52, 120
John o'Groats **210**
Jones, Arthur 72
Joseph of Arimathea 45
Jovial Hunter (Sir Ryalas) 138
Judas Iscariot 152
Jura **204**, *204-5*
Jura Fell Race 204

K

Kaspar the cat 87
kelpies 209
Kemp, Ursula 102
Kempe, Will 105
Kent 61-7
Kentford **108**

Kidderminster **138**
Kieve 23
Kilgwrrwg **191**
Kilve **42**, *43*
Kinder Scout **112**
King Cole 101
King Cole's Kitchen 101
King Otter 210
King Stone 70
King's Cave 205
King's Crag 167
King's Cross Station, London **86**
King's Lynn **106**
King's Men 70
Kingsteignton 29
Kiplingcotes Derby 172
Kirk Yetholm **203**
Kirkby Lonsdale **148-9**
Kirkcudbright **197**, *197*
Kirkton of Largo **200**
Kirkwall **213**
Kissing Friday 128
Kit's Coty House 61
Knaresborough **169-70**
Knightlow Hill 136
Knights Hospitaller 57
Knights Templar 57, 59
Knightsbridge, London **84**
Knutsford **142**
Koh-i-Noor diamond 89
Kolbein Hruga 212
Kynaston, Wild Humphrey 133
Kynaston's Cave *132*, 133
Kynaston's Leap 133

L

Lady Chapel 45
Lady Lovibond 65
Lady's Well 70
Laidly Worm 163
Lambert, Percy 74
Lambton Worm 161
Lamorna 20
Lampeter **179**
Lanark **196**
Lancashire 152-5
Land's End **14**
Langarroc 17
Langholm **196**
Largo Law 200
Last Invasion Tapestry 186
Laxton **130**
Leek **134**
Leicester **120**
Leicestershire & Rutland 120-1
Leighton Buzzard **51**
Leofric, Earl 119, 125, 137
Leominster **119**
Lerwick 198-9, *198-9*
Lewes **78**
Lewis 208, 209
Lewis chess set 208
Liberton **200**
Lightfoot, Lucy 58

Lilliard's Stone 203
Lincoln **124**, *124-5*
Lincoln Imp 124
Lincolnshire 122-5
Lindisfarne **162**, *162-3*
Linton **203**
Little Baddow **101**
Little Comberton **138**
Little Dunmow Priory
  Church 100
Little John 112
Little Salkeld **146**
Little Stretton 133
Little Wittenham **72-3**
Littleport **98**
Liver Building 152
Liverpool **152**
Llanarth **179**
Llanberis **176**
Llandderfel **178**
Llanddewi-Brefi **179**
Llanddulas **183**
Llanddwyn **182**, *182*
Llandeilo **190**
Llanfor **176**
Llangar 182
Llangollen 185
Llangurig **180**
Llanina **179**
Llanrhaeadr-ym-
  Mochnant **180**
Llansilin **181**
Llantrisant **191**
Llanuwchllyn **176**
Llanwonno **190**
Llyn Llech Owain 190
Llyn y Geulan Goch 176
Loch Ness **211**
Loch Ness Monster 211
Loch Rèasort **208**, *208-9*
Lollards 134
London **82-93**
London Bridge **88-9**
London Stone 88
Londonderry, Marquess
  of 160, *160*
Long Man of Wilmington
  78
Long Meg and her
  Daughters 146
Long Pack 167
Long Stone 58
Longrock **16**
Longwick **54**
Lord Mayor's Show 92
Love Feast 126
Lovers' Bridge 170
lover's knots 98
Lovers' Rock 169
Lovett, Edward 92
Lud's Church 134
Luton **51**
lych gates 143
Lyonesse 14

M

Mabinogion **178**
Macclesfield **145**
McKenzie, William 152

McMurdo, Donald 210
Madron **15**
Maen Huail 181
Maes Gwyddno 178
Magdalen College 72
Maid Marion 130
Maiden Stack 215
Maidens' Garlands 56-7
Maid's Head public
  house, Wicken 98
Maid's Money 74
Maidstone **61**
Major Oak 130
Malvern Hills **139**
Mansfield **130**
Marbles Championship
  75, *75*
Margate **64-5**
Marged vch Ifan 176
Mari Lwyd 191
Market Weighton **172**
Marldon **29**
Marsh, George 154
Marshall, Billy 197
Marshfield **117**
Marymass Fair 196
Mathematical Bridge 97,
  97
Maughold **157**
May Day garlands 54, 68
May festivals **30-1**
May Queen Festival 93
Mayburgh Henge 148
Mayor of Ock Street 73
maypoles
  Barwick in Elmet 172
  Belton 120
  Longwick 54
  Padstow 22
mazes
  Breamore Down 56, *56*
  Hilton 98
Mazey Day 14
Medbourne 128
medicinal springs and wells
  Aconbury 118
  Bath 42
  Bodmin 21
  Harbledown 63
  Innerleithen 203
  Liberton 200
  North Marston 54
  Otmoor 72
  Woolpit 108
  see also holy wells
Medmenham Abbey 55
Melbury Osmond 38
Melwas 45
Men-an-Tol 15, *15*
Merbach Hill 119
Merewald 119
Merlin 14, 23, 81, 177
Merlin's Cave 23
Merlin's Rock 14
mermaids
  Benbecula 208
  Conwy 183
  Leek 134
  Rostherne 142
  Tresco 25
  Zennor 16

Mermaid's Pool 112
mermen 161
Michael's Chair 15
Middleton 151
Milk-o-Punch 46
Millbrook 30
Millennium Pie 173
Minehead 30, **39**
Minster Abbey 63, 65
Minster-in-Sheppey **63**
Minster-in-Thanet **65**
miz-maze 56, *56*
mock mayors 73
Moddey Dhoo 156
Moel y Lladdfa 182
molly dancing 105, 155
'Molly Grime' 122
Money Pit 73
Mons Badonicus 38
monsters
  Beast of Bolam 167
  Grey Man of Macdui
    206
  Shug Monkey 96
  see also dragons; water
    monsters
Monti, Raffaelle 160
Montol festival 14
Moor Evil 72
Morgan, Richard 191
Morgawr 17
morris dancing **104-5**,
  150, **155**
  Abingdon 73
  Bacup 154
  Bampton 70
  Border Morris 155
  Cotswold Morris 155
  Hastings 79
  Longwick 54
  molly dancing 105, 155
  Northwest Morris 155
  Oxford 72
  Rochdale 151
  Saddleworth 151, 152
  Thaxted 100, *104*, 105
  Whalton 166
  Whittlesea 99
  Winster 113
Mortimer, Roger 130
Mortimer's Hole 130
Morwenstow **25**
Mother Haggy 60
Mother Redcap 96
Mother Shipton's Cave
  and Petrifying Well 170
Mottistone **58**
Mount Badon 70
Mountain Ash 190
Mousa Broch *214*, 215
Mousehole **14**
Moyle, Sir Thomas 67
Mrs Dee's Rock 139
Much Marcle **118**
Mull of Galloway **195**
mumming
  Abingdon 73
  Abram 151
  Antrobus 143
  Gloucester 116
  Helston 17

Marshfield 117, *117*
Middleton 151
Penzance 14
Whittlesea 99
Murrell, James 103
Music Barrows 35
Mynterne, Conjuror 37
Mynydd Mawr 190
Mystery plays
  Chester 142
  York 172

N

Nantgwynant **177**
Nettle Day 128
Nevern **188**
Nevison, John 169
Nevison's Leap 169
'new' traditions 68-9
Newark-on-Trent **130**
Newbrough **167**
Newington **62**
Newnham Abbey 33
Newton Cross **186**
Newton, Sir Isaac 97
Newtown Linford **120**
Nicholas, Jemima 186
nine men's morris 137
Nippy Hug Day 128
Norfolk 106-7
North Marston **54**
North Uist 209
Northampton **126-7**
Northamptonshire 126-7
Northumberland &
  Tyneside 162-3, 166-7
Norton **126**
Norton in Hales **133**
Nos Galen races 190
Notting Hill Carnival 91
Nottingham **130**
Nottinghamshire 130-1
Nunnington **170**
Nut Dance 154, *154*
Nyren, Richard 58

O

Oak Apple Day 85, 112,
  128
Oakham **121**
Obby Oss 14, 22, *22*, 30
  see also Hobby Horses
Oddington 72
Odell **50**, *50*
Ogo Vair 176
Old Deer **207**
Old Dido 100
Old John's Tower 120
Old Man's Day 60
Old Meg (Cranwell) 124
Old Meg (Newbrough)
  167
Old Mother Jenkins the
  Goose Charmer 100
Old Mother Redcap 102
Old Sun Inn, Saffron
  Walden 101, *101*

Old Walworth Town Hall, London **92**
Old Woodstock 73
Oldhurst **99**
Olliver, John 76
O'Neill, Hugh 27
Ooser 38
open-field system 130
'oranges and lemons' 87
Order of the Garter 119
Orkney Islands 212-13
Orleton **119**
Orlingbury **127**
ossuary 66
Ostrich Inn, Colnbrook 52
Otford **61**
Otford Palace 61
Otmoor **72**
Ottery St Mary **32**, *32-3*
Our Lady's Well, Walsingham 107
Our Lady's Well, Woolpit 108
Oxford **72**
Oxfordshire 70-3
Oxtoby, Praying Johnny 164
Oyster Feast 101
Oyster Festival 101

P

Pace Egging 151
Pack Monday Fair 38
Pack o' Cards inn 27
Padstow **22**, 30
Painswick **115**
Palmer's Churn 119
pancake races 113
Papa Stour **215**
Paperboys 117
Paps 204
pargetting 101
pasture rights 100
pawnbroking 87
Pax Cakes 118
Payne, Anthony 25
Peak Cavern 112
Pearly Kings and Queens 90, *90-1*
Peckover House 96
Peel, John 146
Peel Castle **156**, *156-7*
Penarth **191**
Pencoed **191**
Penfolds Field 76
Penhale Sands **17**
Penmaen **189**
Penmark **191**
Penmynydd **183**
Pennant Melangell **180**
Pennard Castle *188-9*, 189
Penrith **146**
Penryn **17**
Penshaw **161**
Penzance **14**
Perk, Herman 215
Petronius 112

Petting Stone 162
Pezeriez Point **46**, *47*
phantom battles 61
phantom black dogs
  Peel 156
  Uplyme 33
  Wicken 98
phantom ships 65
phantom white horses 60
Picts 195, 211
Pie Village 173
Pie-powder Court 130
pieta 122
Pig Face Day 114
pigbell 66
Pilsdon Pen 34
Pinch-Bum Day 128
Piper's Grave 203
Piper's Hole 25
Pitt Rivers Museum 72
plague burial pits 84
Plague Stone 16
Planting of the Penny Hedge 170
Pleinmont Fairy Ring 46
Plough Monday 105
ploughing contests 213
plygain 180
Pontefract **173**
Pontefract Cakes 173
Pontius Pilate 206
Poole **37**
Poor's Pasture 168
Pop (Eton Society) 53
'pop goes the weasel' 92
Portsmouth **58**
Powderham Castle **29**
Preseli Hills **187**, *187*
Price, Dr William 191
Pritchard, Rhys 179
Puddleford 196
Punky Night 44-5
'puppy-dog pie' 115
Purbeck Marblers 35
Pwll Llygad Ych 182
Pyrford Stone **74**

Q

Quainton **54**
Queen's College, Oxford 72
Queen's Crag 167
Queensferry **200**
Quiet Woman public house, Earl Sterndale 112

R

Raleigh, Sir Walter 38
Ralph of Coggeshall 108
Ram Roasting Fair 29
Rame Head 14
Randwick **114**
Randwick Wap 114
ravens
  Corfe Castle 35
  Tower of London 89

Read, Margaret 106
Reading **52**
Reay, Lord (Donald, Wizard of Reay) 210
Reculver **64**, *64*
Redes Mere 145
Reivers 147, 197
Rhôs-on-Sea **183**
Rhys ap Gruffyd 184
Rhys ap Iestyn 189
Richard III 67
Riding the Black Lad 155
Rillaton **21**
Ring of Brodgar *212-13*, **213**
Ripon **169**
Risca (Rhisga) **191**
River Thames **84**
River Windrush 117
Robin Hood 130, 134, 169, 170
Roch Y Garn **186**
Rochdale 151
Rochester **62**, 69
Rogation Monday 51
Rogation Sunday 72
Rollright Stones **70**
Rose Fair 96
Rostherne **142-3**
Round Meadow 38
Round Table 57
Rousay 212
Royal Hospital, Chelsea **85**, *85*
Royston Cave **59**, *59*
Rudston **172**
rush spreading 54, 150-1, *150-1*, 152
Ruthin **181**
Rye **78**

S

Saddleworth 151, **152**
Saddleworth Rushcart 152
Saffron Walden **101**
St Albans **60**
St Alkmund's Church, Shrewsbury 133
St Andrew's Church, Ashingdon 103
St Andrew's Church, Liverpool 152
St Andrew's Church, Penrith 146
St Andrew's Church, Wickhampton 107
St Andrews, Fife **200**
St Anne, Alderney **46**
St Anne's Well 118
St Asaph's Cathedral **183**
St Bartholomew-the-Great, London **88**
St Bartholomew's Church, Much Marcle 118, *118*
St Bees **146**
St Bega 146
St Blaise 87

St Brannoc 26
St Brélades Bay **46**
St Briavels **114**
St Bride 208
St Brigid 183, 211
St Brynach's Church, Nevern 188
St Buryan **14**
St Catherine's Well 130
St Chad's Church, Saddleworth 152
St Chad's Church, Stafford 134
St Cleer **17**
St Clement Danes, Strand, London **87**
St Columb Major **21**
St Columba 211
St Crispin 63
St Crispinian 63
St Cuthman 76
St David 24, 179, 186
St David's, Pembrokeshire **186**
St Derfel's Shrine 178
St Dogmaels **188**
St Dubricius Church, Hentland 118
St Dwynwen's Church, Llanddwyn 182
St Edmund 108
St Edren's Church, Newton Cross 186
St Etheldreda's Church, Hyssington 180
St Etheldreda's Church, London **87**
St Fagan's National History Museum **190**
St Fillans **206**
St George 70, 151
St George, Conwy **183**
St George's Church, Orleton 119
St Germans **20**
St Guron 21
St Guthlac 125
St Gwynno's Church, Llanwonno 190
St Hilda 170
St Ina's Church, Llanina 179
St Ives (Cambridgeshire) **98**
St Ives (Cornwall) **16**, *16*
St John the Baptist Church, Belton 120
St John the Baptist Church, Tredington 116
St John's Chapel, Isle of Man 156
St John's Wood, London **84**
St Kentigern 196
St Keverne **17**
St Keyne **20**
St Leonard 136
St Leonard's Church, Hythe 66, *66*
St Margaret 200

St Margaret's Fair 188
St Margaret's Hope **213**
St Mark's Eve 96
St Martin's, Guernsey **46**
St Mary, Jersey **46**
St Mary the Virgin
  church, Newington 62
St Mary's Church,
  Ambleside 151
St Mary's Church,
  Fairford 117
St Mary's Church,
  Fishguard 186
St Mary's Church,
  Painswick *114-15*, 115
St Mary's Church,
  Rostherne 142-3
St Mary's Church,
  Stevington 50
St Mary's Church,
  Woodford 127
St Mary's Church,
  Woolpit 108
St Maughold's Well 157
St Melangell 180
St Michael's Mount **15**
St Mungo 196
St Nectan 26
St Nectan's Glen **23**
St Neot **20**
St Nicholas's Church,
  Lanark 196
St Ninian's Cave 195
St Non 24
St Oswald 124, 155, 163
St Oswald's Church,
  Grasmere 151
St Osyth **102**
St Pancras Old Church,
  London **86**, *86*
St Patrick 45, 126, 196
St Patrick's Chapel,
  Heysham 153
St Paulinus 122
St Paul's Church, Jarrow
  167
St Peter and St Paul
  Church, Leominster
  119
St Peter's Church,
  Northampton 126-7
St Petroc 21, 22
St Piran 17
St Ragener 127
St Ronan's Border Games
  203
St Ronan's Well 203
St Senara's Church,
  Zennor 16
St Serf 196
St Swithun 57
St Teath **23**
St Teilo's Well 190
St Thomas Becket
  Church, Brightling 78
St Trillo's Chapel, Rhôs-
  on-Sea 183
St Wilfrid's Chair 167
St Wistan's Church,
  Wistow 121
St Withburga 107

Samhain 44, 206
sanctuary 163, 172
sanding ceremony 142
Sandwich **66**
Santon 157
Savoy Hotel, Strand,
  London **87**
Scarborough **170**
Scarletts Well 21
Schorne, Sir John 54
Schorne's Well 54
Scilly Isles 14, **25**
Seascale **146**
Sedgefield **161**
Selby, Dame Dorothy 61
selkies 212
Selling of the Keep of the
  Wether 120
serpent cults 211
Sewing Shields Castle **167**
Shakespeare, William 137
Shebbear **28**
Sheela na gig 59, 96
shell grottoes 64-5
Shemi Wad (James Wade)
  186
shepherd burials 78
Shepherdess Walk,
  London **92**
Sherborne **38**
Sherborne Castle 38
Shere **74**
Sherwood Forest **130**,
  131
Shetland Islands 214-15
Shiant Isles **209**
Shillingstone 38
shin-kicking 128
Ship Money 102
Shipton, Mother 169-70
shipwrecks
  Goodwin Sands 65
  Veryan Bay 19
Shrewsbury **133**
Shropshire 133
Shrovetide football 113,
  113, 128, 161, 166
Shug Monkey 96
Siamese twins 67
Sidbury **32**
Siddington **145**
Silbury Hill **80**
Sileby **120**, 128
Silent Pool 74
silver balls 16, 21
sin-eating 88
Sinodun Hill 72, 73
Sir Gawain and the Green
  Knight 134
Six Hills 60
Skimmington Riding 38
skipping matches 170
Skuttlebrook Wake 116
Smithills Hall 154
Smith's Arms,
  Godmanstone 37
Smoking of the Fool 122,
  123
Smoo Cave 210
smuggling 25, 76
Snowshill **116-17**

Somerset 39-45
soul-caking 143, *143*
South Baddesley **57**
South Ronaldsay 213
Southcott, Joanna 50-1
Southleigh **32**
Southwold **109**
Spanish Armada 211, 215
Spanish Liquor Day 70
squibbing 40
SS *Violet* 65
Staffa **211**
Stafford **134**
Staffordshire 134-5
Stanion **127**
Stanton Drew **44**
stepping stones 153
Stevenage **60**
Stevington **50**
Steyning **76**
Stilton **99**
Stirling **207**
stocks 136
stone circles
  Aikey Brae 207
  Avebury Stone Circle
    80, *80-1*
  Callanish 209
  Devil's Wedding 44
  Long Meg and her
    Daughters 146
  Ring of Brodgar *212-13*,
    213
Stonehenge **80-1**, 187
Stonehaven 199, **207**
Stonehenge 69, **80-1**, 187
Stratford-upon-Avon **137**
Strathpeffer **211**
Stratton **25**
Straw Bear Day 99, *99*
street cries 90
Stretton-on-Dunsmore
  136
Strumble Head 186
Stuart, Jane 96
Suffolk 108-9
Sule Skerry **212**
summer solstice 69, 81
Summerbridge **169**
Summerdale **212**
Surrey 74
Sussex 75-9
Sutton St Nicholas **119**
Swaffham **107**
Swan, Becky 138
Swarkestone Bridge **113**
Sweeps festival 62, *62*, 69
Swineshead Abbey **125**
Swona **213**
sword dancing 166, 169

Taliesin 178-9
Tame, John 117
Tapsell gates 78
Teampull na Trionaid 209
Tebay **148**
Teddy Roe's Band 38
Teeside 161

Tenby **188**
Tetbury **114**, 128
Thaxted **100**, *104*, 105
Thirst House 113
Thomas the Rhymer 202
Thringstone fault 120
thunder stones 72
Thunor's Leap 65
Thurso **210**
Tin Can Band 127
Tinsley Green **75**
Tintagel **23**
Tobermory **211**
Toller, James 99
Tolven 15
Tom Bawcock's Eve 14
tossing the sheaf 134
Totnes **29**
Toustain 172
Tower of London **89**
trade unionism 164
Traquair House **202**
Tre Taliesin **178-9**
Treacle Market 145
Treak Cliff **112**
Tredington 116
Trencrom Hill 20
Tresco **25**
Trinity Fair 109
Trip to Jerusalem public
  house, Nottingham 130
Tristan and Iseult 18
Truro **18**
Tweedsmuir **202**
Twin Sisters 64
Twm Sion Cati 189
Twmbarlwm Hill 191
Tynwald 156

U

Uffington Castle **70**, *71*
Ulph's Horn 172
Unst 215
Up Helly Aa 196, *196-7*
Uplyme **33**
Up'ards and Down'ards
  113, *113*
Uppies and Doonies 203
Uppies and Downies 146
Uther Pendragon 23, 148

V

Veryan **18-19**, *18-19*
Vintners 92
visard mask 126

W

Wade, Charles Paget 117
Waen Rhydd **179**
Wakeman's Horn 169
Wakes 136
Wakes Week 113, 150
Wall, Matthew 60
Wall Game 53
Wallace, William 196, 207

Wallace Monument 207
Wallasea Island **102**, *102*
Walsall **136**
Walsingham **107**
Wandlebury 96
Wareham **37**
Wars of the Roses 60
Warwickshire 136-7
wassailing 18, 39
Watch Service 136
water monsters
  Afanc 182
  Bownessie 149
  grampus 56
  Loch Ness Monster 211
  Morgawr 17
Wayfarer's Dole 57
Wayland's Smithy 70
Waytyng Hill 128
well-dressing
  Bisley 116
  Endon 134
  Malvern 139
well-worship 70
Wells of Swona 213
Wergin's Stone 119
West Witton **168**, *168*
West Wratting **96**
West Wycombe **55**, *55*
Western Isles 208-9
Weston **60**
Weybridge **74**
Whalton **166-7**
Whalton Bale 166
Whispering Knights 70
Whitby Abbey **170**, *171*
White Hart Inn, Walsall
  136

White Horse of
  Uffington 70
White Horse public
  house, Burnham Green
  60
White Notley **100**
Whitebread Meadow 125
Whitehawk Neolithic
  Camp 76
Whithorn Priory 195
Whittlesea **99**
Whittlesford **96**
Whomerley Wood 60
Whuppity Scoorie 196
Wick **210**
Wicken (Cambridgeshire)
  98
Wicken
  (Northamptonshire)
  126
Wickhampton **107**
Widecombe in the Moor
  29
Widow's Son public
  house, London 93, *93*
Wigston **121**
Wilcote 70
Will Scarlet 130
Wilmington **78**
Wiltshire 80-1
Winchester **57**
Windermere *148-9*, **149**
Wingrave **54**
Winster **113**
Winster Wakes 113
Winterborne
  Whitechurch **38**
Winwick **155**

Wisbech **96**
wishing rings 46
Wistow **121**
witchcraft
  Alderley Edge 144-5
  Anne Jeffries 23
  Bamburgh 163
  Batcombe 37
  Boscastle 23
  Bromsgrove 138
  Ceridwen 178-9
  Conjuror Mynterne 37
  Edmondthorpe 121
  folklore/witch
    museums 92, 97, 102
  Hastings 79
  Horseheath 96
  James Murrell 103
  Kidderminster 138
  King's Lynn 106
  Llangurig 180
  Luton 51
  Mother Haggy 60
  Mother Shipton 169-70
  Newbrough 167
  Old Mother Jenkins the
    Goose Charmer 100
  Old Mother Redcap
    102
  Penshaw 161
  St Osyth 102
  St Teath 23
  Stanion 127
  Summerdale 212
  Swona 213
  Tebay 148
  Tobermory 211
  Witch of Wookey 44

Witness Cairn *194*, 195
Wittenham Clumps 72
Woden 63
Woodford **127**
Woodmancote 75
Wookey Hole **44**
Woolpit **108**
woolsack race 114, 128
Worcester **138**
Worcestershire 138
work-related traditions
  164
Workington **146**
World Tin Bath
  Championships 157
Worm Hill 161
Worthing **75**
Wright, Elsie 173
Wroth Silver 136
Wyatt, Sir Henry 61
Wychwood 70
Wycliffe, John 134
Wyre **212**

Y, Z

yarrow 98
Ychen Bannog oxen 179,
  182
Yetnasteen **212**
York **172**
York Minster 172
Yorkshire 168-73
Ysbaddaden 178
Ystradffin **189**
Zennor **16**
Zennor Quoit 16

Acknowledgements

Front Cover Getty Images/© Philip Kramer (Stonehenge, Wiltshire); **Back Cover** Photolibrary.com/JTB Photo (Thaxted Morris Dance Festival); **1** Getty Images/Gallo Images (Morris Dancer); **2-3** Alamy Images/© Roger Bamber (Burning of the Clocks winter solstice celebration, Brighton beach); **6-7** Photolibrary.com/Jeremy Walker (Silbury Hill); **8** Charles Tait; **9** Alamy Images/© John Robertson; **10** Alamy Images/© Jennifer Hartshorne; **11** Collections/© Roger Scruton; **12-13** Photolibrary.com/Lee Pengelly/Silverscene Photography (St Michael's Mount); **15** Photolibrary.com/ James Osmond; **16** Collections/© Brian Shuel; **18-19** Photolibrary.com/Gavin Hellier; **21-22** Collections/© Brian Shuel; **24** Photolibrary.com/Lee Beel; **26-27** Photolibrary.com/Lee Pengelly/Silverscene Photography; **28** Homer Sykes; **31** Photolibrary.com/Britain On View; **32-33** Homer Sykes; **34-35** Photolibrary.com/Baxter Bradford; **36** Photolibrary.com/Chris Parker; **39** Corbis/© Adam Woolfitt; **40-41** Collections/© Michael St Maur Sheil; **43** naturepl.com/Adam Burton; **44-45** Photolibrary.com/Jeremy Walker; **47** Corbis/© Bertrand Rieger/Hemis; **48-49** Alamy Images/© imagebroker (The Long Man of Wilmington); **50-51** Alamy Images/© Green Planet Photography; **53** Photolibrary.com/Jon Hoffmann; **55** Alamy Images/© Nick Jenkins; **56** Collections/© Robert Estall; **59** Homer Sykes; **62** Collections/© Robert Bird; **64-65** Photolibrary.com/John Miller; **66-67** Collections/© Simon McBride; **68-69** Alamy Images/© Adam van Bunnens; **71** Photolibrary.com/Last Refuge; **73** Homer Sykes/© Network Photographer; **75** Collections/© Brian Shuel; **76-77** Alamy Images/Francesco Carucci; **79** Collections/© Robert Bird; **80-81** Photolibrary.com/James Osmond; **82-83** Photolibrary.com/Symphonie Ltd (London financial district skyline); **85** Alamy Images/© Tim Graham; **86-87** Collections/© Brian Shuel; **89** Alamy Images/© Chris Gomersall; **90-91** Photolibrary.com/E&E Image Library; **93** Homer Sykes; **94-95** Photolibrary.com/Roz Gordon (Blythburgh Church); **97** Corbis/© Alistair Laming/Loop Images; **99** Homer Sykes; **101** Collections/© Oliver Benn; **102-103** rspb-images.com/© Ben Hall; **104** Photolibrary.com/JTB Photo; **106** Photolibrary.com/Last Refuge; **109** Photolibrary.com/Ros Drinkwater; **110-111** Collections/© Robert Estall (Village of Orlingbury); **113** Homer Sykes; **114-115** Photolibrary.com/Nature Picture Library; **117** Collections/© Brian Shuel; **118** Alamy Images/© travelib history; **123** Guzelian/ Lorne Campbell; **124-125** Alamy Images/© Phil Crow; **129** Alamy Images/© Nick Turner; **131** Photolibrary.com/David Sellman; **132** Alamy Images/© David Jones; **135** Collections/© Roger Scruton; **139** Alamy Images/© Jeremy Pardoe; **140-141** Photolibrary.com/Jason Friend (Lake Windermere); **143** Homer Sykes; **144-145** Photolibrary.com/Rod Edwards; **147** Artist: Gordon Young/Typography: Why Not Associates/Implementation: Russell Coleman/Photography:Rocco Redondo; **148-149** Photolibrary.com/Imagesource; **150-151** Martin Rushton; **153** Window On Lost Time/© Mick Sharp; **154** Collections/© Brian Shuel; **156-157** Photolibrary.com/The Irish Image Collection; **158-159** Photolibrary.com/Joe Cornish (Cleveland Hills); **160** Pictures Colour Library/Neil Holmes; **162-163** Window On Lost Time/© Mick Sharp; **165** Alamy Images/© Trinity Mirror/Mirrorpix; **166** Homer Sykes; **168** Collections/© Brian Shuel; **171** Window On Lost Time/© Mick Sharp; **174-175** Photolibrary.com/Adam Burton (Cribyn viewed from Pen-y-Fan); **177** Window On Lost Time/© Mick Sharp; **180-181** Window On Lost Time/© Mick Sharp; **182** Window On Lost Time/© Jean Williamson; **184-185** Alamy Images/© Jeff Morgan 05; **187** Window On Lost Time/© Jean Williamson; **188-189** Photolibrary.com/Tony Howell; **192-193** Photolibrary.com/© Gavin Hellier (The Old Man of Storr, Loch Leathan, Isle of Skye); **194** Gary Waidson/www.waylandscape.co.uk; **197** Window On Lost Time/© Jean Williamson; **198-199** Photolibrary.com/John Coutts; **201** Homer Sykes; **204-209** Window On Lost Time/© Jean Williamson; **212-213** Alamy Images/ Robert Harding World Imagery; **214-215** Charles Tait.

Contributors

Project Editor Jo Bourne
Art Editors Kathryn Gammon, Simon Webb
Sub-editor Marion Paull
Cartographic Consultant Alison Ewington
Feature Writer Christopher Somerville
Additional material Jo Bourne, Marion Paull
Picture Editor Caroline Wood
Proofreader Barry Gage
Indexer Marie Lorimer
Maps European Map Graphics Limited

FOR VIVAT DIRECT
Editorial Director Julian Browne
Art Director Anne-Marie Bulat
Managing Editor Nina Hathway
Trade Editor Penny Craig
Picture Resource Manager
Sarah Stewart-Richardson
Pre-press Account Manager Dean Russell
Product Production Manager
Claudette Bramble
Production Controller Jan Bucil

Origination by FMG
Printing and binding Arvato Iberia, Portugal

The Most Amazing Places of Folklore & Legend in Britain is published in 2011 in the United Kingdom by Vivat Direct Limited (t/a Reader's Digest), 157 Edgware Road, London W2 2HR

The Most Amazing Places of Folklore & Legend in Britain is owned under licence from the Reader's Digest Association, Inc. All rights reserved.

The Most Amazing Places of Folklore & Legend in Britain is based on material taken from **Folklore, Myths and Legends of Britain** published by The Reader's Digest Association Limited, London in 1973.

We are committed both to the quality of our products and the service we provide to our customers. We value your comments, so please do contact us on **0871 351 1000** or via our website at **www.readersdigest.co.uk**

If you have any comments or suggestions about the content of our books, email us at **gbeditorial@readersdigest.co.uk**

ISBN 978 1 78020 005 7
Book Code 400-525 UP0000-1